PROHIBITIONS AND RESTRAINTS IN WAR

PROHIBITIONS AND RESTRAINTS IN WAR

Sydney D. Bailey

Published for

THE ROYAL INSTITUTE OF
INTERNATIONAL AFFAIRS

by

OXFORD UNIVERSITY PRESS

LONDON   OXFORD   NEW YORK

1972

Oxford University Press

LONDON OXFORD NEW YORK

GLASGOW TORONTO MELBOURNE WELLINGTON

CAPE TOWN SALISBURY IBADAN NAIROBI DAR ES SALAAM LUSAKA ADDIS ABABA

BOMBAY CALCUTTA MADRAS KARACHI LAHORE DACCA

KUALA LUMPUR SINGAPORE HONG KONG TOKYO

Paperbound edition ISBN 0 19 285056 3
Hardbound edition ISBN 0 19 215196 7

First published as an Oxford University Press Paperback
by Oxford University Press, London, 1972

Printed in Great Britain by
The Eastern Press Limited, London and Reading

CONTENTS

CONTENTS

ABBREVIATIONS*

ABM	Anti-ballistic missiles
AJIL	*American Journal of International Law*
B agents or weapons	Bacteriological (biological) weapons
C agents or weapons	Chemical weapons
CBW	Chemical and bacteriological (biological) weapons
CEIP	Carnegie Endowment for International Peace
CICR	Comité International de la Croix-Rouge
CN	ω-chloroacetophenone (chemical harassing agent)
CS	Orthochlorobenzylidene malononitrile (chemical harassing agent)
ECOSOC	(UN) Economic and Social Council
ENDC	Eighteen-Nation Committee on Disarmament
ET	English translation
Experts' Rpt	*Report of the Conference of Government Experts on the Reaffirmation and Development of International Humanitarian Law Applicable in Armed Conflicts, Geneva, 24 May–12 June 1971*
FC	Fathers of the Church series published by the Catholic University of America Press.
FM27-10	US Dept of the Army, *Field Manual on The Law of Land Warfare*, 1956
GA	General Assembly
GAOR	*General Assembly Official Records*
Georgetown LJ	*Georgetown Law Journal*
HC Deb.	House of Commons Debates
IAEA	International Atomic Energy Agency
ICBMs	Inter-continental ballistic missiles
ILC	International Law Commission
IRRC	*International Review of the Red Cross*

* Excluding those in everyday use.

ABBREVIATIONS

JBP	Hugo Grotius, *De jure belli ac pacis*
LNTS	League of Nations Treaty Series
MIRV	Multiple independently-targetable re-entry vehicle
MLF	Multilateral Nuclear Force
MML	*The Law of War on Land, being Part III of the Manual of Military Law, 1958,* and subsequent amendments
NPT	Non-Proliferation Treaty
SALT	Strategic Arms Limitation Talks
SC	Security Council
SCOR	*Security Council Official Records*
UKTS	UK Treaty Series
UNESCO	UN Educational, Scientific and Cultural Organization
UNTS	UN Treaty Series
UNRWA	UN Relief and Works Agency for Palestine Refugees in the Near East
WEU	Western European Union
WHO	World Health Organization

Note: In Chapter 1 figures in parentheses following titles of publications denote dates of writing.

PREFACE

THIS book is not part of a campaign to make war more respectable. It seeks, in fact, to do four things. First, to show the close connection between the Just War doctrine as an ethical concept and the Just War doctrine as a legal concept. Secondly, to demonstrate that the Just War doctrine is composed of restrictions rather than permissions. Thirdly, to review three contemporary approaches to preventing excesses in war and protecting the innocent: through humanitarian conventions and the International Red Cross, through the Human Rights machinery of the United Nations, and by means of arms control and disarmament. Finally, I have sought to show that it is no longer practicable to separate the Law of The Hague, which governs the conduct of hostilities, from the Law of Geneva, which provides humanitarian protection for the victims of war. The question must now be posed in different terms. As the world moves hesitantly from arms control to partial disarmament, and even more hesitantly along the tortuous path to total disarmament, are there any weapons or methods of war which violate ethical and legal norms so clearly that they should be unreservedly prohibited? And if, in spite of all efforts at peace-making and peace-keeping, wars still occur, are there any restraints which civilized nations should observe unilaterally, or on a reciprocal basis?

The UN Charter affirms the determination that ' We the peoples ' should 'save succeeding generations from the scourge of war...'. The obligations and activities reviewed in this book are no substitute for the primary goal of the United Nations, which often seems impossible and always is necessary.

July 1971   S. D. B.

ACKNOWLEDGEMENTS

I AM grateful to the following, who read and criticized chapters of the first draft of this book: Dr Johan Bouman, Bishop B. C. Butler, OSB, Professor Georg Schwarzenberger, Professor Jacques Freymond, and Mr William Epstein.

Many others have helped. Father Thomas Gilby, OP, Father Thomas Corbishley, SJ, Colonel Gerald Draper, and Mr John Eppstein elucidated points about the Just War doctrine in Christian ethics. Edward H. Milligan, librarian at Friends House, London, and the staff of the Friends Historical Library, Swarthmore College, Pennsylvania, helped me to track down records of what Quakers call the Holy Experiment. Duncan Wood, Quaker representative in Geneva, was tireless in procuring documents for me, and Mr Sean MacBride, formerly secretary-general of the International Commission of Jurists, gave me a first-hand account of the Human Rights Conference in Teheran in 1968. Mr Constantin Stavropoulos, Mr Marc Screiber, Miss Margaret McAfee, and other members of the UN Secretariat helped me at various times to obtain UN documents.

The staff of the East Finchley Public Library met with equanimity my most unreasonable requests for books, and Mrs Vivian Hewitt of the Carnegie Endowment for International Peace was always willing to trace articles in back issues of obscure journals or to obtain for me books not readily available in Britain. I am also indebted to the staff of the Catholic Central Library in London and the Catholic University of America Press for advice about English translations of Latin works.

Through the good offices of Mr Joseph E. Johnson and Mr Ralph Zacklin, I was invited to become a member of a Panel of the American Society of International Law concerned with International Law and Humanitarian Problems. I am grateful to the Society's Executive Vice President and Director, Mr Stephen M. Schwebel, for his willingness to allow a novice to participate in the work of the Panel. My colleagues in the Conference on Christian Approaches to Defence and Disarmament and a working party of the British Council of Churches discussed an early outline of the book. I learned a great deal from these discussions, especially from those whose opinions differ from my own. I have also been given generous help by officials in the Foreign and Commonwealth Office who, by tradition, must be nameless. The publications of the Stockholm International Peace Research Institute have been invaluable.

ACKNOWLEDGEMENTS

My wife Brenda did not, as is often the case, prepare the index, but in the midst of her busy life she gave unfailing support at all stages. The index was, in fact, prepared by Mr Douglas Matthews of the London Library. I am greatly indebted to Miss Hermia Oliver of Chatham House who has been a most patient and meticulous editor.

Needless to say, none of those mentioned above is responsible for what I have written.

THE JUST WAR IN CHRISTIAN ETHICS

*Let hope keep you joyful; in trouble stand
firm . . .
Call down blessings on your persecutors . . .
Never pay back evil for evil . . . If possible,
so far as it lies with you, live at peace with all
men.*

Paul's letter to the Romans
(*New English Bible*)

The early Church

The doctrine of the Just War had its origin in Christian
ethics more than 1,000 years before Hugo Grotius began to
clothe it in legal forms. Josef Kunz has described the Just War
doctrine as ' a theological, not a legal concept ' and Arthur
Nussbaum has written that the traditional doctrine is ' essentially religious '.[1]

The first Christians were, of course, pacifists, more concerned
with their religious tasks than with the secular affairs of the
Roman Empire. The spirit of Christ was to transform the life
of the individual. The essential social groupings were the family
and the Church; within these, Christian principles were to
have absolute validity. All other elements of human existence,
including the state, belonged to ' the world '. The unbeliever
was in bondage to ' the world ', and only Christ could free him.
Christian hope was based on the faith that individual men and
women would be saved, but the redemption of ' the world '
would not become visible until the return of Christ. This would
inaugurate ' the next world ', when God's perfect rule over all
creation would be established. The earthly life of Christians
was a period of preparation for full sainthood; their real
citizenship was in heaven.[2]

During the period of waiting until the Second Coming of
Christ, Christian believers were to be sober and industrious,

[1] ' Bellum justum and bellum legale ', 45 *AJIL* (1951), 530; Nussbaum, ' Just
war—a legal concept? ', 42 *Michigan LR* (1943), 478.

[2] This and several later paragraphs are adapted from an article, ' Some Reflections on the Use of Force ', *Friends' Q.*, Apr. 1969.

content with their earthly circumstances, in all things submissive—young to old, women to men, servants to masters, and all to Caesar.[3] Governmental authority, although pagan, was accepted as a divine institution and was to be obeyed so long as this did not conflict with Christian conscience.

Almost all Christian writers before the fourth century took it for granted that service in the army was incompatible with Christian principles.[4] 'The Lord . . . in disarming Peter, unbelted every soldier.'[5] If a soldier were converted to Christianity, he was expected to give up military service. 'But, once we have embraced the faith and have been baptized, we either must immediately leave military service (as many have done); or we must resort to all kinds of excuses in order to avoid any action which is . . . forbidden.'[6] Several cases are recorded by both Christian and non-Christian writers of converted soldiers suffering martyrdom.[7]

The early Christians were thus pacifist, in the sense that they did not bear arms; but they did not usually condemn the use of arms by the unconverted if this were necessary for the purpose of maintaining an orderly fabric of society.

Critics of Christianity maintained that the Christian attitude was irresponsible. They argued, first, that Christians accepted the benefits of Imperial Rome but were unwilling to meet the obligations of citizenship. How would the Emperor be defended, asked Celsus (A.D. *c.* 180), if everybody were to embrace such a utopian religion? When asked how Christians should act when others were fighting, Tertullian said that the life of the Christian was to be of the quality that made war unnecessary, and that he

[3] 1 Cor. 14:34–5; Eph. 5:22–33 and 6:1–9; Col. 3:18 and 6:1; 1 Tim. 2:11–12; 1 Tim. 6:1–2; Tit. 2:9–10; Tit. 3:1; 1 Pet. 2:13–18; 1 Pet. 3:1–2; 1 Pet. 5:5.

[4] See Justin Martyr, *First Apology* (153), ch. 14 (ET in FC, vi (1948), p. 47); *Dialogue with Trypho* (155–60), chs 109–10 (ET ibid. pp. 316–19); Origen, *Contra Celsum* (248), iii.7; v.33; vii.26; viii.73–4 (ET H. Chadwick (Cambridge, 1953), pp. 132–3, 289–90, 415–16, 509–10); Lactantius, *Divinae institutiones* (305), v.10 & 17; vi.6, 10, 18, & 20 (ET in FC, xlix (1964), pp. 352, 371, 405–10, 417–20, 443–8, 452); Eusebius Pamphili, *Hist. ecclesiastica* (314), viii.1 (ET in FC, ix (1953), p. 166).

[5] Tertullian, *De idolatria* (198–203), ch. 19, in Ante-Nicene Christian Lib., xi (Edinburgh, 1869), p. 171.

[6] Tert., *De corona militis* (211), ch. 11, para. 4 (ET in FC xl (1959), p. 257).

[7] Pamphili, *Hist. eccles.*, vii.15 (ET pp. 116–17). Other cases are recorded by C. J. Cadoux in *Early Christian Attitude to War* (London, 1919), pp. 149–54.

was to pray for those who served righteously as soldiers.[8] Origen put it like this:

And as we by our prayers vanquish all demons who stir up war . . . and disturb the peace, we . . . are much more helpful to the king than those who go into the field to fight for them. And we do take our part in public affairs, when along with righteous prayers we join self-denying exercises and meditations. . . . And none fight better for the king than we do. We do not indeed fight under him, although he require it; but we do fight on his behalf . . . by offering our prayers to God.[9]

The other charge (and it was one that was to be made against Christian pacifists repeatedly, up to our own day) was that the practice of Christianity actually increased the number of wars. Sometimes the argument was that popular hatred of Christianity was itself a cause of war; in St Augustine's time, and particularly after the sack of Rome by Alaric in 410, it was said that the effect of Christian teaching was to weaken the will and capacity to resist aggression.

Arnobius rebutted the first charge in these words:

Actually, regarding the wars which you say were begun on account of hatred of our religion, it would not be difficult to prove that after Christ was on earth, not only did they not increase but in great measure were reduced as a result of the repression of fierce passions. . . . We have learned from his teachings . . . that it is better to suffer wrong than be its cause.[10]

The situation was to change radically during the fourth century. The first Christians had assumed that the pagan world of Caesar was wicked and doomed, that its redemption had to await the return of Christ. But the Second Coming was delayed and then, to their amazement, Caesar became a Christian. Not only that, the Emperor Constantine ascribed his victories in war to the fact that he had adopted the Christian faith; assuredly those who believed in the God of the Christians would prosper, claimed Constantine, and pagans would suffer nothing but mis-

---

[8] Tert., *Apol.*, paras 29 & 37; *De spectaculis* (198–203), para. 29; *Ad scapulam* (212), paras 2 & 47 (ET in Ante-Nicene Christ. Lib., xi.33–4, 47–8, 109–10, 116).

[9] Origen, *c. Cels.*, viii.73 (ET p. 557).

[10] *Arnobius of Sicca: The Case against the Pagans* (310–14) (ET G. E. McCracken, London, 1949), i.6.64.

fortune.[11] ' The professed object of Constantine was to legislate the millennium in a generation.' [12]

All this was to throw the Church into confusion. Some retreated into monasticism. Some joined utopian sects which were regarded as heretical, and in due course died or were coerced out of existence. The majority took the view that they should seize the opportunity to extend the frontiers of Christianity into the political realm, even if this meant some modification in putting into practice the high ethical standards of the Christian gospel. In 380 the Emperor Theodosius I declared that Catholic Christianity was the state religion of the Roman Empire. Non-Christians were but ' foolish madmen ' and should be ' branded with the ignominious name of heretics '. They would be punished with ' the chastisement of the divine condemnation ' as well as with ' the punishment which our authority . . . shall decide to inflict '.[13] Christians were learning to live with the ambiguities of politics. The emblem of the cross was inscribed on the shields of Roman soldiers,[14] and early in the fifth century non-Christians were excluded from serving in the army.

There has always been a minority of Christians which has believed that the Church made a disastrous compromise at the time of Constantine, and that it can recover its original vitality only by unequivocal loyalty to the total demands of the teachings of Jesus, whatever the consequences. But the mainstream of Christian thinking has held that fourth-century Christians were right, that there can be no going back to the ' innocence ' of the early Church.

St Ambrose and St Augustine

The pioneer in asserting the claims of the Church in the post-Constantinian era was St Ambrose, bishop of Milan (339–97). ' For the first time in history we find a representative

[11] Pamphili, *Life of the Blessed Emperor Constantine* (337–40) (London, 1845), ii.42.86–7.
[12] C. N. Cochrane, *Christianity and Classical Culture* (1st ed. New York, 1940; paperback 1957), p. 211.
[13] The text of the decree is in H. Bettenson, ed., *Documents on the Christian Church* (1943), p. 31.
[14] Pamphili, *Life*, iv.21.191.

of the Church entering the secular arena. . . . Never before had the claims of the Church been asserted in so daring and uncompromising a manner.' [15] Ambrose had been elected bishop of Milan by popular acclamation in 373, although he was a layman and had not at the time been baptized. Indeed, his promotion in the Church from baptism and confirmation, via deacon and presbyter, to bishop took place within the space of a week.[16]

Ambrose had a complex personality. C. N. Cochrane writes that ' he was prepared to use the devil's weapons as a means of realizing the kingdom of God ' (p. 350). His leadership, ' if not invariably wise, was at any rate bold, effective, and transparently honest ' (p. 373). His writings have many affinities with those of Cicero.

Ambrose writes of the blessings of peace,[17] but accepts the necessity of going to war in a just cause and ' when driven to it by wrongs received '.[18] Restraint is to be shown during the conduct of war and after victory. ' [Justice] must even be preserved in all dealings with enemies. . . . But a deeper vengeance is taken on fiercer foes, and on those that are false as well as those who have done greater wrong.' Ambrose lays great stress on justice, which accords with nature, and ' is binding, even in war '. Clergy are to take no part in fighting ' for we have our thoughts fixed more on the duty of the soul than on that of the body '.[19] He assures the Emperor Gratian of his prayers for the victory of Roman arms,[20] but ten years later he does not hesitate to write a stern letter rebuking the Emperor Theodosius for the massacre of seven thousand inhabitants of Thessalonica in retaliation for a seditious

[15] F. Homes Dudden, *Life and Times of St Ambrose* (Oxford, 1935), pp. 497, 499. See also Cochrane, p. 347.

[16] Homes Dudden, pp. 66, 73-4.

[17] *De officiis ministrorum* (prob. later than 386), i.30, para. 155 (ET in *Select Library of Nicene and Post-Nicene Fathers of the Christian Council*, 2nd ser., x: *Select works and letters* . . . , tr. H. de Romestin & others (Oxford, 1896), p. 67.

[18] Ibid. i.27, para. 129; 28, para. 131; 38, para. 176 (ET pp. 22-3 & 30); see also *De Tobia* (prob. later than 385), para. 51 (ET L. M. Zuker (Washington, 1953), p. 67).

[19] *De off.*, i.29, paras 139-40 (ET p. 24); iii.4, para. 24 (ET p. 71); i.25, para. 175 (ET p. 30).

[20] *De fide* (c. 380), i, Prologue, para. 3; ch. 10, para. 136; ii.16, paras 136 & 143 (ET in *Select works* . . . pp. 201, 222-3, 241, & 242).

outbreak which had led to the murder of a number of officers of the garrison.[21] Theodosius was excommunicated by Ambrose until he had shown public penance.

St Augustine (354–430) further develops the ideas put forward by Ambrose, but he did not pretend to be a systematic thinker. ' Like St Paul and unlike St Thomas, Augustine wrote only under the pressure of immediate necessity.' [22] He was essentially a polemicist, and his most important works were written to combat heretical and schismatic tendencies—Manicheans, Donatists, Pelagians. These splinter groups varied greatly, but the one thing they had in common was a rigorous and uncompromising perfectionism, a rejection of the dilution of the ethics of the gospel which seemed inseparable from wholehearted participation in the affairs of ' the world '. They saw themselves as a holy remnant, undefiled and unspotted by the relativisms and moral ambiguities of politics.

Augustine, by contrast, was a wholehearted exponent of involvement and responsibility. He believed, as Peter Brown puts it, ' that the Church might become coextensive with human society as a whole '.[23]

Augustine's ideas of the Just War were by no means original. In rejecting the pacifism of the early Church, he was only giving a Christian flavour to Greek philosophy and Roman practice. Time and again in his writings, he insists that if fighting were contrary to Christian teaching, Christ would have told those soldiers he encountered to lay down their arms.[24]

Augustine starts from the premise that order is a very great good, and is a prerequisite of justice. If order is threatened or disturbed, the Christian is not allowed to kill in a private capacity, but may do so at the command of the lawful authorities: ' I do not approve of killing [in self-defence] unless one happens to be a soldier or public functionary . . . [acting] according to the commission lawfully given him, and in the

[21] Letter li (390) (ET ibid. pp. 450–3).

[22] J. N. Figgis, *Political Aspects of St Augustine's ' City of God '* (1st ed. 1921, repr. Gloucester, Mass., 1963), p. 5.

[23] *Augustine of Hippo* (London, 1967), p. 224.

[24] *Contra Faustum Manichaeum* (398), xxi. para. 74 (ET R. Stothert in *Works of Aurelius Augustine*, v, ed. M. Dods (Edinburgh, 1872), p. 464); Letter 138 to Marcellinus (412) (ET in FC, xx (1953), pp. 47–8).

manner becoming to his office.' Killing is also permitted at God's express command.[25] He attaches great importance to the duty of obedience to the lawful authorities and considers that a soldier is ' innocent ' if he obeys an unrighteous command on the part of the ruler.[26]

The concise definition of a Just War which Augustine gives has been variously translated, but the clearest translation of which I am aware is that given by John Eppstein: ' Just wars are usually defined as those which avenge injuries, when the nation or city against which warlike action is to be directed has neglected either to punish wrongs committed by its own citizens or to restore what has been unjustly taken by it.' It is the adversary's wickedness which makes a cause just: ' If the victory fall to the wicked (as sometimes it may) it is God's decree to humble the conquered, either reforming their sins, or punishing them.' [27] God is at all times sovereign, ' ending [wars] sooner or later as He wills '. The ruler and his subjects are alike to God, ' both in His power '.[28]

Men ought to hate war and desire peace, but real peace will not be achieved in this world, ' because the mutability of human estate can never grant any realm an absolute security '. Real peace will be possible only in the heavenly city ' whose king is truth, whose law is love, whose measure is eternity '.[29] Augustine writes often that, though war is the contrary of peace, peace is achieved by war and that war's only purpose is to secure peace.[30] Yet he is clearly uncomfortable with this paradox, and

[25] Letter 47 to Publicola (398) (ET in FC, xii.230); *De libero arbitrio* (388), i.5, para. 11 (ET M.Pontifex, entitled *The Problem of Free Choice* (London, 1955), pp. 44–7); *c. Faust. Man.*, xxii, paras 74–5, 79 (ET pp. 463–5); Letter 87, to Emeritus (c.405) (ET in FC, xviii (1953), pp. 19–20; *De civitate Dei*, i (413), chs 16, 20, & 25 (ET J. Healey, ed. R. V. G. Tasker, London, 1945); *Quaestiones in Heptateuchem* (419), vi.10 (ET in J. Eppstein, *Catholic Tradition of the Law of Nations* (London, 1935), p. 74).

[26] *De lib. arb.*, 1.5, paras. 11–12; *c. Faust. Man.*, xxii., para. 75 (ET p. 465).

[27] *Quaest. in Hept.*, vi.10 (ET Eppstein, p. 74); *De civ. D*, xix (427), chs 7 & 25.

[28] *c. Faust. Man.*, xxii, paras 75– 6 (ET pp. 464–6); *De civ. D*, v (415), ch. 22; see also xviii (425), ch. 2.

[29] Letter 189, to Count Boniface (c.418) (ET in FC, xxx (1955), p. 269); *De civ. D.*, iii (413), chs 10 & 16; iv (415), ch. 6; vii (417), ch. 14; xvii (425), ch. 13; xix (427), chs 11, 13, 14, 17, & 18.

[30] Letter 189 (ET p. 269); *De civ. D.*, xv (420), ch. 4; xix, chs 12 & 18; Letter 220, to Boniface (427) (ET in FC, xxxii (1956), p. 111).

insists that ' it is a greater glory to destroy war with a word
than men with a sword '.[31]

The Christian is to wage war with moderation, to show
mercy to prisoners and the defeated, ' especially where no
disturbance of peace is to be feared '. If an earthly state observes
Christian teachings, ' even war will not be waged without
kindness '.[32] Augustine makes an interesting distinction between
the possession of weapons (deterrence) and their use (war).
Christ had told Peter to take a sword, but rebuked him when
he used it to cut off Malchus' ear. ' Doubtless it was mysterious
that the Lord should require them to carry weapons, and forbid
the use of them. But it was His part to give the suitable precepts,
and it was their part to obey without reserve.' [33]

Augustine was continually trying to rebut the charge that
Christian doctrine is ' not adaptable to the customs of the
state ', and it is here that his writings are least satisfactory.
How, he asks, is a state which claims to be based on Christian
principles to implement the precept to return evil with good,
to turn the other cheek, to go the second mile? Augustine gives
three answers. First, if the advice of Christ had been followed,
the Roman state would have been ' founded, sanctified,
strengthened, and enlarged ' very much more successfully than
had been the case under non-Christian rulers. Let those who
say that Christian teaching is opposed to the welfare of the
state consider how differently things would have turned out if
only rulers and judges, parents and children, masters and
slaves, tax-collectors and taxpayers, had followed Christian
teaching; the critics would be forced to admit that nothing
would provide more effectively for the safety of the state than
to observe Christian teaching. The Roman Empire had become
rich and famous ' by natural virtues without true religion ';
how much more might have been added if men had been
Christian.[34]

Secondly, the purpose of overcoming evil with good is to
show how temporal things are to be despised for the sake of

[31] Letter 229, to Count Darius (c.429) (ET ibid. pp. 152–3).
[32] Letter 138, to Marcellinus (ET pp. 46–7); Letter 189 (ET p. 270).
[33] c. Faust. Man., xxii, para. 77 (ET p. 468).
[34] Letter 138 (ET pp. 41–8, 50).

faith and justice. The intention must be to win over the offender, so that he will be brought to repentance rather than overcome by force. But, adds Augustine without further explanation, ' we often have to act with a sort of kindly harshness, when we are trying to make unwilling souls yield, because we have to consider their welfare rather than their inclination '.[35]

Thirdly, the precepts of Christ ' refer rather to the interior disposition of the heart than to the act which appears exteriorly '.[36]

St Thomas, Vitoria, and Suárez

For many centuries, the Christian Church had almost nothing but the scattered writings of Ambrose and Augustine as a basis for the Just War doctrine. The Decretals of Gratian of Bologna (twelfth century) provide the beginning of systematic thought about the Christian concept of the Just War, and between the thirteenth and sixteenth centuries the Just War doctrine was further elaborated. Conditions were laid down about the requirements of the doctrine, both as regards the purposes for which a Just War could be fought, the procedure by which it should be initiated, and the manner in which it had to be conducted.

St Thomas Aquinas (1226–74) starts from the assumption that war is opposed to charity, and then asks ' whether it is *always* a sin to wage war ' (my italics). With admirable lucidity, Thomas writes that war may be just (or justified) if three conditions are satisfied.[37]

1. The authority of the sovereign by whose command the war is to be waged. It is not the business of a private individual to declare war, he wrote, because he can seek redress of his rights from a tribunal.

2. A just cause is required, namely that those who are attacked should deserve it on account of some fault.

3. It is necessary that the belligerents should have a rightful intention, so that they intend the advancement of good or the avoidance of evil.

[35] Ibid. (ET pp. 44 & 46).
[36] c. Faust. Man., xxii, para. 76; Letter 138 (ET p. 45).
[37] Summa theologica, II/II, Q. 40, art. 1 (ET London, 1947 ed., ii.1359–60).

Most scholars assume that Thomas was making more explicit what Augustine had written about a just cause being necessary, but one writer finds a difference between them.

While to Augustine the injury itself provides the just cause for war, Thomas Aquinas demands some fault on the part of the wrongdoer: his culpability which deserves punishment is the justifying reason for going to war. The just war is primarily in the nature of a punitive action against the wrongdoer for *his subjective guilt rather than his objectively wrongful act*.[38]

The first explicit requirement in point of time to be added to Thomas's three conditions was that for a war to be just, the ruler ought to be so sure of the degree of his power that he is morally certain of victory. War brings so many evils in its train that it is wicked to cause or permit these evils, and then fail to secure the good ends for which the war is fought.

According to Francisco Suárez (1548–1617), the requirement about certainty of victory had been put forward by Thomas de Vio Cajetan, an Italian Dominican (1469–1534), but Suárez's reference to Cajetan is inaccurate.[39] Suárez considered that Cajetan had been too rigorous in his demand for moral certainty. First, because from a human standpoint, such a degree of certainty is almost impossible of realization. Secondly, because it may be in the interest of a state not to await such certitude, ' but rather to test its ability to conquer the enemy, even when that ability is somewhat doubtful '. Thirdly, because if complete certainty were required, ' a weaker sovereign could never declare war upon a stronger '. Suárez considered that a ruler should avoid an *offensive* war if there was not a ' probable expectation of victory, or one equally balanced as to the chances of victory or defeat '. A *defensive* war might be attempted without such certainty or balance of chances, because in that case ' it is a matter of necessity '.[40]

[38] Joachim von Elbe, ' The Evolution of the Concept of the Just War in International Law ', 33 *AJIL* (1939), 669 (my italics).

[39] Fr Thomas Gilby, OP, tells me that the passage in Cajetan to which Suárez refers does not deal with the Just War doctrine, but with superstitious amulets!

[40] *De triplici virtute theologica: de charitate*, disputation 13, s. 4 (ET G. L. Williams & A. Brown in *Selections from Three Works by . . . Suárez* (Oxford, 1944, repr. New York, 1964), ii.822–3 (in Scott's Classics of Internat. Law)). See also J. B. Scott,

Three further requirements of a Just War were made explicit by a succession of gifted Spanish neo-scholastics, especially the Dominican Francisco de Vitoria [41] (c. 1480–1546) and the Jesuit Suárez.

The first additional requirement was that a serious effort must be made to resolve the matter at issue by peaceful means before resorting to force. Vitoria keeps coming back to the need for caution and prudence. ' Not every kind and degree of wrong can suffice for commencing a war.' Before embarking on war, the ruler must make ' an exceedingly careful examination ' and must listen to the opinions of those who are opposed to going to war. The ruler should reflect that others are his neighbours, whom we are bound to love as ourselves. ' For it is the extreme of savagery to seek for and rejoice in grounds for killing and destroying men whom God has created and for whom Christ died. But only under compulsion and reluctantly should [the ruler] come to the necessity of war.' If a subject is convinced of the injustice of a war, ' he ought not to serve in it, even on the command of the prince '. Vitoria goes even further and insists that those whose conscience is against the justice of a war may not serve in it ' *whether they be right or wrong* ' (my italics).[42]

It might be thought that Vitoria is only emphasizing the requirements of Thomas Aquinas that a just cause and rightful intention are necessary. Suárez, however, carries the argument a stage further. War, he wrote, brings so many misfortunes in its train and is so often carried on in an evil fashion that it requires many justifying circumstances to make it righteous. The only just and sufficient cause is ' a grave injustice which cannot be avenged or repaired in any other way '. Before a

---

' Francisco Suárez: his Philosophy of Law and Sanctions ', 22 *Georgetown LJ* (1934), 405–518; Luis de Molina (1536–1600), *De justitia et jure*, i, treatise 2, disp. 102, quoted in B. Hamilton, *Political Thought in Sixteenth-Century Spain* (Oxford, 1963), p. 145.

[41] J. Scott pointed out that ' in speaking of Francis as a man, his surname is spelled with a " c " . . . whereas in speaking of him as a theologian and jurist, the " c " is eliminated.' *Spanish Origin of International Law: Francisco de Vitoria and his Law of Nations* (Oxford, 1934), p. 70.

[42] *De Indis et de iure belli relectiones*, ss. 14, 20–3, 29, & 60 (ET J. P. Bate, ed. E. Nys, Washington, 1917, repr. New York, 1964), pp. 171, 173, 175, & 187 (in Scott's Classics of Internat. Law); see also Scott, App. B, pp. liv, lvi–vii, lix, lxx.

ruler goes to war, he must call to the attention of the opposing state the existence of a just cause, and must seek suitable reparation. If the other state agrees to make reparation, the ruler ' is bound to accept it, and desist from war, for if he does not do so, the war will be unjust '.[43]

In the light of these requirements, Vitoria and Suárez both raise the question whether a war can be just on both sides. Both answer that, apart from ignorance, this is impossible.[44]

The final requirements relate to the actual conduct of war and comprise two distinct principles: proportion and discrimination. These were implied but not spelled out in the writings of Augustine and Thomas Aquinas. Suárez put it like this: ' The method of its conduct must be proper, and due proportion must be observed at its beginning, during its prosecution and after victory.' [45] When he wrote that the conduct of war should be ' proper ', he mainly had in mind the immunity of the innocent from direct attack, but all writers of the period follow Thomas Aquinas in distinguishing between two effects of an act, one of which is intended, while the other is beside the intention—the law of double effect. ' Now moral acts [wrote Thomas] take their species according to what is intended and not according to what is beside the intention, since this is accidental.' [46]

All Christian theologians agreed that it was unlawful to slay the innocent.[47] Vitoria defined the innocent as including women, children, ' harmless agricultural folk ', ' the rest of the peaceable civilian population ', ' foreigners or guests who are sojourning among the enemy ', clerics, and members of religious orders. Suárez points out that the immunity of religious persons and priests is by canon law; he substitutes ' ambassadors ' for ' foreigners or guests ' (by *jus gentium* rather than natural law); and he adds among those who should be immune ' all unable to bear arms . . . [and] those who are able to bear arms, if it is

---

[43] *De trip. virt.*, ss. 1, 4, 7 (ET pp. 805, 816, 137-8).

[44] Vitoria, *De Indis*, ss. 32 & 35 (ET pp. 177 & 179); Scott, App. V, pp. lx & lxii; Suárez, s. 7 (ET p. 850).

[45] *De trip. virt.*, s. 1 (ET p. 805).

[46] *Summa*, II/II, Q. 64, art. 7 (ET p. 1471).

[47] Ibid. art. 6 (ET p. 1470).

evident that . . . they have not shared in the crime nor in the unjust war '.[48]

The law of double effect was put to some odd purposes in the Middle Ages as, indeed, it is in our own day. Domingo de Soto (1495–1560) held that there were two consequences of self-defence, ' the preservation of one's own life and the destruction of another's, of which the former was intended, the latter was accidental '.[49] But the more usual application has been to say that the killing of enemy *soldiers* is intended, while the accidental killing of *civilians* in the course of military operations is unintended.

The real problem, then as now, was whether it was lawful to engage in a military operation in which the death of innocent people could be *expected*, even though it was not *intended*. The modern version of this question is whether those who hold the Christian version of the Just War doctrine today may, in order to maintain nuclear deterrence, threaten to attack military targets located in or near cities in the knowledge that if deterrence fails and strategic nuclear weapons are used, civilians will be killed as a collateral effect. Paul Ramsey has answered the question in this way: ' Certainly there can be justified destruction of an entire city that is an indirect consequence of the destruction of a military installation. The destruction of a city may be a collateral effect, an accompanying, unavoidable result of bombing military targets.' [50]

Vitoria and Suárez both accept that innocent people may be slain as an indirect effect or collateral circumstance. Vitoria considered that it was permissible to kill innocent people in the course of storming a fortress or city, but this conclusion evidently troubled him, for he added:

Great attention, however, must be paid to the point already taken, namely, the obligation to see that greater evils do not arise out of war than the war would avert. For if little effect upon the ultimate issue of the war is to be expected from the storming of a fortress or

[48] Vitoria, *De Indis*, ss. 13, 35, 36 (ET pp. 170, 178–9); Scott, App. B, pp. liv, lxii; Suárez, *De trip. virt.*, s. 7 (ET pp. 843–50).

[49] *De justitia et jure*, v, qu. 1, art. 8 (ET quoted in Hamilton, p. 137).

[50] In James Finn, *Protest: Pacifism and Politics* (New York, 1968), p. 421; see also Ramsey's ' More Unsolicited Advice to Vatican Council II ', in Finn's *Peace, the Churches and the Bomb* (New York, 1965), esp. pp. 46–7.

fortified town wherein are many innocent folk, it would not be right, for the purpose of assailing a few guilty, to slay the many innocent. . . . In sum, it is never right to slay the guiltless, even as an indirect and unintended result, except when there is no other means of carrying on the operations of a just war. . . .[51]

Vitoria goes on to consider whether it is lawful to kill the innocent from whom some danger is apprehended *in the future*; ' for example, the children of Saracens are guiltless, but there is good reason to fear that when they grow up they will fight against Christians '. He writes that although such killing ' may possibly be defended ', it is in no wise right. It is ' intolerable that any one should be killed for a future fault '. Similarly it is not lawful to kill innocent hostages.[52]

Suárez held that the slaying of the innocent is always illicit. ' No one may be deprived of his life save by reason of his own guilt.' All losses could be inflicted on an enemy ' provided that these . . . do not involve an intrinsic injury to innocent persons, which would be in itself an evil '. The death of innocent people is acceptable only if it is ' not sought for its own sake, but is an incidental consequence '.[53]

A few Catholic writers in the United States have recently questioned whether the principle of non-combatant immunity is an essential part of the Just War doctrine. Dr William O'Brien, for example, argues that the principle that non-combatants are immune from direct intentional attack is not derived from some first principle of natural law, but arose out of the practice of individuals and states in the late medieval and early Renaissance period. The principle was possible, he writes, because of the material facts of war at the time the principle was being made explicit. Strict adherence to it today would mean abandoning both the concept of nuclear deterrence and the possibility of fighting a nuclear war against a nuclear enemy.[54]

Richard Shelly Hartigan has also made the point that non-combatant immunity achieved its present form ' primarily as

[51] *De Indis*, s. 37 (ET p. 179); Scott, App. B, pp. lxii–lxiii.
[52] Ibid., ss. 38 & 43 (ET pp. 179–82); Scott, App. B, pp. lxiii & lxv.
[53] *De trip virt.*, s. 7 (ET pp. 840, 845–6, 848).
[54] See, in particular, his *Nuclear War, Deterrence and Morality* (New York, 1967), pp. 31, 57, 81–3, 85; see also his contribution in Finn, *Protest*, pp. 405–8.

the result of long custom and practice, and only secondarily as the result of deductive moral reasoning '.[55]

O'Brien and Hartigan are a minority, nevertheless, and the weight of opinion is that non-combatant immunity is an integral part of the Just War doctrine. Paul Ramsey would defend the principle not simply because it is implicit in Augustine and Thomas Aquinas, but ' by showing how rooted it is in certain very fundamental principles of moral action '.[56] The principle was reaffirmed by the Second Vatican Council in the following terms: ' Any act of war aimed indiscriminately at the destruction of entire cities or extensive areas along with their population is a crime against God and man himself. It merits unequivocal and unhesitating condemnation.' [57]

The principle of discrimination has in practice meant regarding combatants as guilty and non-combatants as innocent. In insurgency and counter-insurgency warfare, the traditional distinction between soldier and civilian is blurred, and the principle of discrimination is more difficult to apply. Moreover, the invention of weapons of mass destruction introduces a further difficulty, since it is difficult to use these weapons in such a way that only military targets are harmed. Those who believe in the Christian version of the Just War doctrine now lay stress on the second requirement for the conduct of military operations, the principle of proportion. But this is to solve one problem by creating another. What is a proportionate response to the threat of genocide?

Suárez belonged to the generation *after* Luther and Calvin, but the Just War doctrine at the time of the Reformation may be said to have required seven conditions to be satisfied for a war to be justified:

1. War can be decided upon only by the legitimate authorities.
2. War may be resorted to only after a specific fault and if the

[55] ' Noncombatant Immunity: Reflections on its Origins and Present Status ', *R. Politics*, Apr. 1967, pp. 204–20; see also Hartigan's articles ' Saint Augustine on War and Killing: the Problem of the Innocent ', *J. Hist. Ideas*, Apr.–June 1966, pp. 195–204, and ' Noncombatant Immunity: its Scope and Development ', *Continuum*, Autumn 1965, pp. 300–14.

[56] In Finn, *Protest*, p. 423.

[57] Pastoral Constitution on the Church in the Modern World (*Gaudium et Spes*), art. 80, in W. M. Abbott, ed., *Documents of Vatican II* (New York, 1966), p. 294.

purpose is to make reparation for injury or to restore what has been wrongfully seized.

3. The intention must be the advancement of good or the avoidance of evil.

4. In a war other than one strictly in self-defence, there must be a reasonable prospect of victory.

5. Every effort must be made to resolve differences by peaceful means before resorting to the use of force.

6. The innocent shall be immune from direct attack.

7. The amount of force used shall not be disproportionate.

Luther and Calvin

The Christian version of the Just War doctrine entered the Protestant tradition at the time of the Reformation. Luther, like Augustine, was a polemicist and dealt with the problem haphazardly in a series of books, tracts, and sermons, written between 1523 and 1530, with such vivid titles as *Whether soldiers, too, can be saved*. Calvin, in this respect more like Thomas Aquinas, was a systematic thinker and dealt succinctly with the question in a couple of pages of his *Institutes of the Christian Religion* (1536).

Luther with great force, and Calvin with more restraint, start from the assumption that governmental authority is divinely instituted and must be obeyed. The citizen is not bound to obey the ruler if the ruler is in the wrong; but if there arise cases of doubt, and if citizens ' cannot with all diligence find out, they may obey him [the ruler] without peril to their souls '.[58] War should be fought ' at the emperor's command, under his banner, and in his name. Then everyone can be sure in his conscience that he is obeying the ordinance of God.' [59] The magistrate (ruler), wrote Calvin, ' does nothing by himself, but carries out the very judgments of God . . . ; all things are done on the authority of God who commands it '.[60]

Both Calvin and Luther seem to regard as illicit what is

[58] Luther, *Temporal Authority: to what extent it should be obeyed* (1523), in *Luther's Works*, xlv, ed. H. T. Lehmann (ET J. J. Schindel, Philadelphia, 1962), pp. 125–6.
[59] Luther, *On War against the Turk* (1529), ibid. xlvi (ET C. M. Jacobs, rev. R. C. Schultz, Philadelphia, 1967), p. 185.
[60] *Institutes of the Christian Religion*, ed. J. T. McNeill (ET F. L. Battles, London, 1961), iv.20, s. 10, p. 1497.

nowadays called the Just Revolution. Calvin writes that rulers
are ' the guardians and defenders of the laws ' and should overthrow all who seek to undermine the authority of the laws.
Luther maintains that ' war and uprisings against our superiors
[or ' overlords ', as he writes elsewhere] cannot be right'.[61]

Following the Catholic tradition, Luther and Calvin insist
that rulers may resort to war only ' to execute . . . public
vengeance [as Calvin puts it] . . . , to restrain the seditious
stirrings of restless men, to help those forcibly oppressed, to
punish evil deeds . . . , to defend by war the dominions entrusted to their safe-keeping '. Recourse to arms should arise
from ' concern for the people alone '. When men allege that
war is a great plague, wrote Luther, they should consider how
great is the plague that war prevents. It is ' a small misfortune
that prevents a great misfortune '.[62]

Luther expressly makes the point emphasized by the neo-
scholastics on the need to be sure of victory.

If we are not going to make an adequate, honest resistance that will
have some reserve power, it would be far better not to begin a war,
but to yield lands and people . . . without useless bloodshed, rather
than have him [the Turk] win anyhow in an easy battle and with
shameful bloodshed. . . .[63]

Luther and Calvin both insist on the need to seek a peaceful
resolution of disputes before resorting to arms. Calvin warns
the ruler not to seek occasion to take to arms lightly ' unless they
are driven to it by extreme necessity '. Surely, he writes,
' everything else ought to be tried before recourse is had to
arms '.[64]

As to the actual conduct of military operations, Calvin and
Luther give different advice. Calvin warns rulers against
' undue cruelty ' and ' giving vent to their passions '. ' Rather,
if they have to punish, let them not be carried away with head-
long anger, or be seized with hatred, or burn with implacable
severity. Let them also . . . have pity on the common nature in

[61] Ibid. s.11, p. 1499; Luther, *Temporal Authority*, p. 124 and *Whether soldiers, too,
can be saved* (1526), *Luther's Works*, xlvi. 118.
[62] Calvin, *Institutes*, ss. 11 & 12, pp. 1499 & 1501; see also Luther, *Temporal
Authority*, *Works*, xlv.124; *Whether soldiers* . . . , ibid. xlvi.95 f. & 121.
[63] Luther, *War against the Turk*, ibid. pp. 201–2.
[64] Luther, *Temporal Authority*, ibid. xlv.125; Calvin, *Institutes*, s.12, pp. 1501–2.

the one whose special fault they are punishing.' But he also warns against imprudent leniency and quotes a Latin tag to the effect that it is indeed bad to live under a prince with whom nothing is permitted, but much worse under one by whom everything is allowed.[65]

Luther, in more bloodthirsty vein, writes that it is ' both Christian and an act of love to kill the enemy without hesitation, to plunder and burn and injure him by every method of warfare until he is conquered '. Almost as an afterthought, he adds ' except that one must beware of sin, and not violate wives and virgins '.[66]

Both the Reformers accept the need for Christians to bear arms, and Luther urges Christians to offer their services as hangmen, constables, judges, lords, or princes. The profession of the soldier is ' right and godly ', and children are especially urged not to ' despise, reject, or do away with soldiers . . . and those whose business is war '. Every occupation ' has its own honor before God '.[67]

Calvin prefaces his discussion of the problem of war by admitting that it is ' a seemingly hard and difficult question ' since the law of God forbids all Christians to kill. Luther asks why Christ and the apostles did not bear the sword, and answers briskly, ' You tell me, why did Christ not take a wife or become a cobbler or a tailor '.

If an office or vocation were to be regarded as disreputable on the ground that Christ did not pursue it himself, what would become of all the offices and vocations other than ministry, the one occupation he did follow? Christ pursued his own office and vocation, but he did not thereby reject any other.

Although Christ did not bear or prescribe the sword, ' it is sufficient that he did not forbid or abolish it but actually confirmed it '.[68]

The Just War doctrine is today, explicitly or implicitly, the ethical position of almost all non-pacifist Christians, but there has always been a pacifist minority within the Christian

[65] *Institutes*, ss. 10 & 12, pp. 1498–1500.
[66] *Temporal Authority*, xlv.125.
[67] Ibid. p. 95; *Whether soldiers . . .* , xlvi.94; *A sermon on keeping children in school* (1530), xlvi.245–6.
[68] Calvin, *Institutes*, s. 10, p. 1497; Luther, *Temporal Authority*, xlv.100 f.

community. Both the World Council of Churches and the Roman Catholic Church now recognize pacifism as a legitimate Christian position. A Commission appointed by the British Council of Churches reported in 1946 [69]:

Uncompromising obedience to the claims of the kingdom which is not of this world may have a direct political relevance. What the man who thus obeys is asserting is that there are standards of conduct which the State exists to protect and foster, and which for that reason it may not ask to be cast aside in a conflict of naked power. The possibility that an uncalculating refusal to have anything to do with methods of warfare involving wholesale massacre, and the acceptance of the political consequences arising out of such a refusal, is a duty demanded of us by the present historical crisis.

At the first Assembly of the World Council of Churches in 1948, three positions held by Christians were outlined: there is a duty to maintain the rule of law, by force if necessary; ' modern warfare, with its mass destruction, can never be an act of justice ' (a form of nuclear pacifism) [70]; the refusal of all military service as ' an absolute witness against war and for peace ' (total pacifism). The Assembly admitted its ' deep sense of perplexity in the face of these conflicting opinions ' and by implication accepted that any of the three is legitimate for Christians. [71]

The Second Vatican Council noted that if the kind of instruments which can now be found in the armouries of the great nations were to be employed to their fullest extent,

an almost total and altogether reciprocal slaughter of each side by the other would follow, not to mention the widespread devastation which would take place in the world and the deadly aftereffects which would be spawned by these weapons. *All these considerations compel us to undertake an evaluation of war with an entirely new attitude* [my italics].

The Council, in addition to stating and elaborating the Just War position, praised ' those who renounce the use of violence in the vindication of their rights . . . provided that this can be

[69] *Era of Atomic Power* (London, 1946), p. 53.
[70] This was the position adopted by the General Synod of the Netherlands Reformed Church in June 1962.
[71] *First Assembly of the World Council of Churches*, ed. Visser 't Hooft (London, 1949), p. 89.

done without injury to the rights and duties of others or of the community itself'. The Council thought it right that the law should 'make humane provisions for the case of those who for reasons of conscience refuse to bear arms, provided however, that they accept some other form of service to the human community'.[72]

More recently, a number of churches and ecumenical bodies have declared themselves in favour of 'selective' conscientious objection. An expert conference held in Austria in 1970 and reporting jointly to the World Council of Churches and the Pontifical Commission for Justice and Peace had this to say.

The right of conscientious objection also extends to those who are unwilling to serve in a particular war because they consider it unjust or because they refuse to participate in a war or conflict in which weapons of mass destruction are likely to be used. . . . Members of the armed forces have the right and even the duty, to refuse to obey military orders which may involve the commission of criminal offences, or of war crimes or of crimes against humanity.

The same wording was approved by an Inter-Faith Conference on Religion and Peace held in Japan later in 1970.[73]

William Penn's 'Holy Experiment'

What the man in the street wants to know, however, is not whether pacifism is a legitimate position for a Christian, but whether it works. Some pacifists would claim no more than that pacifism is right; probably the majority of pacifists see pacifism as a practicable policy, and indeed the early Quakers tried to build a state on pacifist principles in Pennsylvania—what William Penn and his fellow Quakers called 'The Holy Experiment'.

Penn wished to return to the 'purity' of the early Church,[74] but not by withdrawing from politics. 'True godliness', he

[72] Pastoral Constitution on the Church in the Modern World, arts. 78–80 (Abbott, pp. 290–3).

[73] Peace—The Desperate Imperative (Geneva, 1970), pp. 57–8; Findings of the World Conference on Religion and Peace (New Delhi, Gandhi Peace Foundation, n.d.), p. 41.

[74] See e.g. his writings Quakerism a New Nickname for Old Christianity . . . (1672) and Primitive Christianity Revived . . . (1696).

once wrote, ' don't turn men out of the world, but enables them
to live better in it, and excites their endeavours to mend it.' [75]
His policy received its first major test in 1689—a request that
Pennsylvania should make preparations for defence. The
initial reaction of the Quaker members of the Council was to
belittle the gravity of the threat. Said John Simcock, ' I see no
danger but from the Bears and wolves '. When the issue could
no longer be evaded, the Quakers decided to state their personal attitudes as a matter of conscience and to abstain from
voting, but Simcock made it clear that they did not want to
tie the hands of others; ' they may do every One what they
please '. [76]

In 1693, when the English Crown had resumed control over
Pennsylvania, there came a request for funds for the defence of
New York, but Governor Benjamin Fletcher agreed that those
who had scruples about supporting war could give money which
might be used for other purposes and ' not be dipt in blood '. [77]
The Assembly refused to vote funds until other matters had
been attended to, but in the end a money bill was
approved.

Menwhile, Penn was struggling in London to have Pennsylvania restored to him. He promised that he would transmit
to the Council and the Assembly of the colony all messages
from the English Crown, and he said that he had no doubt that
the colony would supply such men or money as the Crown considered necessary for the safety of America. In 1694 Pennsylvania was restored to Penn.

Requests for money or men continued to trouble the Penn-
sylvanian Quakers. In 1695 the General Assembly in the colony
said they would vote funds only if a new constitution were
adopted, whereupon Fletcher dissolved the two Houses. In
1696 £300 was voted in the expectation that it would be used
to buy food and clothes for distressed Indians. The following
year Pennsylvania was asked to supply 80 men or £2,000 for

[75] Quoted in Soc. of Friends, *Christian Faith and Practice in the Experience of the
Society of Friends* (London, 1960), extract 395.

[76] *Minutes of the Provincial Council of Pennsylvania* (Philadelphia, 1852), i.299, 300,
306, 309 ff.

[77] Ibid. p. 400.

the defence of New York, but a joint committee of the two
Houses replied by drawing attention to the fact that they had
contributed £300 the previous year.[78]

In 1709, the issue arose once again, and the Quakers held
an informal meeting to decide their attitude: '. . . notwithstanding their profession and principles would not by any means
allow them to bear arms; yet it was their duty to support the
Govmt of their Sovereign the Queen . . . and therefore that
they might and ought to present the Queen with a proper sum
of money.'[79] £500 was appropriated, which led to a sharp
response from Governor Charles Gookin: 'Words alone, I
assure you, Gent., are not much valued by the ministry at
Home, and £500 from Pennsylvania will add . . . but little
weight.' The Quakers might have scruples about war, he said,
but that should not prevent them from being generous in their
gifts to the Queen. No conscience could be pleaded to prevent
the grant of a sum 'in some measure worthy of Her Royal
acceptance'.[80]

What is an ad hoc decision the first time it is taken easily
becomes a precedent. When money was requested for military
purposes, the first reaction of Friends in Pennsylvania was to
deny that the situation was dangerous. When this argument had
exhausted its utility, Friends claimed that the measures con-
templated were provocative. If a request for funds were
persisted in, they said that their grievances should be considered
first, or that it was inconvenient for the Assembly to meet, or
simply that they could not afford the money. When prevarica-
tion would no longer suffice, funds were usually voted, at first
on the understanding that they would not be used for military
purposes, but after 1709 simply as a present for Queen Anne
or King George.

The attitude of Friends to military service is illustrated by a
phrase which occurs several times in the laws of Pennsylvania:
'the people called Quakers who, though they do not, as the

[78] Ibid. p. 520 ii.35, 40–1; *Pennsylvania Archives*, 1st ser., i.192.
[79] *Minutes PC*, ii.449, 452, 459, 463, 466–7; *Penn. Arch.*, ii.857–81; *Memoirs
Hist. Soc. Penn.*, x: Corresp. of Penn & Logan (Philadelphia, 1872), pp. 346,
349–50.
[80] *Minutes PC*, ii.459, 460, & 462.

world is now circumstanced, condemn the use of arms in others, yet are principled against it themselves.' [81]

A bare recital of selected facts about Pennsylvania may give a false impression. The Holy Experiment is remembered for its pioneering achievements in such matters as religious toleration, respect for the rights of the Indians, and a humane penal system. But Pennsylvania could not be isolated from the external situation. The colony posed no threat to others, but the Quakers of that day learned, as each generation has learned since, that their task is not to create a peaceable kingdom as a sanctuary into which to escape from the wars and rumours of wars which threaten the rest of mankind. The clear implication of Penn's essay *Towards the Present and Future Peace of Europe* (1693) is that pacifism is not enough. Men must also build the institutions of peace.

[81] Ibid. iv.366 (1739); *Penn. Arch.* ii.516 (1755).

THE JUST WAR IN INTERNATIONAL LAW

> *All things are uncertain the moment men depart from law. . . . War ought not to be undertaken except for the enforcement of rights; when once undertaken, it should be carried on only within the bounds of law and good faith. . . . In order that wars may be justified, they must be carried on with not less scrupulousness than judicial processes are wont to be.*
>
> Hugo Grotius

Hugo Grotius: the father of international law

' The modern law of nations of which Vitoria was the expounder, Suárez the philosopher, and Grotius the systematizer.' [1] It is, indeed, hardly possible to exaggerate the contribution which Hugo Grotius made to the foundation of international law as a subject in its own right, worthy of academic study, distinct from moral theology, and with immediate practical applications in the relations between states. He was a great innovator, not because he disregarded the work of his predecessors and contemporaries, but because he brought their disparate work into coherent relationship. His work to mitigate the practices of warfare ' came to have a great influence in furthering the development of civilised usages and customs '.[2] He was a man of extraordinary scholarship, and in his work on the law of war and peace—*De jure belli ac pacis* [3]—he cites or quotes from the works of Greek, Roman, and Jewish classical writers: Homer, Herodotus, Euripides, Thucydides, Xenophon, Isocrates, Plato, Aristotle, Demosthenes, Polybius, Cicero, Sallust, Virgil, Horace, Strabo, Livy, Ovid, Philo, Seneca, both Plinys, Josephus, Plutarch, and Tacitus. He quotes from fifty-two of the Bible's

[1] Scott in 22 *Georgetown LJ* (1934), 407.

[2] G. I. A. D. Draper, *The Christian and War*, reprinted from *International Relations* and distributed by the Mothers' Union (London, n.d.).

[3] ET F. W. Kelsey & others, Oxford, 1925, sponsored by CEIP in Scott's Classics of Internat. Law; reprinted New York, 1964.

seventy-five books, as well as from the Apocrypha. He wrote a commentary on St Paul's Epistle to Philemon. He was fully acquainted with the writings of the early fathers of the Church: Justin Martyr, Tertullian, Origen, Lactantius, Eusebius, Sts Ambrose, Jerome, John Chrysostom, and Augustine. He was also steeped in the writings of the schoolmen and quotes St Thomas, Cajetan, Domingo de Soto, and Luis de Molina, and he mentions in particular that among the theological works he had studied were those of Vitoria.[4] He refers more than once to the writings of his Spanish Catholic contemporary Suárez, and he tells us that he had obtained the works of Ayala and Gentilis. He was a Protestant, belonging to a moderate Calvinist group, but it is noteworthy that he does not quote from the writings of Calvin or Luther. He warns his readers against the dangers of receiving with approval everything written by famous authors; often they are simply under the influence of their feelings. But ' when the schoolmen agree on a point of morals, it rarely happens that they are wrong '.[5]

Grotius wrote in a way that both shocked and fascinated the traditionalists, for he was a man of independent judgement. He did not look for authority in a church or creed or political ideology, but in the conscience of the individual. His *De jure belli ac pacis* was first published in Paris in 1625. It was on the Roman Catholic Index from 1626 to 1896, but within a century of its first publication, Dutch, French, German, and English translations had appeared. The Latin text, with an abridged English translation by William Whewell, was published by the Cambridge University Press in 1853, but I have used the full (1925) translation published for the Carnegie Endowment for International Peace.

The reason why Grotius wrote this remarkable book was, as he correctly expressed it, that before his time ' no one has treated [the mutual relations among states or rulers of states] in a comprehensive and systematic manner '. These relations he considered were governed by two distinct systems of law,

---

[4] *JBP, Prolegomena*, para. 37. A pamphlet edition of the *Prolegomena* was published in 1957.

[5] *JBP, Proleg.*, para. 52; 1, 3, 5, 6 (the figures standing for book, chapter, section, & para.).

which ' writers everywhere confuse '. First, there is the law of
nature, natural law, which is based on right reason; secondly,
there is the law of nations, which is derived from the law of
nature. This law of nations has received its obligatory force
' from the will of all nations, or of many nations '. Grotius
considered that the very fact of the possibility of a *law of nations*
proved the existence of *the law of nature*. What he wrote ' would
have a degree of validity even if we should concede . . . that
there is no God, or that the affairs of men are of no concern to
Him '.⁶

Grotius also recognizes a third system of law, municipal law,⁷
but he sometimes confuses the reader by referring in addition to
what he calls ' The Law of the Gospel '.⁸

In his early years Grotius had been concerned with a case
before the Prize Court involving the Dutch East India Com-
pany, some of whose members were Mennonites. The Mennonites were then, and are today, pacifists, rejecting all use of
force. From his contact with these worthy people, Grotius
realized that any serious study of the law of war written by a
Christian must come to grips with the question whether it is
possible to wage war without violating Christian principles.
The *practice* of the majority of Christians might have provided
him with a sufficient answer, for Christians seemed to have no
greater scruples about going to war, or about the methods of
waging it, than pagans or adherents of other faiths. Indeed, this
was something which greatly shocked Grotius.

Throughout the Christian world I observed a lack of restraint in
relation to war. . . . I observed that men rush to arms for slight
causes, or no cause at all, and that when once arms have been taken
up there is no longer any respect for law . . . ; it is as if, in accordance
with a general decree, frenzy had openly been let loose for the committing of all crimes.

When good men are confronted with such ruthlessness, he
writes, they are likely to go to the other extreme and forbid all
use of force. If things go too far in one direction, men go to the

⁶ *JBP, Proleg.*, paras 1, 11, 40, & 46; 1, 1, 14, 1.

⁷ *JBP, Proleg.*, para. 41; 1, 1, 14; 2, 2, 5; 2, 5, 7; 2, 14, 7; 2, 14, 8; 3, 9, 10 &
17; 3, 18, 1.

⁸ See e.g. *JBP*, 1, 2, 7–8; 1, 3, 3; 2, 1, 13; 2, 5, 9.

opposite extreme, hoping that this will lead to ' a true middle ground '. He feared that his fellow countryman Erasmus had yielded to this temptation. Grotius was too wise to think that the truth lay at the mid point between extreme opinions.

The very effort of pressing too hard in the opposite direction . . . does harm, because in such arguments the detection of what is extreme is easy, and results in weakening the influence of other statements which are well within the bounds of truth. For both extremes therefore a remedy must be found, that men may not believe that nothing is allowable, or that everything is.[9]

In order to consider the question of the use of force as a matter of Christian ethics, Grotius goes back to the time of Christ and the experience of the early Church. When soldiers came to John the Baptist, ' he did not bid them withdraw from military service, as he must have done if such was the will of God '. If it had been Christ's purpose absolutely to do away with capital punishment and war, ' he would have expressed this purpose with words as plain and explicit as possible '. The reason Christ rebuked Peter for using a sword against Malchus at the time of his arrest was that ' he [Peter] was taking up arms against those who were coming as representatives of the public authority ' [10]—a more plausible explanation than St Augustine's!

Grotius insists that, for the Christian, a greater degree of moral perfection is required than those things enjoined by the law of nature only. The law of the gospel makes it impermissible for the Christian to use force in personal self-defence, ' for Christ bids us submit to a blow rather than do harm to an aggressor '. No true Christian should, of his own accord, enter upon a public office which may require him to have to decide upon the shedding of blood, for Christian goodness is manifested by seizing every opportunity to show mercy.[11]

Grotius does not deny that the early Church was pacifist. ' The early Christians, fresh from the teachings of the Apostles . . . , both understood the Christian rules of conduct better, and lived up to them more fully, than did men of later times.'

[9] *Proleg.*, paras 28–9.
[10] 1, 2, 7, 5; 1, 2, 8, 2; 1, 3, 3, 7.
[11] *Proleg.*, para. 50; 2, 1, 10, 1; 2, 20, 16; 1, 2, 9, 10.

Little by little, he writes, the interpretation of the law of the gospel was adjusted to the customs of the age, and by the time of Constantine, there is no lack of writers who hold the opinion that Christians may lawfully resort to war. Many bishops were very alert guardians of discipline, but ' we do not read that there was a single one who . . . sought to deter either Constantine from inflicting the death penalty and engaging in war, or Christians from military service '.[12]

But ' it was not the intention of Grotius to furnish a System of Ethics ' [13]; he was asking what can be learned from the law of nature and the law of nations about the relations between states and rulers. Grotius takes it for granted that the intentional killing of an innocent person is forbidden; ' it is necessary that he who is killed shall himself have done wrong '. Grotius then asks if there are any exceptions to the general prohibition of taking human life, if it is ' ever lawful ', or ' ever permissible ' to wage war. Grotius answers his own question by saying that it is permissible to use force ' as a just penalty or in case we are able in no other way to protect our life or property '. Such force may be used only in such a way that it ' does not violate the rights of others '. Not all wars, he writes cautiously, are at variance with the law of nature, ' and this may also be said to be true of the law of nations '.[14]

Like the schoolmen, Grotius assumes that a war of self-defence is justified, that a state may respond with force if attacked. ' The right of self-defence . . . has its origin . . . in the fact that nature commits to each his own protection.' [15]

Three other causes are given which may make a war just. First, ' for the enforcement of rights '.[16] Secondly, to seek reparation for injury.[17] Thirdly, to punish the wrong-doer.[18] Yet not every wicked act should necessarily be punished;

[12] 1, 4, 7, 9; 2, 1, 13, 2; 1, 2, 9, 5 & 9. What Grotius wrote may be technically correct, but there were many leading Christians who were faithful to the pacifism of the early Church at the time of Constantine.

[13] Whewell in his introduction (see p. 25 above).

[14] *JBP*, 1, ch. 2 & 1, 1, 1, 1; 3, 11, 2; 1, 2, 1, 6; 1, 2, 4, 1.

[15] 2, 1, 3.

[16] *Proleg.*, para. 25.

[17] 2, 1, 1, 4; 2, 1, 2, 1; 2, 2, 1.

[18] 2, 1, 2, 1; 2, 15, 38; 2, 20, 1, 1; 2, 20, 39, 4.

' many reasons . . . admonish us to forgo punishments '. There may be occasions when ' to refrain from the exercise of one's right is not merely praiseworthy but even obligatory, by reason of the love which we owe even to men who are our enemies '. Love for our neighbour often prevents us from pressing our right to the utmost limit. The obligation to forgive rests upon us with special weight ' when either we too are conscious . . . ourselves of some sin, or when the sin committed against us is the result of some human and pardonable weakness, or when it is sufficiently clear that he who has wronged us is repentant '. All these reasons for leniency have their origin in ' the love which we owe to our enemies '. In any case, there should always be a prudent calculation of likely consequences. If a particular course of action is likely to have both good and bad consequences, ' it is to be chosen only if the good has somewhat more of good than the evil has of evil ' [19]—which is to ask a lot of mere mortals! Moreover, Grotius adds two further warnings. First, there may exist a just cause for going to war, but the war may be unjust because of the wrong intention of the one who engages in hostilities.[20] Secondly, a war may be undertaken for a just cause, but may become unjust because it gives rise to unjust acts.[21]

Grotius follows the majority of medieval theologians by holding that morally a war cannot be just on both sides, except where ignorance is present, but he distinguishes between ethical justice and legal justice. Many things are done ' without right and yet without guilt '. If the word ' just ' is considered in relation to its legal consequences, however, it must be admitted that a war may be just from the point of view of either side.[22]

A war is not just unless it has been sanctioned by the lawful authorities on both sides, and it is also ' necessary . . . that it should be publicly declared ' and proclaimed by one of the parties to the other. The reason why public declarations are required is to avoid resort to war to settle private quarrels. The

[19] 2, 24, 2, 1 & 3; 2, 24, 3, 3; 2, 24, 5, 2 & 3; 3, 1, 4, 2.
[20] 2, 22, 17, 1.
[21] 3, 10, 3.
[22] 2, 23, 13.

twin requirements of the sanction of the lawful authorities and public declarations of war must both be satisfied; ' one without the other does not suffice '.[23]

A prudent ruler will not go to war without a reasonable expectation of victory. Even if the cause is right, it is of the highest importance that the necessary resources should be available. Even if one has made a commitment to an ally, one is not ' bound to render aid if there is no hope of a successful issue '. War ought not to be undertaken ' save when the hope of gain [is] greater than the fear of loss '.[24]

Military alliances are permissible, but not of an unconditional character. Aid should not be rendered ' for any sort of war without distinction of cause ', and it is not permissible to entice or force anyone to anything which it may not be permissible for him to do. A war formally declared against a ruler is declared at the same time against ' all his subjects ' and ' all who will join him as allies '.[25]

Peace is to be highly valued, ' especially by Christians '. Throughout the whole period of war, the soul can be kept serene and trusting in God only if it is always looking forward to peace.[26]

Grotius is reluctant to concede that there can be a just revolution comparable to a just war, except where judicial procedures are not available. It is

much more consistent with moral standards, and more conducive to the peace of individuals, that a matter be judicially investigated by one who has no personal interest in it, than that individuals, too often having only their own interests in view, should seek by their own hands to obtain that which they consider right. . . .

It is not permissible ' for either private or official persons to wage war against those under whose authority they are ', although if the lawful authorities issue an order which is contrary to the law of nature or the commandments of God, it should not be carried out. It is not even permissible for a private citizen to put down by force or kill a usurper of sovereign power,

[23] 1, 3, 1, 1; 3, 3, 5 & 11.
[24] 2, 24, 9; 2, 25, 4, & 2, 25, 7, 1.
[25] 2, 25, 9, 1; 3, 1, 21; 3, 3, 9.
[26] 3, 15, 2 & 3.

except where the usurper has seized power by means of an unlawful war and contrary to the law of nations, and ' no promise
has been given to him, but possession is maintained by force
alone '. It is a weighty question how to choose between independence and peace, between life and liberty, but private
individuals ought not to take it upon themselves to decide such
a question, since it involves the interest of the whole people.
Even when the right of sovereignty is in dispute, the private
citizen should ' accept the fact of possession '. Grotius points
out that although the administration of the Roman Empire
was often in the hands of extremely bad men, and there was no
lack of pretenders who sought to rescue the state, the early
Christians ' never associated themselves with [these] attempts '.
Those who from a lawful cause have come into personal or
political slavery ' ought to be satisfied with their state '. But he
allows one exception: ' Peoples . . . and divisions of peoples,
are to be restored to those who had the right of dominion over
them, *or even to themselves* [if they have been unjustly taken over
by the enemy] ' (my italics).[27]

A ruler desirous of winning friends should strive for a reputation for having undertaken war ' not rashly nor unjustly ' and
of having waged it in ' a manner above reproach '. A nation
is not foolish which does not press its own advantage to the
point of disregarding the law common to all nations, for no
state is so powerful that it may not some time need the help of
others. The state which transgresses the laws of nature and of
nations cuts away the bulwarks which safeguard its own future
peace.[28]

Grotius devotes a great deal of attention to the immunity of
the innocent, and his list of those he regards as innocent is a
long one. It includes children, women (unless they have committed a crime which ought to be punished), old men, all those
whose manner of life is opposed to war such as those performing
religious duties and ' those who direct their energies to literary
pursuits ', farmers, merchants, artisans and other workmen,
prisoners of war, and neutrals. Military commanders are to

[27] 1, 3, 1, 1; 1, 3, 2, 1; 1, 4, 1, 2–3; 1, 4, 5, 1; 1, 4, 15, 1; 1, 4, 16; 1, 4, 19, 1–2;
1, 4, 20; 2, 22, 11; 2, 24, 6, 2; 3, 16, 4.
[28] *Proleg.*, paras 18 & 27.

forbid plundering and 'the violent sack of cities and other similar actions' which cannot take place without harming many innocent people.[29]

Grotius accepts the law of double effect as it had been formulated by St Thomas; 'many things follow indirectly, and beyond the purpose of the doer'. Thus it is permissible to bombard a ship full of pirates or a house full of brigands, even if innocent women and children are thereby endangered. At the same time, we must take care regarding what happens beyond our purpose, 'unless the good which our action has in view is much greater than the evil which is feared, or, unless the good and the evil balance'. In all cases of doubt, we should favour that course which has regard for the interest of another rather than our own.[30]

Among the methods of war which Grotius considers to be expressly forbidden are the use of poison, the use of falsehood or deception, except perhaps to save the life of an innocent person, of deliberate terrorism, and attacks on 'things of artistic value [and] things which have been devoted to sacred uses', including 'structures erected in honour of the dead'. Also forbidden is the harming or killing of hostages. A hostage may try to escape, unless he has given a pledge not to do so in order that he might have more liberty, but prisoners captured in a just war should not try to escape.[31] Rape is contrary to the law 'not of all nations, but of the better ones'. Among Christians, rape should be subject to punishment, even in time of war.[32]

It is not permissible to injure or kill to prevent a future offence, unless the danger to life or property is 'immediate and imminent in point of time'. Those who accept fear of any sort as justifying 'anticipatory slaying' are greatly deceived, and deceive others; while it is permissible to kill him who is making ready to kill, yet the man is more worthy of praise who prefers to be killed rather than to kill. It is quite untenable to take up arms against a power which, if it becomes too great in the

[29] 2, 1, 4, 1; 3, 11, 8–15; 3, 12, 8, 4; 3, 17, 1; 3, 18, 4.

[30] 3, 1, 4.

[31] 2, 21, 12; 3, 1, 18; 3, 4, 15–17; 3, 11, 16, 1; 3, 11, 18, 1; 3, 12, 6–7; 3, 14, 7; 3, 20, 53 & 54.

[32] 3, 1, 16; 3, 4, 19, 1–2.

future, may be a source of danger. The idea that the possibility of being attacked confers the right to attack (a pre-emptive strike) is ' abhorrent to every principle of equity '. Fear of an uncertainty cannot confer the right to resort to force. For protection from uncertain dangers, we must rely on ' Divine Providence and on a wariness free from reproach, not on force '. As for vengeance ' not as a retaliation for the past, but as a preventive for the future ', Christ wishes us to forgo this. ' Nature does not sanction retaliation except against those who have done wrong.' [33]

In a just war, he who takes booty from the enemy becomes its owner ' without limit or restriction '; but in an unjust war, things taken must be restored. Individual soldiers who capture anything acquire it for themselves ' when they are not in formation or engaged in executing an order '. But Grotius again insists that ' the rules of love are broader than the rules of law '. Humanity requires that those who do not share in the guilt of a particular war should be left with their possessions ' particularly if it is quite clear that they will not recover from their own state what they have lost '.[34]

Those rulers who decide to stay out of a war have an obligation to be impartial and, in particular, to avoid increasing the power of him who supports a wicked cause. There are advantages in having one's neutral status recognized by treaty.[35]

A truce does not end a state of war; it is ' an agreement by which warlike acts are for a time abstained from . . . , a period of rest in war, not a peace '. During a truce, all acts of war are unlawful. If one party violates a truce, the other party is ' free to take up arms even without declaring war '.[36]

Although, according to the law of nations, prisoners of war become slaves, both Christians ' among themselves ' and Moslems ' among themselves ' have agreed that prisoners shall not become slaves but shall be exchanged, or freed when an appropriate ransom has been paid or some other agreement has been reached. Innocent prisoners are not to be killed or

[33] 2, 1, 5; 2, 1, 8; 2, 1, 17; 2, 1, 18, 1; 2, 20, 10, 6; 2, 20, 39, 4; 3, 11, 16, 2–3.
[34] 3, 6, 2, 1; 3, 6, 12, 2; 3, 6, 21, 3; 3, 13, 4, 1–2; 3, 16, 1, 1.
[35] 3, 17, 3, 1 & 3.
[36] 3, 21, 1 & 2; 3, 21, 6, 1; 3, 21, 11.

punished with undue severity, nor are tasks to be imposed upon them which are excessively severe.[37]

Those who go to war without a just cause deserve punishment, but they shall not be executed unless they have committed a crime which a just judge would hold punishable by death. Collective punishments are forbidden. ' It is not sufficient that by a sort of fiction the enemy . . . be conceived as forming a single body '. On the other hand, responsibility for a wicked act does not rest solely on him who ordered it; responsibility is shared with those who granted it the necessary consent, or who helped it, or who furnished asylum, or who actually shared in committing the crime, or who gave advice, or praise, or approval, or who did not forbid it, or who failed to help the injured, or who did not dissuade when they ought to have done so, or who concealed facts which they ought to have made known—' all these may be punished, if there is in them evil intent sufficient to deserve punishment '. Like Augustine and Thomas, Grotius attaches importance to the intention behind an act, as well as to its intrinsic nature and likely consequences.[38]

In all these matters, Grotius insists on the supreme authority of the individual conscience. If an act is objectively just but the person who commits it considers it to be unjust, ' the act is vicious '. If those who are ordered to go to war consider that the cause is unjust, ' they should altogether refrain '.[39]

Indeed, Grotius is constantly advising moderation and magnanimity. It is better to acquit a guilty person than condemn one who is innocent. War is such a serious matter that the ruler should not be content with ' merely acceptable causes ' but only ' causes that are perfectly evident '. War is so horrible that ' only the utmost necessity, or true affection ', can render it honourable. It is better to neglect care of our own lives in order to safeguard the life of another. Moderation is often an act of prudence. Even those who deserve punishment should be treated ' with goodness, with moderation, with highmindedness '. A conquered enemy should be shown clemency. When

[37] 3, 7, 1, 1; 3, 7, 9; 3, 14, 3 & 4; 3, 14, 5, 1; 3, 14, 9, 1.
[38] 2, 21, 1, 2; 2, 22, 17, 1; 3, 1, 3; 3, 11, 16.
[39] 1, 4, 1, 3; 2, 23, 2, 1; 2, 26, 3, 1; 3, 1, 21.

crimes have been committed which deserve death, ' it will be
the part of mercy to give up something of one's full right
because of the [large] number of those involved '. We should
consider not only ' what the laws of men permit ' but also
' what is right from the point of view of religion and morals '.
Those displays of strength which are of no use for obtaining a
right or putting an end to war ' are incompatible both with the
duty of a Christian and with humanity itself'. Moderation
' gives the appearance of great assurance of victory '.[40]

Grotius was writing a treatise on the law of war *and peace*,
and much that he has to say about the law of peace lies outside
the scope of the present work. Suffice it to note that Grotius
considers how war may be avoided by creating the appropriate
institutions for the peaceful settlement of disputes. Three ways
of avoiding war are reviewed: a conference (that is to say,
direct negotiations), arbitration, or decision by lot. ' Where
judicial settlement fails, war begins.' [41]

The whole structure of international law depends upon agreements being honoured, which is ' a rule of the law of nature '.
' Faith must be kept even with the faithless.' Whatever may be
the terms on which peace is made, they ought to be preserved
absolutely. If differences arise regarding the interpretation of
an agreement, we should not depart from the natural meaning
of the words, except to avoid an absurdity.[42]

Much could be written by way of commentary on this
fascinating treatise, but I will confine myself to two remarks.
First, Grotius does not fail to remind his readers of the perfectionism of ' Sermon on the Mount ' Christianity. For thirteen
centuries, this emphasis has been confined to a few utopian
sects, while the mainstream of Christian theology had been
more concerned with accommodating ' the law of the gospel '
to the requirements of the secular world. Yet here was Grotius,
a Christian and a humanist, a man of the world, a professional
bureaucrat, formulating a theory of international law ' from

[40] 2, 23, 5, 1; 2, 23, 13, 4; 2, 14, 1, 1; 2, 25, 9, 3; 3, 11, 7, 1 & 4; 3, 11, 17 & 19;
3, 12, 8, 2; 3, 15, 7, 1; 3, 15, 12, 1.
[41] 2, 1, 2, 1; 2, 23, 7–9; 3, 20, esp. 46–7.
[42] *Proleg.*, para. 15; 3, 14, 13; 3, 23, 11; 3, 25, 7.

an entirely secular point of view ' [43] and yet constantly re-
iterating the need to love the enemy, to give him the benefit of
the doubt, to be killed rather than to kill.

Secondly, the work of Grotius has well stood the test of time.
Three and a half centuries later, the main thrust of his book is
commonplace among international lawyers. There are, of
course, aspects where the work of Grotius has been elaborated
or refined or overtaken by events. Perhaps he should have taken
a stronger line against looting. Perhaps he should have paid
more attention to the problem of reprisals. In an age which
emphasizes ' the inadmissibility of the acquisition of territory
by war ',[44] perhaps Grotius gives too much weight to the fact
of possession. His discussion of what is now called ' the just
revolution ' is perhaps too much influenced by his passion for
order and certainty. But criticism of particular defects does not
detract from the seminal value of the work as a whole.

Total war and absolute weapons

It is impossible, within the scope of this book, to survey even
in the most sketchy form the way others have built on the
foundations laid by Hugo Grotius. His main contribution was to
secularize what, until his day, had been considered to be in
theory a matter of moral theology or Christian ethics, but a
matter in which practice had increasingly disregarded theory.
In any event, there are two respects in which technical developments during the past century have made it increasingly
difficult to apply one of the main principles which Grotius had
taken over unaltered from Christian teaching: the idea that
' the innocent ' should be immune from direct attack, ' the
innocent ' comprising all those who take no direct part in the
actual conduct of hostilities.

The first development was that of total war, the idea that
entire populations should be mobilized in the war effort, the
transformation of war ' from a contest between aristocracies
into a struggle of peoples '.[45] Wartime armies in the so-called

[43] Ernst Troeltsch, *Social Teaching of the Christian Churches* (first published in
Germany in 1911), trans. Olive Wyon (New York, 1960), ii.636.

[44] SC res.242 (S/8247), 22 Nov. 1967.

[45] A/C.3/SR.1780 (mimeo.), 5 Nov. 1970, p. 16.

developed countries are formed by conscripting all those who are physically fit and not engaged in activities essential to the war effort. In this century, conscription has been applied to women as well as to men. The productive capacity of the community is geared wholly to winning the war, or at least avoiding defeat. Government-controlled propaganda is directed towards the unity of the national effort and towards under-mining the will of the enemy. Party politics, normally regarded as essential to the democratic system, are put into cold storage for the duration of the war, so that the energies of the nation may be fully concentrated on military victory. If territory is occupied by the enemy, underground resistance movements operate under cover of normality. Brave men and women infiltrate into enemy society to disrupt essential activities or to stiffen the will of the underground movement to continue resistance. So-called fifth columns prepare the way for a take-over of further territory.

In situations of this kind, what happens to the traditional distinction between civilian and combatant, innocent and guilty? It is only too easy to assume that the adversary is not the enemy's armed forces, but his whole society. And if his whole society is the adversary, it is argued, his whole society becomes a legitimate target for attack. If this results in injury to those who are unquestionably ' innocent ', such as young babies, this is justified by recourse to the law of double effect: the harm done to ' the innocent ' was not intended, even though it was expected and indeed inevitable.

During the past generation, what had become increasingly acceptable in international armed conflicts has become commonplace in internal wars, in wars of national liberation, in insurgency and counter-insurgency. Thus we have the phenomenon of the man or woman, even the child, who is a peasant by day and a guerrilla fighter by night.[46]

Accompanying this trend towards total war has been the invention of absolute weapons, by which I mean weapons which by their nature (range and power) have no military function except to threaten, or if necessary use, against enemy cities.

[46] Wolfgang von Weise, ' Terror als Methode Moderner Kriegführung ', *Allgemeine Schweiz. Militärzeitschrift*, Aug. 1969, pp. 437–47.

Even before the discovery of nuclear power and long-range missiles, this ability to attack enemy cities had made modern war different in kind, and not simply in degree, from the traditional war between professional volunteer armies about which Sts Augustine and Thomas, and Grotius, had written. ' The most radical and significant change of all in modern warfare ', wrote Father John Ford in 1944, ' is . . . the enormously increased power of the armed forces to reach behind the lines and attack civilians indiscriminately.' [47] It is not denied that both sides during the second world war resorted to terror-bombing against civilians, and one writer claimed in 1945 that the traditional distinction between combatant and non-combatant had been ' so whittled down by the demands of military necessity ' that it had become ' more apparent than real '.[48] When the decision had to be made about the first use of nuclear weapons, the advice offered to President Truman by a group of ' exceptionally thoughtful and humane men ', which included Henry Stimson and George Marshall, was to use the first nuclear weapon as soon as possible against a previously undamaged Japanese city containing ' a military installation surrounded by houses ' and without explicit prior warning (advice of the Interim Committee of the US War Department after its meetings on 31 May and 1 June 1945).[49] The current doctrine of nuclear deterrence includes a conditional intention to use nuclear weapons against enemy cities.

To make a threat does not necessarily mean that one will carry it out. ' The fact that it is wise to make a threat does not mean that if our attempt fails it will always be wise to carry it out. . . . But we cannot bluff every time without making future threats worthless.' [50] If one is told that nuclear deterrence does not include any conditional ' intention ' along the lines suggested above, that states ' only pretend to prepare nuclear reprisal ', that the threat is only a matter of semantics and will never have to be implemented, the private citizen can only

[47] ' The Morality of Obliteration Bombing ', *Theolog. Stud.*, Sept. 1944, p. 281.
[48] Lester Nurick, ' The Distinction between Combatant and Non-combatant in the Law of War ', 39 *AJIL* (1945), 680.
[49] Frisch, ' Scientists and the Decision to Bomb Japan ', *B. Atomic Scientists* (spec. issue ' Trinity +25 years '), June 1970, pp. 109–10 & 114.
[50] Roger Fisher, *International Conflict for Beginners* (London, 1970), p. 40.

reply that he knows 'nothing of such a well-intentioned subterfuge '.[51] The fact is that the credibility of deterrence depends on a firm resolve not to shrink from taking the action which one has declared one will take in defined circumstances. In this situation, the ' traditional theological teaching on war . . . seems hopelessly inadequate '.[52]

It is the realization of these facts which has given rise during the past twenty-five years to a sort of nuclear pacifism. Those who take this view do not renounce all use of force; what they reject is the strategic use of nuclear weapons, the power of which is measured in thousands or millions of tons of TNT, and which cannot be threatened or used with discrimination exclusively against military targets, but only against cities or large areas. Pacifism, whether a selective pacifism limited to particular weapons or particular methods of waging war, or the full-blooded and complete rejection of all use of force whatever the consequences for oneself or others, provides a way of escape from one set of dilemmas, only to face the pacifist with another set of dilemmas which are no less acute. Perhaps the most poignant fact with which the pacifist must come to terms is not that he may suffer as a consequence of his rejection of force, but that many of the victims will be totally innocent. But this is part of the human condition and is as true for the non-pacifist as it is for the pacifist.

Attempts to outlaw war

It will seem to many a utopian dream to try to get rid of war simply by fiat, without first building the institutions of peace and eliminating the instruments of war. The League Covenant and the UN Charter recognize the interconnection between the three processes. Members of the League agreed ' to respect and preserve as against external aggression the territorial integrity and existing political independence of all Members ' (Art. 10). States agreed not to resort to war without first trying to settle their disputes peacefully. War, or the threat of war, was not

---

[51] A. L. Burns, *Ethics and Deterrence: a Nuclear Balance without Hostage Cities?* (Adelphi Paper 69) (London, 1970), p. 14.

[52] *Peace: the Desperate Imperative*, p. 20.

declared to be illegal but 'a matter of concern to the whole League' (Art. 11 (1)). Any resort to war in disregard of the Covenant was to be deemed 'an act of war against all other Members of the League' (Art. 16 (1)).

The UN Charter also seeks to distinguish between the legal and illegal use of force.[53] It contains a commitment that 'Members shall refrain in their international relations from the threat or use of force against the territorial integrity or political independence of any State, or in any other manner inconsistent with the Purposes of the United Nations' (Art. 2 (4)). Members agree to settle their disputes by peaceful means (Art. 33 (1)), and Chapter VII of the Charter provides for enforcement machinery, which has largely remained a dead letter, for dealing with threats to or breaches of the peace, or acts of aggression. The last article (51) of the Chapter declares that the right of individual or collective self-defence remains unimpaired. Both the League and the UN pay their respects to disarmament—in the case of the League to 'the reduction of national armaments' (Art. 8 (1)) and in the case of the UN to 'disarmament and the regulation of armaments' (Art. 47 (1)).

Recently, a committee of the UN General Assembly has elaborated the principles of international law contained in the UN Charter regarding friendly relations and co-operation among states, and the Declaration containing this elaboration was approved by the Assembly during the UN's silver jubilee in 1970.[54] Seven principles were chosen for progressive development and codification, namely:

(a) The principle that States shall refrain in their international relations from the threat or use of force against the territorial integrity or political independence of any State, or in any other manner inconsistent with the purposes of the United Nations;

(b) the principle that States shall settle their international disputes by peaceful means in such a manner that international peace and security and justice are not endangered;

(c) the duty not to intervene in matters within the domestic jurisdiction of any State, in accordance with the Charter;

[53] Kunz, in 45 *AJIL* (1951), p. 533.
[54] Res. 2625 (XXV), 24 Oct. 1970.

(d) the duty of States to cooperate with one another in accordance with the Charter;

(e) the principle of equal rights and self-determination of peoples;

(f) the principle of sovereign equality of States;

(g) the principle that States shall fulfil in good faith the obligations assumed by them in accordance with the Charter.

That part of the Declaration regarding the renunciation of force is given in full in Appendix 1 (h), pp. 160-1.

The most ambitious, if least realistic, attempt to outlaw war was the Pact of Paris of 27 August 1928 (often known as the Kellogg Pact or the Briand-Kellogg Pact).[55] This effort has been described by Dean Acheson as ' simple and painless ' but of ' negligible ' effect.[56] It committed the parties to a total renunciation of war as an instrument of national policy. Its significance was not that it would or could or did prevent resort to war; it was that the initiative for it had come from the United States, which had decided to stay out of the League.

Individual responsibility under international law

If the international community is to prohibit all war, or aggressive war, or war in defiance of obligations arising from treaties and other sources of international law, or crimes against the peace, or methods of waging war which do not conform to the usages established among civilized peoples, or are contrary to the laws of humanity, or violate the dictates of the public conscience, then more is needed than simple promises by governments that neither they nor their citizens will use force for illegal purposes or in an illegal way. In the conditions of the second half of the twentieth century, to resort to war against another state except in self-defence or under the enforcement provisions of the UN Charter is a crime, in both the moral and legal senses of the word. Crimes within national societies are deterred by three kinds of force: the force of personal conscience, the force of public opinion, and the force of the police. In order that the community should accept the Rule of Law, those who are responsible for maintaining law and order are themselves subject to law; ' no man is above the law, but . . . every man,

[55] 94 LNTS, 57.
[56] ' The Eclipse of the State Department ', *Foreign Affairs*, July 1971, p. 600.

whatever be his rank or condition, is subject to the ordinary law of the realm and amenable to the jurisdiction of the ordinary tribunals '.[57]

Comparable institutions are slowly being created for the international community, but it is increasingly accepted that international law is not confined to the relations among states, that an individual who commits an act which is a crime under international law is responsible therefor and consequently liable to punishment. Almost the first act of the UN General Assembly was to ask Members to arrest war criminals who had committed atrocities and ' cause them to be sent back to the countries in which their abominable deeds were done, in order that they may be judged and punished according to the laws of those countries '. At the suggestion of Secretary-General Lie, the Assembly affirmed ' the principles of international law recognized by the Nuremberg Charter Tribunal and the judgment of the Tribunal '.[58] The International Law Commission, which had been set up by the General Assembly to promote the progressive development and codification of international law,[59] was asked to formulate the principles of international law recognized in the Charter of the Nuremberg Tribunal and to prepare a draft code of offences against the peace and security of mankind.[60]

It hardly needs stressing that the Nuremberg Tribunal was established by the victors to try the vanquished. If Allied nationals committed crimes under international law during the second world war, they were not brought to trial before any international tribunal. It is notable, moreover, that the accused at Nuremberg were not charged with aerial bombardment of cities, possibly because this would have exposed the prosecutors to the *tu quoque* argument.[61] The Nuremberg Tribunal itself considered that its Charter was ' not an arbitrary

[57] A. V. Dicey, *Introduction to the Study of the Law of the Constitution*, 10th ed. (London, 1959), p. 193.

[58] Res. 3 (1), 13 Feb. 1946 & 95 (1), 11 Dec. 1946; *GAOR*, 1st sess., 35th mtg, 24 Oct. 1946, pp. 699–700. The wording of res. 3 (1) was based on the Moscow Declaration of 30 October 1943 on German Atrocities (see RIIA, *UN Documents 1941–5* (1946), pp. 15–16).

[59] UN Charter, Art. 13 (1) (a); GA res. 174 (11), 21 Nov. 1947.

[60] GA res. 95 (1), 11 Dec. 1946, 175 (II) & 177 (II), 21 Nov. 1947.

[61] Georg Schwarzenberger, *International Law as applied by International Courts and Tribunals*, ii: *Law of armed Conflict* (London, 1968), pp. 151, 510, & 525.

exercise of power on the part of the victorious nations but . . . the expression of international law existing at the time of its creation; and to that extent is itself a contribution to international law'. Nevertheless, a number of jurists considered that the Nuremberg procedure was partially defective.[62] It is no doubt for this reason that the General Assembly was careful not to endorse the entire Nuremberg procedure, but only to affirm those ' principles of international law ' which are to be found in the Charter [63] and the judgment of the Tribunal.

In accordance with the directive of the General Assembly, the ILC formulated seven principles, as indicated in italic type below.[64] The comments of the ILC on the Principles are reproduced in Appendix II, pp. 163-70.

1. *Any person who commits an act which constitutes a crime under international law is responsible therefor and liable to punishment.*

The general rule is that international law may impose duties on individuals directly without any interposition of internal law. ' Crimes against international law [said the judgment of the Tribunal] are committed by men, not by abstract entities, and only by punishing individuals who commit such crimes can the provisions of international law be enforced.' ' The authors of . . . acts [which are condemned as criminal by international law] cannot shelter themselves behind their official position in order to be freed from punishment in appropriate proceedings ' (A/CN. 4/5, 31 Mar. 1949, pp. 41-2).

2. *The fact that internal law does not impose a penalty for an act which constitutes a crime under international law does not relieve the person who committed the act from responsibility under international law.*

Once it is admitted that individuals are responsible for crimes under international law, it is obvious that they are not relieved from their international responsibility by the fact that their acts are not held to be crimes under the law of any

[62] A/CN.4/5 (memo. submitted by the Secretary-General), 3 Mar. 1949, pp. 23-9 & 37-8. The ILC drew on this material in forming their own comments.
[63] Cmd 6903 (1945), UKTS no. 27, pp. 4-9.
[64] A/1316 (*GAOR*, 5th sess., suppl. 12) paras 95-127. See also MML, paras 624-41 and FM27-10, paras 499 & 504.

particular country. 'The very essence of the [Nuremberg] Charter is that individuals have international duties which transcend the national obligations of obedience imposed by the individual State' (p. 42).

3. *The fact that a person who committed an act which constitutes a crime under international law acted as Head of State or responsible government official does not relieve him from responsibility under international law.*

This wording is based on Article 7 of the Nuremberg Charter.

4. *The fact that a person acted pursuant to order of his Government or of a superior does not relieve him from responsibility under international law, provided a moral choice was in fact possible to him.*

This wording is based on Article 8 of the Nuremberg Charter. The Tribunal rejected the argument of the defence that there could not be any responsibility since most of the defendants acted under Hitler's orders.

That a soldier was ordered to kill or torture in violation of the international law of war [declared the Tribunal] has never been recognized as a defence. . . . The true test, which is found in varying degrees in the criminal law of most nations, is . . . whether moral choice was in fact possible (pp. 41–2).

5. *Any person charged with a crime under international law has the right to a fair trial on the facts and law.*

Article 16 of the Nuremberg Charter set out the procedure to be followed to ensure fair trial for the defendants.

6. *The crimes hereinafter set out are punishable as crimes under international law.*

The Tribunal was careful not to equate all internationally illegal acts or violations of international law as *crimes*. A criminal act is certainly an illegal act, but not every illegal act is criminal. Nevertheless, the Tribunal held that acts prohibited by a treaty can be crimes even if they are not expressly designated as such in the treaty (pp. 45–6).

a. *Crimes against peace:*

(i) *Planning, preparation, initiation or waging of a war of aggression or a war in violation of international treaties, agreements or assurances;*

(ii) *Participation in a common plan or conspiracy for the accomplishment of any of the acts mentioned under* (i).

The above wording is essentially the same as that of Article 6 (a) of the Nuremberg Charter. The Tribunal refuted the argument of the defence that aggressive war was not an international crime, relying primarily on the Briand-Kellogg Pact, which in 1939 was in force between 63 states.

In the opinion of the Tribunal, the solemn renunciation of war as an instrument of national policy necessarily involves the proposition that such a war is illegal in international law; and that those who plan and wage such a war . . . are committing a crime.

Resort to aggressive war is not merely illegal; it is criminal. ' To initiate a war of aggression . . . is not only an international crime; it is the supreme international crime.' The Tribunal reinforced its understanding of the Briand-Kellogg Pact by citing other international documents as evidence of the intention of the vast majority of civilized states and peoples to brand aggressive war as an international crime (pp. 45–6, 58).

In its comments on Principle 6 (a), the ILC understood the expression ' waging of a war of aggression ' to refer only to high-ranking military personnel and high state officials (A/1316, para. 117).

b. *War crimes:*

Violations of the laws or customs of war which include, but are not limited to, murder, ill-treatment or deportation to slave-labour or for any other purpose of civilian population of or in occupied territory, murder or ill-treatment of prisoners of war, of persons on the seas, killing of hostages, plunder of public or private property, wanton destruction of cities, towns or villages, or devastation not justified by military necessity.

This is essentially Article 6 (b) of the Nuremberg Charter.

The law of war [stated the Tribunal] is to be found not only in treaties, but in customs and practices of States which gradually obtained universal recognition, and from the general principles of justice applied by jurists and practiced [*sic*] by military courts. This law is not static, but by continual adaptation follows the needs of a changing world. Indeed, in many cases treaties do no more than express and define for more accurate reference the principles of law already existing.

The Tribunal stated that war crimes were covered by specific provisions of the Regulations annexed to the Hague Convention of 1907 and of the Geneva Convention of 27 July 1929 on the Treatment of Prisoners of War. By 1939 the rules laid down in the 1907 Hague Convention ' were recognized by all civilized nations, and were regarded as being declaratory of the laws and customs of war '. Violations of the provisions of the Hague and Geneva Conventions ' constituted crimes for which the guilty individuals were punishable ' (A/CN. 4/5, pp. 44 & 61-5).

c. *Crimes against humanity:*

Murder, extermination, enslavement, deportation and other inhumane acts done against any civilian population, or persecutions on political, racial or religious grounds, when such acts are done or such persecutions are carried on in execution of or in connexion with any crime against peace or any war crime.

This wording is a revision of Article 6 (c) of the Nuremberg Charter. The Tribunal itself was careful to distinguish between acts committed before 1939, and acts committed during the war.

To constitute crimes against humanity, the acts relied on before the outbreak of war must have been in execution of, or in connexion with, any crime within the jurisdiction of the Tribunal. . . . The Tribunal therefore cannot make a general declaration that the acts before 1939 were crimes against humanity within the meaning of the Charter.

In other words, the Tribunal found that crimes against humanity are accessory to crimes against peace and war crimes (A/CN. 4/5, pp. 66 & 68).

When the ILC came to draft Principle 6 (c), it decided to omit the words ' before or during the war ', which were included in the Nuremberg Charter, and emphasized that ' crimes against humanity . . . may take place also before a war in connexion with crimes against peace ' (A/1316, paras. 120-3).

The wording of the Nuremberg Charter makes it clear that crimes against humanity can be committed both against the perpetrator's own compatriots and against populations of other nationalities (Art. 6 (c)). While the Tribunal affirmed that the planning and waging of an aggressive war and war crimes are international crimes under international law, it made no corresponding statement in regard to crimes against humanity. On the other hand, the Tribunal held that its Charter, including the reference to crimes against humanity, was ' the expression of international law at the time of its creation ' (A/CN. 4/5, p. 70).

7. *Complicity in the commission of a crime against peace, a war crime, or a crime against humanity as set forth in Principle 6 is a crime under international law.*

This wording is a paraphrase of the last paragraph of Article 6 of the Nuremberg Charter. All the stages in the bringing about of a criminal act are declared to be crimes. The Tribunal did not impose a collective responsibility on the members of any organization, based solely on the fact of membership. To hold a member responsible for the criminal activities of his organization, the Tribunal required some conduct on the part of the member which established his complicity in the activity (pp. 56 & 79).

These, then, were the seven Nuremberg Principles as formulated by the ILC and presented to the General Assembly in 1950. But the Commission had by then been invited to undertake two other tasks: to prepare a draft code of offences against the peace and security of mankind [65]; and to study the desirability and possibility of establishing an international judicial organ for the trial of persons charged with genocide or other crimes over which jurisdiction would be conferred by international conventions. [66]

During its fifth regular session, which opened on 19 September 1950, the General Assembly took four decisions which bear on the subject matter of this book. First, it invited governments to submit written observations on the ILC's formulation of the Nuremberg Principles (res. 488 (V), 12 Dec. 1950). Secondly, it deferred consideration of that part of the ILC report relating

[65] GA res. 177 (II), 21 Nov. 1947.
[66] GA res. 260B (III), 9 Dec. 1948.

to a draft code of offences against the peace and security of mankind and requested the Commission, in its further work on the draft code, to take account of the observations made in the Assembly as well as any written observations by governments (res. 488 (V). Thirdly, it established a committee of seventeen states to prepare one or more preliminary draft conventions and proposals relating to the establishment and statute of an international criminal court (res. 489 (V), 12 Dec. 1950). Finally (although first in point of time), it remitted to the ILC a Soviet proposal on the need to define aggression (res. 378B (V), 17 Nov. 1950).

From this point onwards, the four subjects were so inextricably intertwined that it seemed impossible to make progress on one aspect until progress was also possible on the other three. The General Assembly has neither accepted nor rejected the seven Nuremberg Principles, on the ground that the formulation of them by the ILC raises problems closely related to that of defining aggression.

As for a possible code of offences against the peace and security of mankind, the ILC prepared a draft for consideration by the sixth session of the General Assembly, which opened on 6 November 1951. The draft stated that among the offences against the peace and security of mankind are ' acts in violation of the laws or customs of war ', and that every such violation should be regarded as a crime even if the existence of a state of war is not recognized by any of the parties. The Commission reiterated that the fact that a person acted pursuant to order of his government or of a superior does not relieve him from responsibility ' provided a moral choice was in fact possible to him '.[67] The Assembly decided in 1951 to postpone the draft until its next session. It did not, however, take up the draft in 1952 or 1953, and in 1954 the ILC submitted a revised draft. There had been some criticism of the expression ' provided a moral choice was in fact possible to him ' (which is, in fact, taken from the fourth of the Nuremberg Principles). The expression was accordingly replaced by the words ' if, in the circumstances at the time, it was possible for him not to comply

---

[67] A/1858 (*GAOR*, 6th sess., suppl. 9), p. 13.   See also FM27-10, paras. 509-11.

with that order '.[68] The Assembly deferred consideration of
the new draft in 1954 and again in 1957,[69] and since then the
question seems to have sunk into oblivion.

The third of the four items, relating to international criminal
jurisdiction, suffered a similar fate. The Committee appointed
by the Assembly in 1950 itself established a subcommittee,
which prepared a number of drafts for consideration by the
full Committee; several governments submitted written comments on these drafts. All this material was submitted to the
General Assembly in 1952. A wide divergence of view was
expressed, and a new Committee was appointed to review the
documentation and, in particular, to explore the implications
and consequences of establishing an international criminal
court (res. 687 (VII), 5 Dec. 1952). The Assembly, in other
words, was asking to be told what would be the consequences
of implementing the decision which it had taken in principle
two years previously.

The new Committee duly prepared a fresh report. In 1953 the
Assembly postponed a decision of substance, and in 1954 it
postponed consideration of the report pending progress on
related issues. The matter was again deferred in 1956 and
1957,[70] since when nothing was heard of it until 1968, when
the basic idea of the earlier work was resuscitated by Saudi
Arabia.[71]

The fourth item of the 1950 quartet was the Soviet proposal
regarding the definition of aggression, and this has prospered,
in the limited sense that a variety of committees have looked
into the matter and the issue is still actively before the
Assembly.[72] Apart from the intrinsic difficulties of defining
aggression, direct and indirect, in such a way as not to lay up
difficulties for the future, there was some suspicion of Soviet
motives on the part of Western governments. The issue was

[68] A/2693 (*GAOR*, 9th sess., suppl. 9), paras 41–54.
[69] Res. 897 (IX), 4 Dec. 1954 & 1186 (XI), 11 Dec. 1957.
[70] Res. 898 (IX), 14 Dec. 1954 & 1187 (XII), 11 Dec. 1957.
[71] A/7342 (*GAOR*, 23rd sess., annexes, agenda item 55), para. 104.
[72] Res. 599 (VI), 31 Jan. 1952; 688 (VII), 20 Dec. 1952; 895 (IX), 4 Dec. 1954;
1181 (XII), 29 Nov. 1957; 2330 (XXII), 18 Dec. 1967; 2420 (XXIII), 18 Dec.
1968; 2549 (XXIV), 12 Dec. 1969; 2644 (XXV), 25 Nov. 1970; 2781 (XXVI), 3
Dec. 1971

first raised in 1950, soon after the North Korean attack on South Korea, and it was alleged that the Soviet move was diversionary in character. The matter lay dormant for a decade but was revived in 1967, at a time when the war in Vietnam was escalating. But there may also be present, even if only at a subconscious level, a realization that if ever agreement is reached on a definition of aggression it will no longer be plausible to postpone action on the Nuremberg Principles, the draft code of offences against the peace and security of mankind, and the question of international criminal jurisdiction.

It might have been possible for the Assembly to have reaffirmed the seven Nuremberg Principles when they were first formulated more than twenty years ago; but if the matter were raised in the atmosphere prevailing in the General Assembly of the 1970s, there would undoubtedly be great pressure to extend the definitions in the sixth Principle to cover inhumane acts resulting from the more virulent forms of racism. That, in itself, might be unobjectionable, but it would change the character of the Nuremberg Principles, which were intended to deal with *war* crimes and related offences, and not simply with grave violations of human rights.

In 1965 the question of the punishment of war criminals arose in a new context as a result of a proposal by Poland. The event which sparked off this event (or non-event, as it turned out) was the fear that the Federal Republic of Germany was on the point of enacting a law which would have provided that no further prosecutions for war crimes could begin after 1965. The law which was finally enacted in West Germany extended from 8 May 1965 to 31 December 1969 the period during which prosecutions could take place of previously undetected offences of the most serious kind, and in 1969 the deadline was further extended to 31 December 1979.

When Poland first raised the matter in 1965, these West German actions lay in the future. The Polish proposal was dealt with in the normal fashion. Studies were undertaken by the UN Secretary-General,[73] and there were debates and decisions

[73] See, in particular, E/CN.4/906, 15 Feb. 1966, E/CN.4/928, 25 Jan. 1967, & E/CN.4/983 & Adds., 13 Jan.–25 Feb. 1969 (mimeo.).

in the Commission on Human Rights,[74] ECOSOC,[75] and the General Assembly.[76] The Polish initiative had three results.

First, a Convention was prepared on the Non-Applicability of Statutory Limitations to War Crimes and Crimes against Humanity, and this Convention came into force on 11 November 1970.[77] The original intention was to prepare a convention with the single object of ensuring that no statutory limitation should apply to war crimes, with the hope that this would act as a deterrent to the recurrence of the atrocities committed during the second world war. As the work of drafting proceeded, however, the definition of ' Crimes against Humanity ' was extended to apply not only to those mentioned in the Nuremberg Charter, and to genocide as defined in the Genocide Convention of 1948, but also to ' eviction by armed attack or occupation and inhuman acts resulting from the policy of *apartheid* '. A British attempt to amend the definition to read ' War crimes of a grave nature and crimes against humanity as defined in international law ' was heavily defeated, and the Convention was approved in plenary by 58 votes in favour, 7 against (including the UK), with 61 states abstaining or absent.[78]

Secondly, a proposal was initiated by Saudi Arabia whereby persons accused of war crimes or crimes against humanity should be tried by a tribunal consisting of judges from states not parties to the conflict, and that the right of asylum should be denied to a person found guilty of such crimes.[79] The General Assembly considered that this proposal raised ' issues that are closely related to the general question of international criminal jurisdiction ', and decided that the proposal should

[74] Res. 3 (XXI), 9 Apr. 1965; 3 (XXII), 4 Apr. 1966; 4 (XXIII), 20 Mar. 1967; & 13 (XXIV), 7 Mar. 1968.

[75] Res. 1074D (XXXIX), 28 July 1965; 1158 (XLI), 5 Aug. 1966; 1220 (XLII), 6 June 1967.

[76] Res. 2338 (XXII), 18 Dec. 1967 & 2391 (XXIII), 26 Nov. 1968.

[77] For text see, annex to GA res.2391 (XXIII), 26 Nov. 1968. Ten ratifications were needed to bring it into force, and these were forthcoming from the East European UN Members. In July 1971 there were 14 parties to the Convention.

[78] A/7342 (*GAOR*, 23rd sess., annexes, agenda item 55), paras 22 & 39.

[79] A/C.3/L.1570/Rev. 2(ibid. para. 104).

be taken up ' at such time as it [the Assembly] resumes consideration of the question . . . or at such other time as it deems
appropriate' (res. 2392 (XXIII), 26 Nov. 1968). In 1971 a group
of non-governmental organizations proposed that there should
be set up a permanent Commission of Inquiry which would be
responsible for investigating all complaints of violations during
armed conflicts of the Hague Conventions of 1899 and 1907,
the Geneva CBW Protocol of 1925, and the four Geneva Red
Cross Conventions of 1949. The proposed Commission of
Inquiry would report jointly to the Security Council and
General Assembly.

Thirdly, the General Assembly decided on 15 December 1969
to call upon states ' to take the necessary measures for the
thorough investigation of war crimes and crimes against
humanity . . . and for the detection, arrest, extradition and
punishment of all war criminals and persons guilty of crimes
against humanity ', and asked Secretary-General Thant to
submit to its 1970 session a progress report on the implementation of its 1969 decision.[80]

U Thant's report took the form of replies received from 25
UN Members, as well as from West Germany, to a note verbale
which he had issued to ' all the States concerned ' on 20 March
1970.[81] After considering these replies, on 15 December the
Assembly adopted a long resolution (2712 (XXV)) by 55 votes
to 4, with 68 states abstaining or absent; one can speculate on
the basis of the voting in committee a week before the
Assembly's decision that support for the resolution came mainly
from Communist or Afro-Asian states plus Israel, and that the
4 negative votes were probably cast by Australia, Portugal, the
UK, and the United States.[82]

The resolution, *inter alia*, encouraged states to take measures
against war criminals and again asked them to become parties

[80] Commission on Human Rights res.9 (XXV), 7 Mar. 1969 & 5 (XXVI), 4
& 5 Mar. 1970; ECOSOC res.1416 (XLVI), 6 June 1969 & 1500 (XLVIII), 27
May 1970; GA res.2583 (XXIV), 15 Dec. 1969.

[81] A/8038, 19 Aug. 1970; A/8038/Add. 1, 6 Nov. 1970; A/8038/Add. 2, 7 Dec.
1970 (mimeo.). The reply from W. Germany (Annex to A/8038, pp. 6–16) gives a
useful summary of the action taken to prosecute war criminals by the Occupying
Powers and by W. Germany.

[82] Voting in the Third Committee is given in A/8233, 11 Dec. 1970, para. 15 (i)
(mimeo.).

to the Convention on the Non-Applicability of Statutory Limitations to War Crimes and Crimes against Humanity; the UN Secretary-General was asked ' to continue . . . the study of the question of the punishment of war crimes and crimes against humanity, and also of the criteria for determining compensation to the victims of such crimes ', and to report to the General Assembly in 1971. A resolution in similar terms was adopted by the Human Rights Commission in 1971.[83]

Whatever may be the final fate of the question of defining aggression, on which hangs further action on the Nuremberg Principles, a possible code of offences against the peace and security of mankind, and the question of international criminal jurisdiction; however many or however few states may decide to accede to the Convention on the Non-Applicability of Statutory Limitations; whatever may be the results of the study of the punishment of war crimes and crimes against humanity which the Secretary-General has been asked to undertake, the question of penal sanctions against individuals who commit crimes against international law remains before the international community. U Thant has emphasized that breaches of the laws and customs of war involve the personal responsibility of those committing them; he has suggested that those who violate humanitarian instruments should be liable to penal sanctions after a fair trial ' on the national level '; and he has expressed the view that future humanitarian instruments will be more effective if they expressly provide for penal sanctions against violators.[84]

Retribution and reprisals

Military retribution is an act of counter-attack, punishment, or revenge. Any particular act of retribution may be open to question on prudential or humanitarian grounds, but so long as it conforms to the laws and customs applicable in armed conflicts, it is not illegal. Reprisals, by contrast, are acts which in ordinary circumstances would be regarded as violations of

[83] Commission on Human Rights res. 16(XXVII), 26 Mar. 1971.
[84] A/7720, 20 Nov. 1969, paras 122–7; A/8052, 18 Sept. 1970, para. 110 (mimeo.).

international law. The only justification for resorting to such unlawful acts in reprisal arises from the prior commission of an illegal act by the enemy; ' reprisals can be exercised only to stop a violation or prevent its repetition '.[85] The rationale behind reprisals has been that a belligerent should not be put at a disadvantage because the enemy breaks the rules.

Certain acts of reprisal are illegal. The Geneva Conventions of 1949 expressly forbid reprisals against protected persons, namely, wounded and sick in the armed forces; wounded, sick, and shipwrecked members of the armed forces at sea; prisoners of war; and civilian persons in occupied territory in time of war.[86] The Hague Convention of 14 May 1954 on the protection of cultural property in the event of armed conflict also contains an absolute ban on reprisals (Art. 4 (4)).[87] A resolution (2675 (XXV)) of the General Assembly of 9 December 1970 has affirmed that ' civilian populations or individual members thereof, should not be the object of reprisals ' (para. 7).

U Thant has drawn attention to the risk that under the stress of armed conflict, the notion of reciprocity may lead to reprisals ' which may be themselves contrary to internationally proclaimed objectives of the humane treatment of civilians, prisoners and combatants, and the application of which should be forbidden or, to say the least, strictly circumscribed '. The international community should direct its efforts towards the development of ' internationally agreed standards '. In a later report, he suggested a total prohibition ' in all circumstances ' of the use of the civilian population as an object of reprisal.[88]

The question of reprisals was considered by the UN Special Committee on Friendly Relations and Co-operation among States, and the Declaration adopted by the General Assembly without dissent on 24 October 1970 affirmed that ' States have a duty to refrain from acts of reprisal involving the use of force' (res. 2625 (XXV)). The United Kingdom accepted this unqualified wording on the understanding that the term

[85] Denise Bindschedler-Robert, *Law of Armed Conflicts* (New York, CEIP, 1970), p. 58. See also MML, paras 642-9; FM27-10, para. 497; Experts' Rpt., paras 573-5.

[86] Conv. I, art. 46; II, 47; III, 13; IV, 33.

[87] 249 UNTS, 215.

[88] *Respect for Human Rights in Armed Conflicts*, A/7720, 20 Nov. 1969, para. 203 (mimeo.) & A/8052, 18 Sept. 1970, para. 42 (c) (mimeo.).

'force' denotes physical or armed force; this would accord with Britain's consistent interpretation of the term 'force' as used in Article 2 (4) of the UN Charter.[89]

It is not difficult to see how the admissibility of the notion of reprisals opens the way to abuse, and one scholar has raised the question whether 'the doctrine [of reprisals] in application makes a contribution to the maintenance of law and order sufficiently great to outweigh its potentialities for abuse'.[90] Moreover, it is the view of a great many international lawyers that the UN Charter 'abolished the traditional right of reprisals', as Quincy Wright puts it. E. S. Colbert maintains that 'the right to determine when an illegal action has occurred and to decide on and direct the methods of punishment is transferred from the individual State to the Security Council which becomes itself the author of reprisals'.[91] This view is strengthened by the general condemnation of reprisals by the Security Council on 9 April 1964 ('*Condemns* reprisals as incompatible with the purposes and principles of the United Nations'), as well as the Council's condemnation of particular acts of reprisal.[92]

The International Committee of the Red Cross (CICR) has taken the view that the only position it can adopt is to call for a complete prohibition of reprisals, with procedures for investigating alleged violations. But realizing that an immediate prohibition of reprisals is not possible, the CICR has drawn attention to 'limits ... formulated in the texts of qualified writers or in the publications of specialized institutions'.[93]

[89] A/7326 (*GAOR*, 23rd sess., agenda item 87), para. 119.

[90] E. S. Colbert, *Retaliation in International Law* (New York, 1948), p. 200. See also Julius Stone, *Legal Controls of International Conflict* (London, 1954), pp. 289–90, 354, & 366; Morris Greenspan, *Modern Law of Land Warfare* (Berkeley, 1959), pp. 407–13; E. C. Stowell, ' Military Reprisals and the Sanctions of the Laws of War ', 36 *AJIL* (1942), 643–50.

[91] Wright, ' Legal Aspects of the Viet-Nam Situation ', 60 *AJIL* (1966), 750–70; Colbert, p. 202; see also Ian Brownlie, *International Law and the Use of Force by States* (Oxford, 1963), pp. 223, 265, & 281.

[92] Res.188 (S/5650), 9 Apr. 1964; 228 (S/7598), 25 Nov. 1966; 248, 24 Mar. 1968; 256, 16 Aug. 1968; 262, 31 Dec. 1968; 265 (S/9120/Rev.1), 1 Apr. 1969; 270 (S/9410), 26 Aug. 1969; 280 (S/9807), 19 May 1970.

[93] *Reaffirmation and Development of the Laws and Customs applicable in Armed Conflicts*, report submitted to the 21st Internat. Conf. of the Red Cross (doc.DS 4a, b, e) (1969), pp. 83–7 (hereafter cited as *Istanbul Rep.*).

(a) Reprisals cannot be exercised unless the Party alleging violation have offered the possibility of an enquiry and impartial observation of the facts;

(b) The scale of reprisals must not be out of proportion to that of the violation they aim at stopping;

(c) They must be carried out, so far as possible, only in the same field as that of the violation;

(d) They should in any case not be contrary to the laws of humanity.

It is when one tries to apply these unexceptionable principles to particular cases that difficulties begin to arise. The original illegality may vary in scale from a minor border raid by a small force of irregulars to a massive thermonuclear attack on cities. Richard Falk has studied the events surrounding Israel's attack on Beirut airport on 28 December 1968 and has suggested the following framework of principles concerning reprisals *in time of peace*.[94]

(1) That the burden of persuasion is upon the government that initiates an official use of force across international boundaries;

(2) that the governmental user of force will demonstrate its defensive character convincingly by connecting the use of force to the protection of territorial integrity, national security, or political independence;

(3) that a genuine and substantial link exists between the prior commission of provocative acts and the resultant claim to be acting in retaliation;

(4) that a diligent effort be made to obtain satisfaction by persuasion and pacific means over a reasonable period of time, including recourse to international organizations;

(5) that the use of force is proportional to the provocation and calculated to avoid its repetition in the future, and that every precaution be taken to avoid excessive damage and unnecessary loss of life, especially with respect to innocent civilians;

(6) that the retaliatory force is directed primarily against military and paramilitary targets and against military personnel;

(7) that the user of force make a prompt and serious explanation of its conduct before the relevant organ(s) of community review and seek vindication therefrom of its course of action;

[94] ' The Beirut Raid and the International Law of Retaliation ', 63 *AJIL* (1969), 441–2 (footnotes omitted).

(8) that the use of force amounts to a clear message of communication to the target government so that the contours of what constituted the unacceptable provocation are clearly conveyed;

(9) that the user of force cannot achieve its retaliatory purposes by acting within its own territorial domain and thus cannot avoid interference with the sovereign prerogatives of a foreign state;

(10) that the user of force seek a pacific settlement to the underlying dispute on terms that appear to be just and sensitive to the interests of its adversary;

(11) that the pattern of conduct of which the retaliatory use of force is an instance exhibits deference to considerations (1)–(10), and that a disposition to accord respect to the will of the international community be evident;

(12) that the appraisal of the retaliatory use of force take account of the duration and quality of support, if any, that the target government has given to terroristic enterprises.

What is the relevance of the four ' limits ' of the CICR or the 12-point framework of Professor Richard Falk to the kinds of instant response or ' launch on warning ' implied in some versions of the doctrine of nuclear deterrence? The man in the street, unschooled in the niceties of international law, may well agree with Professor Telford Taylor that ' resort to crime in order to reform the criminal is an unappetizing method '.[95]

---

[95] *Nuremberg and Vietnam: an American Tragedy* (Chicago, 1970), p. 54.

INTERNATIONAL HUMANITARIAN LAW AND THE INTERNATIONAL RED CROSS

Until a more complete code of the laws of war has been issued . . . the inhabitants and the belligerents remain under the protection and the rule of the principles of the law of nations, as they result from the usages established among civilized peoples, from the laws of humanity, and the dictates of the public conscience.
Preamble to the Hague Conventions of 1899 & 1907 (the Martens Clause)

The Law of Geneva and the Law of The Hague

The international humanitarian law applicable in armed conflicts has been codified in two parallel streams known, somewhat confusingly, as the Law of Geneva and the Law of The Hague. The Law of Geneva is designed ' to ensure respect, protection and humane treatment of war casualties and non-combatants ', while the Law of The Hague ' lays down the rights and duties of belligerents in conducting [military] operations and limits the methods of warfare '.[1] Part of the confusion to which I refer arises from the fact that the Law of The Hague includes two instruments identified with other cities (the St Petersburg Declaration of 29 November—11 December 1868 and the Geneva CBW Protocol of 17 June 1925).

The codification of the Law of Geneva began just over a century ago. The Geneva Conventions have been as follows:

22 August 1864	For the amelioration of the condition of the wounded in armies in the field
6 July 1906	For the amelioration of the condition of the wounded *and sick* in armies in the field [my italics]
27 July 1929	For the relief of the wounded and sick in armies in the field
,,	Treatment of prisoners of war.

[1] Jean Pictet, ' The Need to restore the Laws and Customs relating to Armed Conflicts ', *R. Internat. Commiss. Jurists*, Mar. 1969, p. 23.

These conventions were superseded by the four Geneva (Red Cross) Conventions of 12 August 1949,[2] as follows:

1. Amelioration of the condition of the wounded and sick in armed forces in the field.

2. Amelioration of the condition of wounded, sick, and ship-wrecked members of the armed forces at sea.

3. Treatment of prisoners of war.

4. Protection of civilian persons in time of war.

In 1971 Lesotho became the 129th state to be expressly bound by the provisions of the four Geneva Conventions of 1949.[3] The Fourth Convention of 1949 was the first designed to protect civilians, but it applies only to persons who, in case of armed conflict or occupation, find themselves ' in the hands of a Party to the conflict or Occupying Power *of which they are not nationals* ' (Art. 4, my italics).

Some scholars consider that states are bound by both the Hague and Geneva Conventions, whether they are parties or not.[4] As regards the Geneva Conventions, however, the United Kingdom has rejected the view that the principles of the Conventions ' must be strictly observed by all Governments whether or not they signed them '. Such an assumption, according to the UK, is ' legally wrong and in practice completely futile '. The Conventions, in the British view, are ' binding only on the signatory States '.[5]

The four Geneva Conventions of 1949 were prepared at a diplomatic conference convened by the Swiss Federal Council. The First Convention replaces the Geneva Conventions of 1864, 1906, and 1929 in relations between the parties.[6] The Second Convention replaces the Tenth Hague Convention of 1907 for the adaptation to Maritime Warfare of the principles of

---

[2] 75 UNTS, 31 (I), 85 (II), 135 (III), & 287 (IV).

[3] *IRRC*, Oct. 1971, pp. 549-550

[4] Taylor, p. 30. See also FM27-10, p.i.

[5] A/C.3/SR.1799, 26 Nov. 1970, p. 3; A/C.3/SR.1804, 1 Dec. 1970, p. 10. The CICR considers that ' even without a declaration of continuity, *newly independent States* are implicitly bound by the participation of the States to which they succeed, unless they explicitly repudiate these [Geneva] Conventions ' (my italics)(*Ann. Rep. Internat. Cttee . . . 1965* (1966), p. 53). For an examination of the question of the succession of states to humanitarian treaties, see the study by the UN Secretariat in A/CN.4/200, 21 Feb. 1968, paras. 128-32 (mimeo.).

[6] Conv. I, Art. 59.

the Geneva Convention of 1906.[7] The Third Convention replaces the Geneva POW Convention of 1929; in relation to parties to the Hague Conventions of 1899 or 1907 which also become parties to the Third Geneva Convention, the latter shall be complementary to the relevant provisions of the two Hague Conventions.[8] The Fourth Geneva Convention broke new ground, in that it was the first expressly to protect civilians who, in case of conflict or occupation, find themselves in the hands of a state of which they are not nationals.[9] Like the Third Convention, the Fourth supplements the relevant provisions of the Hague Conventions of 1899 and 1907.[10]

There are certain provisions common to the four Geneva Conventions. The parties undertake ' to respect and to ensure respect for ' the Conventions ' in all circumstances ' (Art. 1). This obligation is not subject to ' military necessity ' except when the Conventions allow for such a consideration in specific provisions. The Conventions apply to ' all cases of declared war or of any other armed conflict . . . even if the state of war is not recognized by one of [the parties] ', and also to cases of partial or total occupation (Art. 2). Certain minimum provisions apply in the case of armed conflict not of an international character (Art. 3). There are provisions about the duration of application,[11] special agreements which the parties may conclude,[12] the inalienability of the rights of protected persons,[13] the duties of Protecting Powers or their substitutes,[14] the activities of the CICR,[15] and conciliation procedures.[16] All four Conventions contain provisions for the repression of abuses and infractions.[17] The final provisions define the procedure for signature, ratification, and entry into force of the Conventions, and for subsequent

[7] II, 58.
[8] III, 134–5.
[9] IV, 4.
[10] IV, 154.
[11] I, 5; III, 5; IV, 6.
[12] I, 6; II, 6; III, 6; IV, 7.
[13] I, 7; II, 7; IV, 8.
[14] I, 8 & 10; II, 8 & 10; III, 8 & 10; IV, 9 & 11.
[15] I, 9; II, 9; III, 9; IV, 10.
[16] I, 11; II, 11; III, 11; IV, 12.
[17] I, 49–52; II, 50–3; III, 129–31; IV, 146–9.

accessions to them.[18] Denunciation takes effect one year after notification, except when the party is involved in an armed conflict, in which case denunciation shall not take effect until peace has been concluded and until all protected persons have been repatriated. In any case, denunciation in no way impairs the obligations which the parties are bound to fulfil ' by virtue of the principles of the law of nations, as they result from the usages established among civilized peoples, from the laws of humanity and the dictates of the public conscience '.[19] The parties agree to disseminate the text of the Conventions and to include the study of them ' in their programmes of military and, if possible, civil instruction, so that the principles thereof may become known to the entire population '.[20]

The Conventions are based on the principle that those who are placed *hors de combat* or who are taking no active part in hostilities shall have their lives spared and shall in all circumstances be treated humanely. The taking of hostages, executions without regular judgment, torture, cruel or degrading treatment, and reprisals against persons protected by the Conventions, are prohibited.[21]

Wounded and sick, both military and civilian, shall be respected, as shall all medical personnel, hospitals sheltering wounded and sick, vehicles transporting them, and medical equipment allotted to them. The emblem of the red cross, the red crescent, or the red lion and sun, is the sign of this protection, and it shall be used for no other purpose. Chaplains must also be protected. Medical personnel and chaplains are, for their part, bound to observe strict military neutrality.[22]

Military personnel and auxiliaries who are captured or who surrender must have their lives spared. They must at all times be treated humanely and in particular must receive the necessary food, clothing, and medical care. They shall be permitted to correspond with their families. The capturing authority will communicate the names of POWs to the Central Tracing

[18] I, 55–64; II, 54–63; III, 133–43; IV, 150–9.
[19] I, 63; II, 62; III, 142; IV, 158.
[20] I, 47; II, 48; III, 127; IV, 144.
[21] I, 3 & 46; II, 3 & 47; III, 3 & 13; IV, 3 & 32–4.
[22] I, 12, 15, 19–20, 24–7, 32–6, 38–44; II, 12, 18, 22–4, 36–9, 41–5; IV, 16–22.

Agency of the CICR, which will be allowed to visit prisoners and arrange for them to receive relief. If penal sanctions are taken against POWs for offences committed before their capture, the CICR (in the absence of the Protecting Power) is to be informed. The CICR is authorized to follow the judicial proceedings and to assist POWs in their defence. In the event of the death penalty being pronounced, the sentence shall not be carried out until at least six months after the CICR has been notified of the sentence.[23]

Civilian wounded and sick, as well as civilian hospitals and their personnel, shall be the object of particular respect and may be placed under the protection of the red cross or equivalent emblem. Civilians in occupied territory must, in so far as circumstances permit, be enabled to live in a normal manner. Deportations, pillage, and indiscriminate destruction of property in occupied territory are prohibited. Civilians may be interned only for imperative reasons of security, and conditions shall be of no less a standard than those in POW camps.[24]

The Law of The Hague comprises the St Petersburg Declaration of 1868, the Hague Conventions of 1899 and 1907, the Geneva CBW Protocol of 1925, and the Hague Convention of 1954. I deal with the St Petersburg Declaration of 1868 and the 1925 Geneva Protocol in Chapter 5.

Convention II with respect to the laws and customs of war on land, with the annexed Regulations, was signed at The Hague on 29 July 1899. It was replaced, as between the contracting parties, by Convention IV, signed at The Hague on 18 October 1907. The 1899 Convention ' remains in force as between the Powers which signed it, and which do not also ratify the present Convention ' (1907, Art. 4).[25] Britain ratified the 1899 Convention on 4 September 1900, and the 1907 Convention on 27 November 1909.

The Hague Conventions affirm three important principles

[23] III, 4, 13–30, 70, 72, 78, 101, 123, & 126. See also MML, paras 226, 228, & 235.
[24] IV, 16–22, 33, 41–3, 49, & 53.
[25] *The Hague Conventions of 1899 (II) and 1907 (IV), respecting the laws and customs of war on land* (Washington, CEIP, 1915, pam. No. 5). In summarizing the Conventions, I have used the 1907 wording.

which still remain valid. The parties state in the Preamble to the Conventions their wish to preserve peace and prevent armed conflicts. But when, in the wording of the Conventions, ' events ' bring about an ' appeal to arms ', the parties still desire to serve the interests of humanity and the needs of civilization. The parties therefore consider it important to revise the general laws and customs of war, either by defining them more precisely or by confining them within ' such limits as would mitigate their severity as far as possible '. The Conventions are designed ' to diminish the evils of war, as far as military requirements permit . . .'. The Conventions, in other words, seek to do the impossible—to reconcile the interests of humanity with the demands of military necessity.

The Preamble then goes on to record the failure of the parties to find agreement covering all the circumstances which arise in practice, and yet they do not intend that when unforeseen cases occur, the absence of a written agreement should mean that ' the arbitrary judgment of military commanders ' should be decisive. The Preamble then sets out the so-called Martens Clause, named after the Russian jurist F. F. Martens:

Until a more complete code of the laws of war has been issued, the high contracting Parties deem it expedient to declare that, in cases not included in the Regulations adopted by them, the inhabitants and the belligerents remain under the protection and rule of the principles of the law of nations, as they result from the usages established among civilized peoples, from the laws of humanity, and the dictates of the public conscience.

This is the first basic principle of the Hague Conventions. The code the parties adopted was recognized to be incomplete; it was to be supplemented by rules applied in the interests of humanity and civilization, even when these are not expressed in treaty form.

The second basic principle of the Hague Conventions is to be found in Article 22 of the annexed Regulations: ' The right of belligerents to adopt means of injuring the enemy is not unlimited.' This principle had been affirmed in Article 12 of the Brussels Declaration of 27 August 1874.[26] (Britain signed

[26] *Documents relating to the Program of the First Hague Peace Conference* (Oxford, CEIP, 1921), p. 34. See also MML, para. 107, and FM27-10, para. 33.

the Brussels Declaration but it never received enough ratifications to enter into force.)

The third basic principle is stated in Article 23 (e) of the Regulations: 'It is especially forbidden . . . to employ arms, projectiles, or material calculated to cause unnecessary suffering.' This, too, had been derived from the Brussels Declaration, Article 13 (e).

The Regulations define those who qualify for belligerent status (Arts 1–3) and also contain specific rules for POWs (Arts 4–20). The obligations of belligerents with regard to the sick and wounded are to be governed by the Geneva Convention of 22 August 1864 (Art. 21).

The Regulations especially forbid the use of poison or poisonous weapons; the killing or wounding ' treacherously ' of individuals belonging to the hostile nation or army, although ' ruses of war ' and the employment of ' measures necessary for obtaining information about the enemy and the country ' are permitted; the killing or wounding of ' an enemy who, having laid down his arms, or having no longer means of defence, has surrendered at discretion '; the declaration that no quarter will be given; the improper use of a flag of truce, of the national flag or of the military insignia and uniform of the enemy, or of the red cross emblem; and the destruction or seizure of enemy property ' unless . . . imperatively demanded by the necessities of war ' (Arts 23–4).

It is prohibited to attack or bombard ' by whatever means ' undefended towns, villages, dwellings, or buildings. The officer commanding an attacking force must do all in his power to warn the authorities before beginning a bombardment, ' except in cases of assault '. The pillage of a town or place is prohibited, even when taken by assault. In the event of siege or bombardment, ' all necessary steps must be taken to spare, as far as possible ', buildings dedicated to religion, art, science, or charitable purposes, historic monuments, hospitals, and places where the sick and wounded are being collected, ' provided they are not being used at the time for military purposes ' (Arts 25–8).

A section dealing with ' military authority over the territory

of the hostile state' contains provisions for protecting the
inhabitants of occupied territories. The occupying power must
'take all the measures in his power to restore and ensure, as
far as possible, public order and safety, while respecting, unless
absolutely prevented, the laws in force in the country' (Art. 43).
Respect must be paid to family honour and rights, the lives of
persons, private property (which must not be confiscated), as
well as religious convictions and practice (Art. 46). No 'general
penalty' shall be inflicted upon the population on account of
'the acts of individuals for which they can not be regarded as
jointly and severally responsible' (Art. 50). The provisions in
the 1899 Convention on the internment of belligerents and the
care of wounded in neutral countries (Arts 57–60) were
transferred in 1907 to Convention V respecting the rights and
duties of neutral Powers and persons in case of war on land.

There are 46 parties to the Hague Convention of 1899 and 33
to that of 1907 (April 1971), and 6 members or former members
of the British Commonwealth consider themselves bound by
the Conventions. Altogether 56 states have ratified or acceded
to or consider themselves bound by one or both of the Conventions.[27] But what is perhaps of greater importance is the
judgment of the Nuremberg Tribunal of 1946, to the effect that
'by 1939 the rules of land warfare laid down in the 1907
Convention had been recognized by all civilized nations and
were regarded as being declaratory of the laws and customs of
war'; the International Military Tribunal for the Far East
declared in its judgment of 1948 that the 1907 Convention was
'good evidence of the customary law of nations' (A/7720,
para. 49).

The Hague Convention for the protection of cultural
property in the event of armed conflict of 14 May 1954 [28]
elaborates some of the provisions of Article 27 of the Hague
Convention of 1907; it was prepared at an intergovernmental
conference convened by UNESCO.

As in the case of the Hague Conventions of 1899 and 1907
and the Geneva Conventions of 1949, it applies in the event of

[27] Schwarzenberger, *Internat. Law*, ii.788–91.
[28] 249 UNTS, 215. The text is in MML, pp. 309-20, but in the Table of Contents (p. xxiii) the Convention is incorrectly ascribed to Geneva.

international armed conflicts (Art. 18), but it follows the Geneva Conventions in providing also for the application in non-international armed conflicts of certain provisions, as a minimum (Art. 19). The parties undertake to refrain from using cultural property for purposes which are likely to expose it to destruction or damage, and to refrain from hostile acts against such property. They further undertake to prevent theft, pillage, or misappropriation of cultural property, and acts of vandalism. They agree not to requisition ' movable cultural property ', and there is an unconditional ban on ' any act directed by way of reprisals against cultural property ' (Art. 4).

Article 8 of the Convention grants special protection to ' a limited number of refuges [zones of sanctuary] intended to shelter movable cultural property . . . and [to] immovable cultural property of very great importance '. These refuges must be situated at ' an adequate distance ' from any large industrial centre or important military objectives, and they are not to be used for military purposes.

The Convention, Regulations, and Protocol create machinery for implementation, and provide for the function of Protecting Powers, for conciliation procedure and assistance of UNESCO. As soon as a party is engaged in an armed conflict a Commissioner-General for Cultural Property is to be appointed from an international list of qualified persons. In April 1971 there were 61 parties to the 1954 Hague Convention.

Both the Law of Geneva and the Law of The Hague ' impose direct personal obligations on individuals '[29]; the Law of Geneva (also sometimes known as the Law of the Red Cross) has been drawn up ' solely for the benefit of the individual '.[30]

Telford Taylor (p. 32) has rightly commented that the laws of war ' although a long-established reality . . . are very fuzzy round the edges '. While the Law of Geneva has been codified in comparatively recent times, the Law of The Hague has been overtaken by military technology and ' has remained in a state of neglect often called chaotic '.[31] Except to the extent that existing law was codified by the Geneva CBW Protocol of 1925

[29] D. Bindschedler-Robert, p. 7.

[30] Pictet, *Principles of International Humanitarian Law* (Geneva, n.d.), pp. 11 & 12.

[31] Pictet, in *R. Internat. Commiss. Jurists*, Mar. 1949, p. 23.

and the Hague Convention of 1954 on the protection of cultural property, the Law of The Hague has not been codified since 1907, and war has been transformed during the past sixty-four years. The St Petersburg Declaration of 1868 solemnly affirmed that ' the progress of civilization should have the effect of alleviating as much as possible the calamities of war '. Unfortunately the progress of civilization has not had that beneficial effect: it has, on the contrary, provided man with more effective instruments of slaughter—submarines, aircraft, ICBMs, nuclear explosives, nerve gases, and the like. Mankind is no more secure than it was in 1907; what has changed is that the price of failure has increased. The experts agree, nevertheless, that for a state to declare that existing law is outdated owing to the invention of new methods of warfare is ' entirely contrary to reason and to any accurate legal conception '.[32]

Slaughter on the scale now feasible is beyond the human imagination. Such killing is possible only because modern war, ' with its impersonal methods of killing that operate at ever-increasing distances, is eliminating our instinctual restraint to kill, because quite literally it has removed every single one of the factors that stimulate the killing inhibition '.[33]

For the private citizen with humanitarian impulses and an optimistic outlook, the division of humanitarian law into two streams had a certain logic. For the pacifist minority, and for those like the CICR who simply reject ' the very idea of war ', as one CICR document puts it,[34] the obvious task has been to strengthen the Law of Geneva, which is concerned with the protection of the ' innocent ', i.e. those not able to take a direct part in hostilities (wounded, sick, and shipwrecked members of the armed forces, prisoners of war, civilians), and at the same time to do what is possible towards the abolition of war itself. Andrew Carnegie was so sure that war could be abolished in a foreseeable future that when he set aside $10 m. to promote

---

[32] *Istanbul Rep*, p. 39.

[33] Konrad Lorenz, ' On Killing Members of One's Own Species ', *B. Atomic Scientists*, Oct. 1970, p. 55.

[34] *Draft Rules for the Limitation of the Dangers Incurred by the Civilian Population in time of War*, 2nd ed. (1958), p. 3.

F

world peace, he was careful to instruct the trustees about what should be done with the money when that goal had been achieved.[35]

When civilized nations enter into such treaties as named, and war is discarded as disgraceful to civilized men, as personal war (duelling) and man selling and buying (slavery) hav been discarded within the wide boundaries of our English-speaking race, the Trustees will pleas then consider what is the next most degrading remaining evil or evils whose banishment—or what new elevating element or elements if introduced or fosterd, or both combined—would most advance the progress, elevation and happiness of man, and so on from century to century without end, my Trustees of each age shall determin how they can best aid man in his upward march to higher and higher stages of development unceasingly, for now we know that man was created, not with an instinct for his own degredation, but imbued with the desire and the power for improvement to which, perchance, there may be no limit short of perfection even here in this life upon erth.

For the non-pacifist majority, on the other hand, who may be less sanguine about achieving perfection at an early date, it has not been enough simply to develop and strengthen the Law of Geneva; there has been the further task of strengthening the Law of The Hague, which seeks to restrain belligerents in the actual conduct of military hostilities, to make war less brutal. It is true that some ' unbending pacifists assert that . . . it is vain to imagine that war can be made more humane, when it is of its nature opposed to humane sentiments '.[36] But the mainstream of humanitarian opinion considers this to be a mistaken point of view,[37] and Denise Bindschedler-Robert (p. 10) insists that the unlawfulness or immorality of the resort to force does not negate the legitimacy of the law of armed conflicts, which seeks to lessen the consequences of the inability of the international community to prevent the use of force. No one questions the need for an efficient health organization or a

[35] *Ann. Rep. CEIP 1958–9*, p. 62 (the spelling is Carnegie's).
[36] Pictet, *Red Cross and Peace* (Geneva, 1951), pp. 3–4. See also André Beaufre, ' Wie lässt sich die Kriegführung humanisieren? Die Tendenzen des 20 Jahrhunderts und die Rolle des Roten Kreuzes ', *Schweizer Monatshefte*, Dec. 1968, pp. 861–8.
[37] C. F. von Weizsäcker, *Ethical Problem of Modern Strategy* (Adelphi Paper 55) (London, 1969), p. 1.

fire brigade, ' but it is not for any love of disease or fire '. It is a basic assumption of all humanitarian efforts that evils which cannot be immediately suppressed should, if possible, be attenuated. The Red Cross considers that it combats war by making it more humane, and that all Red Cross work ' is a protest against violence'. The endeavours to abolish war and to protect its victims ' *complete one another and must be conducted on a parallel* '.[38]

The International Red Cross

The International Red Cross consists of three elements. There is, first of all, the CICR, a body founded by five citizens of Geneva in 1863 following the publication of Henry Dunant's *A Souvenir of Solferino*. Secondly, there are 115 national Red Cross, Red Crescent, or Red Lion and Sun Societies.[39] Thirdly, there is the League of National Red Cross and similar societies. These three elements meet together every four years as the International Conference of the Red Cross.[40]

Sometimes people speak loosely of the International Red Cross when in fact they should say ' the International *Committee of* the Red Cross '. Article 4 of the CICR Statute, as amended on 25 September 1952, defines its role as follows:

(a) to maintain the fundamental and permanent principles of the Red Cross, namely: impartiality, action independent of any racial, political, religious or economic considerations, the universality of the Red Cross and the equality of the National Red Cross Societies;

(b) to recognize any newly established or re-constituted National Red Cross Society which fulfils the conditions for recognition in force, and to notify other National Societies of such recognition;

(c) to undertake the tasks incumbent on it under the Geneva Conventions, to work for the faithful application of these Conventions and to take cognizance of any complaints regarding alleged breaches of the humanitarian Conventions;

[38] Pictet, *Red Cross & Peace*, p. 10; *Red Cross as a Factor in World Peace* (report of Round Table conference held in The Hague, 28 Aug. 1967), (1968), p. 9; *Istanbul Rep.*, p. 11.

[39] There is a similar society in Israel, but its emblem—the Jewish Star—has not been accepted by the CICR. See MML, para. 30, n. 1 & FM27-10, para. 238b.

[40] The Conference was founded in 1919.

(d) to take action in its capacity as a neutral institution, especially in case of war, civil war or internal strife; to endeavour to ensure at all times that the military and civilian victims of such conflicts and of their direct results receive protection and assistance, and to serve, in humanitarian matters, as an intermediary between the parties;

(e) to contribute, in view of such conflicts, to the preparation and development of medical personnel and medical equipment, in co-operation with the Red Cross organizations, the medical services of the armed forces, and other competent authorities;

(f) to work for the continual improvement of humanitarian international law and for the better understanding and diffusion of the Geneva Conventions and to prepare for their possible extension;

(g) to accept the mandates entrusted to it by the International Conferences of the Red Cross.

The ICRC [CICR] may also take any humanitarian initiative which comes within its role as a specifically neutral and independent institution and consider any questions requiring examination by such an institution.

The CICR is a self-perpetuating body in that membership is only by co-optation and is limited to Swiss citizens.

The Red Cross movement was initially concerned with sick and wounded combatants on the field of battle. It later extended its concern to prisoners of war, and in 1949 there was adopted for the first time a Convention designed to ensure humane treatment of civilians in occupied territories. By custom rather than by treaty, the CICR now makes its services available for a wide range of humanitarian activities—relief in case of disasters, visiting political prisoners, and even humanitarian assistance in the event of kidnappings, the taking of hostages, or the hijacking of aircraft.[41] In 1962 the Soviet Union suggested that the CICR should check on the withdrawal of Soviet missiles from Cuba; although this was acceptable to the United States, the Cuban government rejected any form of unilateral inspection on Cuban territory.[42] The Soviet Union has vetoed

---

[41] Max Petitpierre, ' A Contemporary Look at the International Committee of the Red Cross ', *IRRC*, Feb. 1971, pp. 63–81; *Reaffirmation and Development of International Humanitarian Law applicable in Armed Conflict* (prelim. report on the Consultation of Experts, doc. D 1153, 1970), p. 37 & Ann. 1, p. 5 (hereafter cited as *Prelim. Rep.*).

[42] A/5502 (*GAOR*, 18th sess., suppl. 2), p. 7; Petitpierre, p. 71.

two proposals in the Security Council which would have conferred functions on the CICR: the first in connection with
allegations of the use of bacterial warfare in Korea (3 July
1952) and the second in connection with the shooting down of
a US RB-47 aircraft (26 July 1960).[43]

The CICR has to act with great discretion in situations of
political delicacy. During the conflict between Federal Nigeria
and former Biafra, for example, the CICR was engaged in its
largest humanitarian effort since the second world war—and
also ' the most thankless '. After the Nigerian air force had shot
down a Swedish aircraft operating under CICR responsibility,
the CICR's activity was ' almost completely paralysed '.
Fourteen CICR delegates or pilots were killed on duty during
this conflict.[44]

In the five-year period covered by the CICR's annual
reports 1965-9, representatives of the Committee had visited
political detainees in no fewer than 36 states or territories:
Angola, Bolivia, Bulgaria, Burundi, Chad, Congo (Kinshasa),
the Dominican Republic, El Salvador, West Germany, Greece,
Guatemala, Haiti, Honduras, Hong Kong, India, Indonesia,
Israel, Libya, Malawi, Malaysia, Mexico, Mozambique,
Nigeria, Pakistan, Panama, Peru, the Philippines, Portuguese
Guinea, Rhodesia, South Africa, Southern Yemen (Aden),
Syria, Thailand, Venezuela, the Republic of Vietnam (South),
and Yemen.

The CICR acts on its own initiative by reminding states of
their humanitarian responsibilities in particular cases, whether
these responsibilities derive from specific instruments or, in the
words of the Martens Clause, ' result from the usages established among civilized peoples, from the laws of humanity, and
the dictates of the public conscience '.

The CICR can undertake its unique responsibilities only if
it acts with great tact and discretion. Its relief and related
activities are given reasonable publicity but, when the CICR
undertakes more delicate tasks (such as visiting political

---

[43] For text of the vetoed proposals, see my *Voting in the Security Council* (Blooming-
ton, 1969), pp. 175-6 & 188.

[44] Petitpierre, pp. 69-71.

prisoners), the general rule is that it seeks no publicity and reports only to the government concerned.[45] An exception to this general rule was the publication in 1970 of a report on its activities in the Middle East for the period June 1967 to June 1970.[46] According to a UN report, the publication of this CICR report was due to ' leakage of the contents . . . which it [the CICR] hoped would remain secret '.[47]

The CICR found that, following the June War, problems relating to the treatment of the wounded and the prisoners of war were settled ' relatively quickly '. Matters were different in the case of the Fourth Convention of 1949 concerned with civilians in occupied territories. The CICR informed the government of Israel in July 1967 that ' in its opinion the Fourth Convention was applicable '. The government of Israel replied a year later (16 June 1968) that it wished ' to leave the question . . . open for the moment '.[48] This hindered the CICR in seeking to prevent such prohibited activities as the destruction of houses and the deportation of protected persons.

The Fourth Convention prohibits any destruction of property ' except where such destruction is rendered *absolutely necessary by military operations* ' (Art. 53, my italics). It also prohibits the punishment of any protected person except for an offence which he or she has *personally* committed (Art. 33, my italics); in other words, indiscriminate or collective punishments are banned. The CICR found that three kinds of destruction were in fact carried out by Israel as measures of punishment: the destruction of villages or town quarters, the destruction of houses, and the so-called ' punishment of neighbours ' policy, which was directed against ' the houses of persons helping members of al-Fatah '. When the CICR delegate made representations to the Israel Ministry of Defence, he was told ' that it was not for the ICRC [CICR] to intervene in a question that affected directly the security of the State '. The CICR took the view that, while deploring all terrorist attacks against civilians, such attacks were in themselves no justification for

[45] Ibid. pp. 64–5 & 75–6.
[46] *IRRC*, Aug. & Sept. 1970, pp. 424–59 & 485–511.
[47] A/8089, 26 Oct. 1970 (mimeo.), paras 51–2 & 149.
[48] *IRRC*, Aug. 1970, p. 427.

resorting to reprisals or any other form of collective penalties.[49]

None of the parties to the Geneva Conventions directly involved in the Middle East conflict had availed themselves of the possibility of requesting a state or a neutral organization to assume the functions of a Protecting Power. Indeed, when the CICR communicated with the states concerned with regard to the application of the Geneva Conventions, only the government of Jordan replied, and then simply to say that ' it did not accept the ICRC's viewpoint '.[50]

CICR delegates were usually given freedom of movement to visit prisoners of war. All applications for information with regard to missing prisoners rapidly received official answers from the Israel military authorities, and requests and suggestions were met in most cases by a positive response. The CICR was able to arrange for the repatriation of all seriously wounded casualties before the end of 1967. After delay in some cases, 5,638 Arab POWs and 19 Israeli POWs were exchanged on a bilateral basis. Detainees and internees were visited, but CICR delegates encountered difficulties in 1969 and 1970 in visiting Israeli prisoners held in Egypt; in 1970 the same problem was encountered in Syria.[51]

There were greater difficulties over the repatriation of civilians, but ' some twenty-thousand persons were enabled to return to their homes on one side or other of the cease-fire lines '. Some 3,700 family reunions were permitted on compassionate grounds.[52]

The CICR had evidence of deportations from the Golan Heights, the West Bank of the Jordan, and the Gaza Strip. The Israel authorities stated that in the case of the Golan Heights there had been no deportations, only ' voluntary departures '. As for the West Bank, those deported were Jordanian citizens engaged in activities detrimental to the interests of the state:

[49] Ibid. Sept. 1970, pp. 485–9. Under Art. 50 of the Hague Regulations, collective punishment was permitted against a population which could be held collectively responsible, but collective punishments are now prohibited by Arts 33 & 53 of the 4th Geneva Convention.

[50] *IRRC*, Aug. 1970, pp. 428–30.

[51] Ibid. pp. 435–44; Sept. 1970, pp. 499–506 & 511.

[52] Ibid. pp. 445–54; Sept. 1970, p. 510.

deportation, in Israel's view, was more humane than internment. There had been transfers of population within the Occupied Territories, and in most cases the persons transferred had accepted compensation.[53]

The CICR took the view that ' at least by analogy ' the provisions of the Fourth Convention should apply to Jewish communities in Arab countries. The CICR delegate was able to visit Jews ' assigned to residence in camps ' in Libya, and was in ' more or less constant touch ' with three communities of Jews with Syrian nationality. The Egyptian government, on the other hand, would not permit CICR delegates to visit interned Jews.[54]

As the CICR has not published comparable reports of other situations during and following armed conflict, it is impossible to judge whether its experience in the Middle East was in any way typical. No country complied fully with the obligations it had assumed, yet no country was totally impervious to the appeals of the CICR. It is easy for the cynic to dismiss the Geneva Conventions as mere ' paper promises ', but there can be no doubt that they act as a measuring rod against which to assess a state's conduct at a time when its national security is at stake. It is interesting that Max Petitpierre, a former President of the Swiss Confederation, concluded that ' on the whole the Geneva Conventions had been applied '.[55]

The CICR has no power other than the power of reason. It can appeal to a government's sense of compassion, but conscience is a very personal attribute; ' society as an entity has no conscience and no feeling of responsibility '.[56] All governments see some interest in respect for law and would like if possible to implement their legal obligations, if for no better reason than a hope that they can rely on other governments to do likewise.

There are many defects in the present system of humanitarian law applicable in armed conflict. There is, unfortunately, widespread ignorance of its basis principles. There are gaps in

[53] Ibid. Aug. 1970, pp. 454–9.
[54] Ibid. Sept. 1970, pp. 508–9.
[55] In *IRRC*, Feb. 1971, p. 66.
[56] Paul Roubiczek, *Ethical Values in the Age of Science* (London, 1969), p. 53.

the law itself. What law there is could be more rigorously applied, and there should be more effective action in the case of grave breaches.

Limitations applicable in armed conflict

One difficulty of securing full implementation of the Law of Geneva is that the Law of The Hague is so out of date. Indeed, the CICR has come to the conclusion that a clear distinction between the Law of Geneva and the Law of The Hague can no longer be maintained; 'belligerents necessarily consider this law as a single whole, and the inadequacy of the [Hague] rules relating to the conduct of hostilities has a negative impact on the observance of the Geneva Conventions'. Max Petitpierre, who writes from a wealth of experience, also insists that the law of war and humanitarian law 'cannot be dissociated'.[57] The General Assembly has, by implication, taken the same view, in regarding 'Respect for Human Rights in Armed Conflicts' as a single subject and in calling in one paragraph for states to become parties to the Hague Conventions of 1899 and 1907 and the Geneva CBW Protocol of 1925 (which belong to the Law of The Hague) and to the Geneva Conventions of 1949.[58] The humanitarian effort now must encompass both fields of law.

The present state of humanitarian law has paradoxical results. The crew of a bombing plane may direct their weapons against a military target in a built-up area and, as an indirect consequence, may kill or injure tens or hundreds of thousands of 'innocent' civilians. If the plane is later hit by anti-aircraft fire, the crew may eject or bail out, and then claim the full protection of the Hague and Geneva Conventions from those who may have survived their attack.[59] It is for this kind of reason that the CICR has been pressing for more than twenty years for a new international agreement on the protection of civilians against indiscriminate warfare. In 1955 it issued a set of draft rules designed to protect civilians in time of war; these

[57] Pictet, in *R. Internat. Commiss. Jurists*, Mar. 1969, p. 8; Petitpierre, in *IRRC*, Feb. 1971, p. 77.

[58] Res. 2444 (XXIII), 19 Dec. 1968, 2674 (XXV) & 2677 (XXV), 9 Dec. 1970.

[59] *Prelim. Rep.* App. 1, p. 28.

were revised and, in 1957, submitted to the International Conference of the Red Cross as *Draft Rules for the Limitation of the Dangers incurred by the Civilian Population in Time of War* (for text, see, App. III), together with a Commentary. The draft was approved in principle by the International Conference ' but had no practical effect at government level '.[60]

The CICR issued a new memorandum in 1967. In it, the CICR urgently called on governments to develop an adequate instrument of international law, and offered its assistance in drawing up such an instrument.[61] It emphasized that the Red Cross ' cannot take direct action to prevent or stop wars, except by rejecting the very idea of war; but it does at least strive continuously to limit their tragic consequences '.[62]

The fundamental humanitarian rule which forms the second basic principle of the Hague Conventions is expressed in double negative form: ' The right of belligerents to adopt means of injuring the enemy is not unlimited ' (Regulations, Art. 22).[63] This general rule may be made concrete in three ways: limitations for the benefit of persons, target limitations, and limitations on weapons and their use.

The limitations for the benefit of persons proceed from the basic principle of the Just War doctrine, namely, that combatants are the main force of resistance and a legitimate target of military operations, and that non-combatants shall neither participate in nor be subject to hostilities. Rousseau expressed the principle in his *Social Contract*:

The object of war being the destruction of the enemy State, a commander has a perfect right to kill its defenders so long as their arms are in their hands: but once they have laid them down and have submitted, they cease to be enemies . . . and revert to the condition of men pure and simple, over whose lives no one can any longer exercise a rightful claim.[64]

[60] *Questionnaire on the Protection of the Civilian Population against the Dangers arising from Hostilities* (doc. D 1157 b, 1970), p. 2.

[61] *Memo. on the Protection of Civilian Populations against the Dangers of Indiscriminate Warfare*, 19 May 1967.

[62] *Draft Rules*, p. 3.

[63] This was reaffirmed in res. XXVIII of the 20th Internat. Conference, Oct. 1965, and by GA res. 2444 (XXIII), 19 Dec. 1968, para. 1 (a).

[64] *Social Contract: Essays by Locke, Hume, and Rousseau* (London, 1947), p. 251.

If combatants who surrender are to be immune from attack, how much more those who never took up arms.

In October 1965 the 20th International Conference of the Red Cross reaffirmed (res. XXVIII) that a distinction must at all times be made between persons taking part in the hostilities and members of the civilian population, to the effect that the latter be spared as much as possible, and that to launch attacks against the civilian populations as such is prohibited; this was reaffirmed by the General Assembly in 1968 and again in 1970.[65] In the *Draft Rules* prepared by the CICR, ' the civilian population ' was defined (Art. 4) as ' all persons ' other than:

(a) Members of the armed forces, or of their auxiliary or complementary organizations.

(b) Persons who do not belong to the [armed] forces referred to above, but nevertheless take part in the fighting.

The CICR, after mature consideration, concluded that if the principle of the protection of the civilian population is to be maintained, it should apply even to civilians engaged in ' non-peaceful ' activities, such as scientists and workers in industries closely connected with the war effort. The CICR admits that this would open the way to abuses, but holds that ' these are minor drawbacks compared with the danger of excluding the above categories from the civilian population '.[66]

The CICR has pointed out that belligerents, in addition to their general obligation to refrain from deliberately attacking non-combatants, should take every precaution to reduce to a minimum the damage inflicted on non-combatants during attacks against military objectives, and should not commit acts of destruction in such a way as to cause harm to the civilian population disproportionate to the importance of the military objective under attack. For the attacking side, this requires careful choice and identification of military objectives, precision in attack, abstention from area bombing unless the area is exclusively military, abstention from attacking civil defence organizations, and (as required by Article 26 of the Hague

[65] Res. 2444 (XXIII), 19 Dec. 1968, para. 1 (b) and (c); 2675 (XXV), 9 Dec. 1970, para. 2. See also MML, paras 13, 88, & 288.

[66] *Draft Rules*, pp. 46–50.

Regulations) the giving of warning in specified cases. Belligerents attacking military objectives should do so in such a way as not to ' risk causing civilian populations harm out of all proportion to the military advantage expected '. For the side being attacked, it requires the evacuation of civilians from the vicinity of military objectives; civilians staying in or near military objectives or threatened areas do so at their own risk.[67]

Some legal writers consider that the practice of belligerents and trends since the second world war ' suggest that the immunity of the civilian population from intentional attack is reaching vanishing point ' and that traditional distinctions have been ' so whittled down . . . as to cease to offer any reliable guidance '.[68] The CICR admits the difficulty of maintaining civilian immunity, but does not for that reason consider that the principle should be abandoned; it points out that the principle ' is implicit in several texts '.[69]

Target limitations constitute a corollary of the group of limitations referred to above. The accepted rule is that attacks may be directed only against military objectives, that is to say, those of which the total or partial destruction would confer a distinct military advantage. The rule is stated in the Hague Regulations in the following terms: ' The attack or bombardment, *by whatever means*, of towns, villages, dwellings, or buildings which are undefended is prohibited ' (Art. 25).[70] This requires that before an objective is attacked, the attacking force shall identify it and ascertain that it is military.[71] Belligerents also have a particular obligation to spare charitable, religious,

[67] *Memo. on Protection*, Annex 2, pp. 1–2; *Questionnaire*, pp. 13–16; Art. 26 of the Regulations annexed to the Hague Conventions of 1899 and 1907; GA res. 2675 (XXV), 9 Dec. 1970, paras 3–4.

[68] Schwarzenberger, *Legality of Nuclear Weapons* (London, 1958), pp. 19 & 48, and his *International Law and Order* (London, 1971), pp. 191–2.

[69] *Questionnaire*, p. 8. In 1971 a conference of government experts drafted a protocol to the 4th Geneva Convention concerning the protection of sick and wounded civilians in time of war (for text, see App. IV). An important feature of this draft is that it would apply not only to persons specifically protected by the four Geneva Conventions but to ' the whole of the populations of the countries in conflict ' (Art. 1).

[70] The italicized words were not in the 1899 Convention. See also GA res. 2675 (XXV), 9 Dec. 1970, paras 5 & 6; MML, paras 284–90, and FM27-10, para. 39.

[71] *Draft Rules*, pp. 76–90.

scientific, cultural, and artistic establishments, and historic monuments.[72]

Not all international lawyers would maintain the rigid standards of the CICR. Schwarzenberger, on the one hand, emphasizes that ' the scope of legitimate objects of warfare is considerably wider than combatants . . . [and that] legitimate target areas are no longer limited to military objectives '.[73] Denise Bindschedler-Robert, on the other hand, points out (pp. 18 & 20) that the great majority of writers, while recognizing that the distinction between lawful and unlawful objectives is difficult to apply, ' believe that it continues to be legally valid '. Moreover, in all recent conflicts, ' each belligerent party has periodically accused the other of having bombed non-military objectives and the accused party has denied the facts without calling into question the cogency of the distinction '.[74]

Opinions differ as to whether it is preferable to seek international agreement on targets which may lawfully be attacked or on targets which may not lawfully be attacked. Certain targets are expressly mentioned as illicit in the Hague Regulations, the Geneva Conventions, and the Hague Convention on the protection of cultural property. The CICR *Draft Rules* include an Annex listing categories of military objectives which are ' generally acknowledged to be of military importance ' (see App. III, pp. 177-9).

The CICR considers that there are two rules which should limit weapons and their use. The first, which is the third basic principle of the Hague Conventions, is that it is forbidden to use weapons ' calculated to cause unnecessary suffering ' (*propres à causer des maux superflus*).[75] The aim when this text was adopted was not primarily to spare civilians, but to avoid causing suffering to combatants in excess of what is essential to place an adversary *hors de combat*. This is a very subjective test. What may seem ' necessary ' to the attacker may seem

[72] Annex to Hague Conventions, Art. 27; 1st Geneva Conv. 1949, Art. 19; 4th Geneva Conv. 1949, Art. 18; Hague Conv. 1954, Art. 4.

[73] *Legality of Nuclear Weapons*, p. 21.

[74] See also MML. paras 86 & 650, n. 1.

[75] Hague Regulations, Art. 23 (e). See Experts' Rpt, para. 597.

quite 'unnecessary' to those attacked. Some of the most effective weapons, such as napalm, are also the most cruel.[76] The British *Manual of Military Law* states that fire weapons shall be directed solely against 'inanimate military targets' and that it is illegal to use them 'solely against combatant personnel'.[77] The CICR points out that although the use of napalm has not been expressly prohibited, it does cause enormous suffering. It considers that the use of fire weapons 'should be accompanied by *special precautions* to prevent them unduly affecting members of the civilian population or disabling members of the armed forces, or causing unnecessary suffering. . . . This is a *minimum* solution'.[78] Nuclear weapons, because of the radiation effects, are viewed by Denise Bindschedler-Robert as 'particularly cruel and out of proportion to any military effect'; their use 'violates the prohibition against causing unnecessary injuries'.[79]

The CICR *Draft Rules* would prohibit the use of radioactive agents, as well as 'incendiary, chemical, bacteriological . . . or other agents'; the CICR considers that 'on the moral level it should continue to proclaim that the employment of atomic weapons is incompatible with the respect due to the persons protected by the Geneva Conventions and to noncombatants in general'.[80] The 20th International Conference of the Red Cross declared in 1965 that the general principles of the Law of War apply to 'nuclear and similar weapons' (res. XXVII). The Conference also invited governments which had not already done so to accede to the Geneva Protocol of 1925 (res. XIV), and this appeal was renewed at the Istanbul Red Cross Conference in 1969.

I refer in Chapter 5 to certain efforts within the UN context to ban the use of nuclear weapons by means of an international convention, but I should add that some distinguished international lawyers have been less than enthusiastic about

---

[76] *Memo. on Protection*, Annex 2, p. 4; CICR, *Reaffirmation and Development of the Humanitarian Laws and Customs applicable in Armed Conflicts* (D 1055b, 1969), p. 12.

[77] Greenspan, pp. 360–2; MML, paras 109, n. 1, & 110, n. 1.

[78] *Istanbul Rep.*, pp. 62–3; *Memo. on Protection*, Annex 2, p. 4.

[79] D. Bindschedler-Robert, p. 31; see also MML, paras 107, n. 1(b) and 113.

[80] *Draft Rules*, Art. 14; *Istanbul Rep.*, p. 54.

such efforts. Schwarzenberger, for instance, considers that such a convention would be a ' grotesquely incongruous ' response to the challenge confronting the world.[81]

The second limitation which the CICR would impose on the use of weapons would be to prohibit the use of ' blind ' weapons, which not only cause great suffering ' but do not allow of precision against specific targets or have such wide-spread effect, in time and place as to be uncontrollable '.[82] The prohibition would apply to chemical and bacteriological weapons (which are, in any event, prohibited under the Geneva CBW Protocol of 1925), floating mines, and delayed-action weapons. The CICR has emphasized that the special danger in using poison gas is the risk of escalation.[83]

It hardly needs to be stressed that the CICR considers that any bombing or other actions undertaken ' with the object of terrorizing [the civilian population] . . . are prohibited '.[84] Indeed, terror bombing, ' far from shattering the enemy's morale, may even [during the second world war] have encouraged a spirit of resistance which prolonged the war '.[85]

Some of the limitations which the CICR would wish to see enforced presuppose that a distinction can be made between combatants and civilians. The fact is that the immunity of civilians is still one of the pillars of international law. Although there have been many examples of blatant disregard of the rule, no government has claimed that to do so is lawful. To the extent that violations have been defended, the argument has been that it was a reprisal for an unlawful act of an enemy or an exceptional measure dictated by overriding considerations, such as the saving of human lives by putting an end to the war quickly.

On the initiative of Norway, the General Assembly on 9 December 1970 adopted a resolution (2675 (XXV)) affirming eight ' basic principles for the protection of civilian populations

[81] *Legality of Nuclear Weapons*, p. 59, and his *Internat. Law & Order*, pp. 193–207.
[82] *Memo. on Protection*, Annex 2, p. 4.
[83] *Questionnaire*, p. 26.
[84] Ibid. p. 24; see also D. H. N. Johnson, ' Legality of Modern Forms of Aerial Warfare ', *Aeronautical J.*, Aug. 1968, p. 689.
[85] D. Bindschedler-Robert, p. 24.

in armed conflict ',[86] but the *Draft Rules* prepared by the CICR have not yet been acted upon.

Irregular fighters and internal wars

It is necessary to start this section with some definitions. The Hague Regulations are declared to apply ' not only to armies, but also to militia and volunteer corps fulfilling [certain] conditions ' (Art. 1). The first three Geneva Conventions of 1949 apply to ' members of the armed forces of a Party to the conflict as well as members of militias or volunteer corps forming part of such armed forces '. In addition, the Geneva Conventions cover ' members of other militias or other volunteer corps, including those of organized resistance movements . . . [fulfilling] the following conditions '.[87] The General Assembly has, in a number of resolutions, called for the application of the Geneva Conventions to ' freedom fighters ',[88] ' participants in resistance movements and freedom fighters ',[89] and ' people captured during their struggle for freedom '.[90] I will use the portmanteau words *irregulars* or *irregular fighters* for all such clandestine underground fighters, partisans, guerrillas, or resistance groups.

The Geneva Conventions of 1949 refer in common Article 3 to ' armed conflicts not of an international character '. I will usually use a shorter expression, such as ' internal armed conflicts ' or ' internal wars '.

Both the Hague Regulations and the Geneva Conventions list four conditions which must be fulfilled by irregular fighters if they are to qualify for the protection afforded by the Conventions. In addition, the Geneva Conventions refer to two other conditions not expressly mentioned in the Hague Regulations.

The two conditions included only in the Geneva Conventions are that irregulars must be ' organized ', and that they must belong to ' a Party to the conflict '. The four conditions

[86] For text, see App. V, pp. 187-8.
[87] Conv. I & II, Art. 13; III, 4.
[88] Res. 2446 (XXIII), 19 Dec. 1968; 2506A (XXIV), 21 Nov. 1969; 2621 (XXV), 12 Oct. 1970; 2707 (XXV), 14 Dec. 1970.
[89] Res. 2674 (XXV), 9 Dec. 1970.
[90] Res. 2678 (XXV), 9 Dec. 1970.

common to both the Hague Regulations and the Geneva
Conventions are:

1. Irregulars must be ' commanded by a person responsible
for his subordinates '.

2. They must have ' a fixed distinctive sign recognizable at a
distance '.[91]

3. They must carry their arms ' openly '.

4. They must conduct their operations ' in accordance with
the laws and customs of war'.

The four conditions common to both the Hague Regulations
and the Geneva Conventions were first formulated in Article 9
of the Brussels Declaration of 27 August 1874.[92] The purpose
was to avoid a situation in which marauders or bandits, on
capture, might claim POW status.

Irregular fighting has been a feature of many conflicts since
the second world war, and this has raised acute legal problems.
An important study of the legal status of irregular fighters,
conducted for the World Veterans' Federation, reached the
following conclusions.[93]

1. The laws of war (*jus in bello*) must be applied regardless of
the cause of war. The question whether a war is lawful or not
is therefore irrelevant with respect to the legal status accorded
to members of resistance groups.

2. Articles 1 and 2 of the Hague Regulations and Article 4 of
the Geneva Convention relative to the Treatment of Prisoners
of War 1949, lay down the conditions which members of resistance groups must meet in order to be treated as privileged
combatants.

3. Members of resistance movements who do not conform to
the requirements mentioned in 2 above cannot be considered
as privileged combatants. In case of capture they will be treated
as common criminals and not as prisoners of war. They may
claim a certain amount of protection by virtue of the Fourth
Geneva Convention and of general principles of law.

[91] This is the wording of the Geneva Conventions; the Hague Regulations have
' emblem ' instead of' sign '.

[92] *Docs re. 1st Hague Peace Conference*, p. 34.

[93] W. J. Ford, ' Resistance Movements and International Law ', *IRRC*, Jan.
1968, pp. 14–15. See also MML, paras 91–5 and 634, & FM27-10, para. 64.

4. For the opposing party in armed conflicts not of an international character a minimum protection has been included in Article 3 common to the four Geneva Conventions of 1949.

5. International law does not forbid the civilian population to commit acts of resistance, but leaves the Occupying Power free to punish these acts.

6. A study of the legal conviction underlying the laws of war relative to the conditions included in Articles 1 and 2 of the Hague Regulations and Article 4 of the Geneva Convention relative to the Treatment of Prisoners of War is necessary. The results of such a study should be made known.

7. The military manuals in the respective countries should be adjusted to each other as much as possible in order to eliminate difficulties arising from different texts.

It is clear from paragraphs 2 and 3 above that many irregular fighters, if captured, run the risk of being treated as common criminals. Consider, for example, the following account of irregular fighting in Southern Africa.[94]

In Rhodesia, the joint forces [of the Zimbabwe African People's Union and the African National Congress of South Africa] wear uniforms. But so far, the rebel [Smith] régime has executed its prisoners of war, and ZAPU does the same. Eventually the nationalist intention is to institutionalize uniformed warfare under Geneva Convention rules. ZAPU will then borrow Viet Cong techniques—such as mobile cages—to keep prisoners alive. They will be prepared to exchange them for their own captured comrades or for political prisoners. Taking civilians as hostages is also envisaged, but only if this appears to be the only way to open the concentration camps . . . ZANU forces [Zimbabwe African National Union] . . . wear civilian clothes, carry forged *situpas* (identity cards) and are mainly concerned with sabotage (though they have so far eschewed terror). The ANC troops operating with ZAPU shed their uniforms at the Limpopo [frontier with South Africa], but their objectives in South Africa are similar to those of the Zimbabweans in Rhodesia: the establishment of bases.

The development of new techniques of rebellion, insurgency, and counter-insurgency has raised in acute form the question whether the requirements mentioned above are all necessary if

[94] R. W. Howe, ' Wars in Southern Africa ', *Foreign Affairs*, Oct. 1969, pp. 151 & 153.

irregular fighters are to qualify for protection under the Hague and Geneva Conventions.

Irregular fighters must be ' organized ', and must belong ' to a Party to the conflict '

These two conditions from the Geneva Conventions seem essential if the public authorities are to distinguish between irregular fighters entitled to protection and marauders or bandits operating for private gain.

Irregulars must be ' commanded by a person responsible for his subordinates '

An Advisory Group of the World Veterans' Federation has commented that

in the minds of those who drafted the Convention ' organized resistance movements ' were deemed to be formations with a hierarchy of command; that being so, it was sufficient if the responsible person was the one responsible for the resistance movement at the highest level and was recognized as such by one [*sic*] of the parties to the conflict.

In any case, the requirement could perhaps be modified to provide simply that irregulars should be subject to military penal law.[95]

Irregulars must have ' a fixed distinctive sign [or emblem] recognizable at a distance '

This stipulation was included in the Geneva Conventions of 1949 ' in full knowledge of the fact that during the Second World War it was frequently violated '; it ' does not by any means signify that the guerrilla may not camouflage himself as any regular soldier may, but he may not camouflage himself as a civilian '.[96] The Advisory Group of the World Veterans' Federation understood the requirement to mean that such a sign

ought to be distinctive in order to make it possible to distinguish the wearer from the peaceful population, that it should be fixed in the sense that the wearer should wear it throughout the whole

---

[95] *Istanbul Rep.*, Annexes, p. 070.
[96] D. Bindschedler-Robert, pp. 43-4, and Experts' Rpt, paras 381 & 521.

operation, and that it should be recognizable at a distance in the same way as the uniforms of regular forces.[97]

Irregulars must carry their arms ' openly '

This requirement could be interpreted to mean that ' when the resistance fighter was engaged on operations, he should carry the weapons in his possession in a similar way to members of the regular forces '.[98]

Irregulars must conduct their operations ' in accordance with the laws and customs of war '

This last requirement seems to me to raise the most difficult questions of all. There is, in the first place, uncertainty and disagreement among the experts as to precisely what are ' the laws and customs of war '. Regular armed forces, operating in accordance with manuals of military law, have been known to disregard ' the laws and customs of war '; irregular fighters, with no such manuals, and in some cases with minimal education and training, are likely to have no more than a rudimentary idea of ' the laws and customs of war '. Moreover, their opponents may be flouting these laws and customs.

On the other hand, it would be an entirely retrograde step to introduce the idea that ' the laws and customs of war ' are losing or have lost their validity. These laws and customs, which are for the protection of combatants as well as non-combatants, should be made more precise and strengthened, not dispensed with. ' It is not possible, nor is it desirable, to adapt these laws to the " military necessities " of the guerrillas.' [99]

It can hardly be disputed that in insurgency and counter-insurgency warfare, civilians may be ' more severely affected than in other forms of war '.[100] The purpose of the irregular fighter is often to demonstrate that the public authorities are incapable of governing. This can be accomplished by fostering discontent but also by resorting to acts of terrorism such as the assassination of the élite on the other side. The fact that this

[97] *Istanbul Rep.*, Annexes, p. 070.
[98] Ibid.
[99] D. Bindschedler-Robert, p. 44.
[100] CICR, *Reaffirmation and Development of Humanitarian Laws*, p.30; see also *Prelim. Rep.*, Annex, p. 8.

may be done in a righteous cause, as in a struggle for equal rights and self-determination of peoples, does not alter the fact that deliberately to kill an innocent person is murder.

During the past quarter of a century, the problem of irregular fighters has arisen mainly in connection with internal wars, but the Geneva Conventions of 1949, born of the experience of the second world war, were primarily designed to deal with wars ' between two or more of the High Contracting Parties ', that is to say, inter-state wars (Art. 2). But the four Conventions also contain common Article 3, which sets out certain minimum standards in the case of ' armed conflict not of an international character ' occurring in the territory of one of the parties. This article has been described by Tom J. Farer as composed of ' affectionate generalities ',[101] but as it is of great importance, I give the text in full:

In the case of armed conflict not of an international character occurring in the territory of one of the High Contracting Parties, each Party to the conflict shall be bound to apply, as a minimum, the following provisions:

(1) Persons taking no active part in the hostilities, including members of armed forces who have laid down their arms and those placed *hors de combat* by sickness, wounds, detention, or any other cause, shall in all circumstances be treated humanely, without any adverse distinction founded on race, colour, religion or faith, sex, birth or wealth, or any other similar criteria.

To this end, the following acts are and shall remain prohibited at any time and in any place whatsoever with respect to the above-mentioned persons:

(a) violence to life and person, in particular murder of all kinds, mutilation, cruel treatment and torture;

(b) taking of hostages;

(c) outrages upon personal dignity, in particular humiliating and degrading treatment;

(d) the passing of sentences and the carrying out of executions without previous judgment pronounced by a regularly consti-tuted court, affording all the judicial guarantees which are recognized as indispensable by civilized peoples.

[101] ' Laws of War 25 Years after Nuremberg ', *Internat. Conciliation*, May 1971, p. 32.

(2) The wounded and sick shall be collected and cared for.

An impartial humanitarian body, such as the International Committee of the Red Cross, may offer its services to the Parties to the conflict.

The Parties to the conflict should further endeavour to bring into force, by means of special agreements, all or part of the other provisions of the present Convention.

The application of the preceding provisions shall not affect the legal status of the Parties to the conflict.

It should be emphasized that there is no necessary connection between irregular fighters and internal wars. Irregulars have in the past taken part in inter-state conflicts of the classical kind. Internal wars have been conducted solely by regular forces. But if one reviews the armed conflicts since the second world war, one finds that a large number of them have been internal, and that irregulars have often taken part on one or both sides. These internal wars have, in the words of a CICR report, been ' frequent and deadly '.[102]

In an internal war, common Article 3 is to be applied ' as a minimum '. Both regular and irregular forces must conduct their operations in accordance with the laws and customs of war. There is, moreover, a strong body of legal opinion which considers that the humanitarian Conventions do not simply bind states, but that they also bind people. In other words, irregular fighters have the same obligation to apply international humanitarian law as do the official governmental authorities which they seek to undermine or supplant. ' There are good reasons to admit that conventions binding the State govern . . . all legal or insurgent authorities which claim to be connected with the State.' [103] The CICR has made this point even more bluntly. ' Adherence to these [Geneva] Conventions is binding not only on the government, but also on the population of the State concerned.' Article 3 must be applied even by ' authorities which were not in existence when the State . . . became a party to the Conventions '.[104]

It is evident from recent history that the frontier between

---

[102] *Istanbul Rep.*, p. 8.
[103] D. Bindschedler-Robert, pp. 53–4, & MML, para. 131, n. 1.
[104] *Protection of Victims of Non-International Conflicts* (DS 5 a–b, 1969), p. 4.

internal and international wars is not always clear. Many legal experts would regard the intervention of foreign personnel as transforming an internal conflict into an international one,[105] but there are ways of providing disguised aid by means of 'volunteers' and mercenaries.[106] The fact is that states are reluctant to admit that armed conflict is taking place within their borders and consequently that Article 3 comes into force. There have been no formal ultimatums or declarations of war since 1945.[107]

There is now a widespread feeling that the standards set forth in Article 3 'as a minimum' could usefully be elaborated. The 21st International Conference of the Red Cross went on record in 1969 as favouring action to make Article 3 more specific, or to supplement it. It also asked the CICR to make a thorough study of the legal status of persons taking part in internal wars and expressed the hope that such persons, if captured, should be 'protected against any inhumanity and brutality and receive treatment similar to that which . . . [the third] Convention lays down for prisoners of war'.[108]

Among the changes in regard to internal wars for which there is a widespread demand are the following [109]:

1. More specific provisions regarding judicial procedures for captured personnel and the punishment of offenders, with the possibility of penal proceedings against war criminals [110];

2. No punishment of combatants or civilians solely for having espoused the cause of a party to the conflict;

3. Deferment of executions during hostilities.[111]

4. General amnesty at the end of hostilities.

5. Specific provision for respect of the Red Cross sign, and of hospitals and similar medical units and establishments.

6. Provision for 'the free passage of all consignments of

[105] *Prelim. Rep.*, Annex 1, p. 15.

[106] Ibid. pp. 11–12, & 21.

[107] *Reaffirmation & Development of Humanitarian Laws*, p. 22.

[108] Res. XVII & XVIII; Michel Veuthey, 'The Red Cross and Non-International Conflicts', *IRRC*, Aug. 1970, p. 414; *Prelim. Rep.*, Annex 1, pp. 19 & 29.

[109] *Prelim. Rep.*, p. 57.

[110] Relevant in this connection are the Standard Minimum Rules for the Treatment of Prisoners, approved by res. 663 C(XXIV) of ECOSOC, 31 July 1957.

[111] *Istanbul Rep.*, p. 121; *Prelim. Rep.*, Annex 1, p. 20.

medical and hospital stores and objects necessary for religious worship intended only for civilians . . . [and] essential food-stuffs, clothing and tonics for children under fifteen, expectant mothers and maternity cases '.[112]

7. Arrangements for both material relief and ' moral comfort ' for captured personnel.[113]

8. The granting to captured combatants of a status analogous to that provided for POWs in the Third Geneva Convention.

9. Strengthening of the provisions whereby the CICR can undertake its humanitarian tasks.

The change which is most difficult to bring about, and yet which has been called for in a considerable number of resolutions of the General Assembly, is no. 8 above.[114] I have referred earlier to the six conditions with which irregular fighters must comply if they are to come within the terms of the POW Convention. The dilemma is that the wider the definition of persons entitled to POW status, the wider the definition of those who may lawfully be attacked.

At a conference of government experts held in Geneva in 1971, considerable attention was devoted to the possibility of elaborating the provisions of Article 3, and a draft protocol was adopted setting out the protection to be afforded to the wounded and sick (see App. IV, pp. 184-6). This was a useful advance, though it left many matters for future attention.

[112] This is the wording used in Art. 23 of the 4th Convention.
[113] Veuthey, in *IRRC*, Aug. 1970, p. 417.
[114] Res. 2383 (XXIII), 7 Nov. 1968 (Rhodesia); 2395 (XXIII), 29 Nov. 1968 (Portuguese Territories); 2396 (XXIII), 2 Dec. 1968 (South Africa); 2446 (XXIII), 19 Dec. 1968 (race discrimination and apartheid); 2506A (XXIV), 21 Nov. 1969 (South Africa); 2508 (XXIV), 21 Nov. 1969 (Rhodesia); 2547A (XXIV), 11 Dec. 1969 (Southern Africa); 2621 (XXV), 12 Oct. 1970 (Colonial Countries and Peoples); 2652 (XXV), 3 Dec. 1970 (Rhodesia); 2674 (XXV), 9 Dec. 1970 (human rights in armed conflicts); 2678 (XXV), 9 Dec. 1970 (Namibia); 2707 (XXV), 14 Dec. 1970 (Portuguese Territories). See also *Istanbul Rep.*, p. 121. See MML, para. 124, n. 1; FM27-10, paras 61, 64, & 80; and Experts' Rpt, paras 113 & 385.

HUMAN RIGHTS IN ARMED CONFLICTS

Everyone has the right to life, liberty and
security of person.
Universal Declaration of Human Rights

A RECENT UN report refers to the reluctance which has been shown by UN organs to consider ' questions which presuppose the persistence of war or even the occurrence of hostilities '.[1] At its very first session, the ILC rejected a proposal that it should attempt to codify the laws of war. The majority of the members of the Commission considered that as war had been outlawed, the regulation of its conduct had ceased to be relevant.

The majority of the Commission declared itself opposed to the study of the problem at the present stage [1949]. It was considered that if the Commission, at the very beginning of its work, were to undertake this study, public opinion might interpret its action as showing lack of confidence in the efficiency of the means at the disposal of the United Nations for maintaining peace.[2]

The UN, after all, was created to keep the peace, and its Members have agreed to refrain from the threat or use of force in their international relations.[3] But this does not mean that armed conflict has ceased. In the first place, the UN Charter does not impair the right of self-defence ' until the Security Council has taken measures necessary to maintain international peace and security ' (Art. 51). Secondly, the UN is itself permitted to use armed force (Art. 42). Thirdly, armed conflict can occur between factions within a state, or between the authorities of a state and dissident groups; such conflict will not necessarily be contrary to any provision of the Charter.

---

[1] A/7720, *Report of Secretary-General on Respect for Human Rights in Armed Conflict*, 20 Nov. 1969, para. 19. See also his 2nd report with the same title, A/8052, 18 Sept. 1970, paras 12–13, and Kunz, ' The chaotic Status of the Laws of War and the Urgent Necessity for their Revision ', 45 *AJIL* (1951), 42–3.

[2] A/925 (*GAOR*, 4th sess., suppl. 10), para. 18.

[3] Art. 2 (4) of the Charter.

Finally, it hardly needs to be noted that states have resorted to the use of armed force against the territorial integrity or political independence of other states in disregard of their Charter obligations. The *Yearbook of World Armaments and Disarmament 1968–9* of the Stockholm International Peace Research Institute lists over 100 conflicts during the period 1945–68, and many of these have been in violation of the UN Charter.

Since 1968 attempts have been made to reinforce the humanitarian work of national and international Red Cross agencies by resort to the human-rights machinery of the UN. Secretary-General Thant has pointed out that a common feature of the four Geneva (Red Cross) Conventions of 1949 and UN human-rights instruments is that they ' appear to belong to the category of treaties setting forth " absolute obligations " '. The obligations, in his view, do not depend on reciprocity (A/7720, para. 82).

Teheran Conference on Human Rights and UN General Assembly, 1968

The first substantial discussion of the role of the UN regarding respect for human rights in armed conflicts took place in 1968 at the International Conference on Human Rights at Teheran, one of the chief events of Human Rights Year. A resolution on the subject was proposed by India and co-sponsored by Czechoslovakia, Jamaica, Uganda, and the UAR. The resolution had a long preamble which, besides referring to various international legal instruments, noted that ' racist or colonial regimes . . . frequently resort to executions and inhuman treatment ', and considered that persons who struggle against such regimes ' should be protected against inhuman or brutal treatment and . . . if detained should be treated as prisoners of war or political prisoners under international law '. The substance of the resolution called on states to accede to the relevant instruments; invited the General Assembly to initiate a study of existing agreements and the need for new ones; and asked the Secretary-General, after consultation with the CICR, to urge governments to respect existing rules of international law.[4]

[4] Final Act of Internat. Conference on Human Rights, 1968, ch. 3, res. XXIII, 12 May 1968.

The British representative at the conference expressed 'serious doubts' about the reference to colonial or racist regimes. He thought it was a mistake to make a direct link between 'freedom fighters' and prisoners of war, in the strict sense in which the CICR had understood the latter expression. He asked for a separate vote on this part of the proposal, but it was approved by 68 votes to none, with 15 abstentions (mainly Western countries). The British representative then voted in favour of the resolution as a whole, which was adopted by 67 votes in favour, no negative votes, and 2 abstentions. Switzerland abstained on the ground that the CICR, the guardian of the Red Cross Conventions, had not been consulted; the Republic of Vietnam (South) gave no public explanation of its abstention.

The substance of the Teheran resolution was raised during the General Assembly later in 1968 in the form of a draft resolution sponsored by sixteen states. One paragraph of the proposal, which would have affirmed that the general principles of the Law of War apply to nuclear and similar weapons, was deleted at the request of the Soviet Union. The amended proposal was then approved by the Assembly (res. 2444 (XXIII), 19 Dec. 1968). The operative part of the resolution affirmed resolution XXVIII of the International Red Cross Conference of 1965 to the effect that:

1. The right of the parties to a conflict to adopt means of injuring the enemy is not unlimited (as noted earlier, this is the essence of Article 12 of the Brussels Declaration of 1874 and Article 22 of the Regulations annexed to the Hague Conventions of 1899 and 1907).

2. It is prohibited to launch attacks against the civilian populations as such.

3. Distinction must be made at all times between persons taking part in the hostilities and members of the civilian population to the effect that the latter be spared as much as possible.

The Secretary-General was asked to do three things:

1. Study steps which could be taken to secure the better application of humanitarian conventions and rules in all armed conflicts.

2. Study the need for additional humanitarian conventions or other legal instruments.

3. 'Take all other necessary steps to give effect to . . . the present resolution and to report to the General Assembly at its twenty-fourth [1969] session.'

States which had not already done so were called upon to become parties to the Hague Conventions of 1899 and 1907, the Geneva Protocol of 1925, and the Geneva Conventions of 1949.

It is interesting to speculate about the intentions of the 111 UN Members who voted for this resolution, since more than half of them have not responded to their own appeal to become parties to the Hague Conventions.[5] On the other hand, as noted in Chapter 5, there has been a steady increase in the number of parties to the 1925 CBW Geneva Protocol. As for the Red Cross Conventions of 1949, the UN Secretary-General reported in 1969 that all but twelve UN Members had adhered to them,[6] and there have been two accessions since 1969.

The Secretary-General was a little slow off the mark in following up the 1968 decision of the General Assembly, but on 19 May 1969 he communicated the provisions of the Assembly's resolution to member states, specialized agencies, UN bodies, and ' a number of non-governmental organizations '. Twenty-one of the 126 member states had replied to his letter by the time his report went to press on 20 November 1969, some merely endorsing the Assembly's resolution or giving factual information about the conventions to which they were parties, others going into detail about steps which they suggested might be taken in the future. Many of the replies reflected the preoccupations of the government concerned: Britain sent the text of her draft convention to ban biological weapons (A/7720, pp. 86–90); Mexico commended the treaty on the denuclearization of Latin America (A/7720, p. 80); the United States complained that North Vietnam had been disregarding the Geneva POW Convention (A/7720, pp. 90–3); Finland proposed that a study be undertaken of neutrality and the status of neutral nationals (A/7720, p. 76); UNESCO

---

[5] Of the 56 states which are parties to or consider themselves bound by one or both of the Hague Conventions, 53 are UN Members.

[6] A/7720, p. 40, n. 49 & pp. 112–14.

suggested a study of the factors which contribute to the inadequacy of existing rules of international law, an appraisal of major innovative legal ideas regarding better application of existing rules, and a study of the range of conditioning processes necessary to ensure human rights in armed conflicts (A/7720, p. 95). WHO, the UN Children's Fund, and the UN High Commissioner for Refugees also sent letters. The number of non-governmental organizations which replied is not disclosed. The CICR sent a letter and later communicated the text of six resolutions adopted at the 21st International Red Cross Conference. Three UN Members responded later, and their replies were annexed to the Secretary-General's Supplementary Report (A/8052) in 1970.

U Thant's preliminary report, 1969

U Thant's first report (A/7720) did not pretend to be more than preliminary, and dealt with only a limited number of questions. He commented that constructive suggestions for remedial action had been relatively few, and that what was required was ' a relatively long-term United Nations endeavour ' (para. 13). Annexed to the report were replies from governments, UN organs and agencies, and the CICR.

The first chapter makes the interesting point that the second world war ' gave conclusive proof of the close relationship which exists between outrageous behaviour of a Government towards its own citizens and aggression against other nations '. The Secretary-General then provides a historical survey of international humanitarian instruments, starting with the Geneva Convention of 1864 (sick and wounded in time of war) and going up to the nuclear non-proliferation treaty (NPT) of 1968. The next chapter compared the four Red Cross Conventions of 1949 and UN instruments in the field of human rights. But the most important chapter was concerned with the substance of the task entrusted to the Secretary-General. He emphasized that the whole problem of humanitarian protection had become very difficult to handle because recent developments had threatened to blur traditional distinctions. The distinction between combatants and civilians was threatened by advances in military technology, and the distinction between international and internal wars had been becoming less clear (paras 16 & 131).

In 1963, following the fighting in Katanga, the Council of Delegates of the CICR had passed a resolution recommending (a) that the UN should be invited to adopt a solemn declaration accepting that the Geneva Conventions apply equally to UN Emergency Forces as they apply to the forces of parties to the Conventions; (b) that the governments of countries providing contingents to the UN should, as a matter of prime importance, give their contingents ' adequate instructions on the Geneva Conventions as well as orders to comply with them '; (c) that the authorities responsible for UN contingents should agree to take all necessary measures to ' prevent and repress ' any infringements of the Conventions.[7]

This matter was raised again in 1969 in the letter of the CICR to U Thant, in which it proposed that the UN should itself formally undertake to apply the Geneva Conventions and other humanitarian rules in operations in which UN forces are engaged. ' Such a gesture would have value as an example.' In issuing regulations for UN forces in the Middle East, the Congo, and Cyprus, the Secretary-General has stipulated that such forces should observe ' the principles and spirit of the general international conventions applicable to the conduct of military personnel '. At the same time he has insisted that training and discipline of troops in UN operations ' has thus far rested with each national contingent ', and that progress would come from a wider acceptance of humanitarian conventions by contributing states rather than by having the UN undertake ' obligations whose discharge would involve the exercise of an authority it has not been granted ' (A/7720, paras 9 & 114 & p. 102). It seems to me a pity that het Secretary-General has not found it possible to evolve a formula that would go at least part of the way to meeting the long-held views of the CICR in this respect.

The 1969 report contained a number of proposals of the Secretary-General of ' areas where it would appear that useful studies might be undertaken ' and the annexes contained other

[7] CICR, *Ann. Rep. 1963* (1964), pp. 49–50.

proposals of UN organs and agencies, and governments. Most of the proposals referred to such matters as the clarification or strengthening of existing instruments; the preparation of new instruments for the better protection of civilians, prisoners, and combatants; the problem of internal armed conflicts; the use of napalm and other weapons alleged to cause unnecessary suffering; and relief activities. These were all discussed in greater detail in the Secretary-General's Supplementary Report in 1970.

U Thant's 1969 report did not become available until the first week of December, by which time the General Assembly had almost completed its 24th session. It was considered rather hurriedly at three meetings of the Assembly's Third Committee. There was general appreciation for the preliminary report and a wish that the study should be continued. Pakistan and Tanzania proposed that in any future work ' special attention ' should be given to the protection of those engaged in ' conflicts which arise from the struggle of peoples under colonial and foreign rule for liberation and self-determination '. This was approved by 48 votes (Afro-Asian and Communist countries) to 17 (West plus Japan), with 28 abstentions (about half of the abstainers being Latin Americans).[8] There was a minor skirmish—one of many on the issue during the 1969 session of the Assembly—on whether the request to states to co-operate in future studies should be addressed to UN Members only or to all states, but an Algerian proposal to replace ' States Members of the United Nations ' by ' Governments ' was defeated.[9] The draft resolution of the Third Committee was approved in plenary meeting by 91 votes to none. The UK was among 23 abstainers, who were presumably the opponents of the Pakistani-Tanzanian amendment.[10]

The resolution asked the Secretary-General to continue his study, to consult and co-operate with the CICR, and to present a further report in 1970; UN Members were asked to extend all possible assistance to him. U Thant's 1969 report was to be transmitted to both the Human Rights Commission and

[8] A/C.3/SR.1733 (mimeo.), 11 Dec. 1969, pp. 5 & 10.
[9] A/C.3/SR.1732 (mimeo.), 10 Dec. 1969, p. 14; A/C.3/SR.1733 (mimeo.), p. 11.
[10] Cmnd. 4363 (1970), para. 313.

ECOSOC 'for their comments'.[11] The comments of the Human Rights Commission were duly annexed to the Supplementary Report in 1970.[12]

U Thant's Supplementary Report, 1970

The Secretary-General's Supplementary Report, issued on 18 September 1970, was in many ways a model of how the UN Secretariat should conduct studies and, on the basis of those studies, put forward proposals for action or further research. Some of his proposals went beyond what governments will now accept, but this is not in itself a reason to refrain from reviewing the consequences of implementing, or failing to implement, various proposals for action.

It may be useful to start with one matter which was dealt with in a preliminary way in 1969 and more conclusively in 1970.[13] While it is true that the UN and regional instruments on human rights on the one hand, and the four Geneva Conventions of 1949 on the other hand, complement each other, the protection afforded by the two sets of instruments is not identical. Common Article 3 of the Geneva Conventions of 1949 sets out minimum standards to be applied in conflicts not of an international character. This goes further in some respects than the UN Covenant on Civil and Political Rights (which has not yet entered into force) in that it provides for judicial guarantees which may not be suspended in periods of armed conflict, and expressly prohibits the taking of hostages. The UN Covenant, on the other hand, goes further than common Article 3 in that it would apply at all times, in all places, and to all individuals without distinction as to nationality or status. The Covenant would also expressly prohibit retroactive penal legislation.[14]

The Secretary-General concluded that the four Geneva Conventions should, as far as possible, remain untouched. He considered, however, that they show 'certain imperfections, inadequacies and gaps' and he suggested that the UN should

[11] GA res. 2597 (XXIV), 16 Dec. 1969; see also E/CN.4/1033, 20 Jan. 1970 (mimeo.).

[12] A/8052, Annex II, pp. 114–16.

[13] A/7720, paras 70–108; A/8052, Annex 1, pp. 87–113.

[14] A/8052, para. 16 and Annex 1, paras 32–4 & 76–8.

be willing to act ' specially in fields in which the International Committee [of the Red Cross] cannot operate '.[15]

The Secretary-General considered what could be done to ensure better humanitarian protection for three groups of persons: civilians, prisoners, and combatants. Civilians are especially exposed if they find themselves close to the battle zone, which may itself be constantly fluctuating.[16] The Secretary-General tentatively suggested in 1969, as did Austria, that sanctuaries or zones of refuge should be established for those civilians not taking part in hostilities,[17] and this idea was elaborated in more detail in his 1970 report. The proposals for verification of civilian sanctuaries were to some extent adapted from the arrangements in the Hague Convention of 14 May 1954 for the Protection of Cultural Property. U Thant suggested that such civilian sanctuaries should be registered with an international authority and be subject to ' an effective system of control and verification '. They should bear ' special markings and insignia, clearly visible and recognizable '. Free access should be granted to official inspectors at all times, and the inspectors would be empowered to order an investigation of a suspected violation of the obligations entered into. The inspector should be permitted to fix a time-limit for rectification which, if not complied with, could lead to the lifting of the protection and immunity. Shelter should be given in such sanctuaries to ' civilians taking no part in hostilities and in no way contributing to the war effort '. The zones would be ' completely disarmed and demilitarized ' and should contain no large industrial or administrative establishment, no important communications or transport facilities, and no installations which might be put to military use. They should be demarcated in such a way that belligerents would secure no military advantage from their existence. Sanctuaries should be immune from attack, possibly even in conflicts not of an international

[15] Ibid. paras 14–17; see also A/7720, paras 180–2.

[16] A/7720, paras 137–8; A/8052, para. 32; see also the CICR's *Prelim. Rep.*, Annex 1, p. 28.

[17] A/7720, paras 145–52 & p. 73. The Geneva Conventions provide for hospital and safety zones, and neutralized zones for sick and wounded combatants and civilians (I, 23; IV, 14–15). See also MML, paras 26-7, and FM27-10, paras 45b and 253-4.

character. The Secretary-General suggested that the matter should be given ' a comprehensive analysis and study in depth ... by a group or committee of qualified experts ' with a view to the preparation of a Protocol to the Geneva Conventions of 1949 or a separate international instrument (A/8052, paras 45–87).

The other main proposal for the better protection of civilians would involve the setting out of a code of standard minimum rules, complementary to the obligations which states have already assumed; this would necessarily require a review of the Hague Regulations (paras 34–44). Such a code would need to define those entitled to protection as civilians, but such definition should be irrespective of nationality and should expressly apply to refugees and stateless persons.[18] A detailed set of norms was proposed in the Secretary-General's 1970 report.[19] The main intention would be to prohibit attacks directed against civilians as such, indiscriminate terrorizing or destruction, and the use of civilians as an object of reprisal. There would, of course, need to be arrangements to prevent abuse, such as using civilians as a shield for military attacks or permanently placing armed forces or military installations in cities or areas with large civilian populations.

In 1969 the Secretary-General had mentioned the problem of ' terror bombing ' and suggested a study of ' the effects of this kind of military operation within their legal context ... and the question of defining limits '. In the suggested minimum code put forward a year later, he included ' the specific prohibition of the use of " saturation " bombing as a means of intimidating, demoralizing and terrorizing civilians by inflicting indiscriminate destruction upon densely populated areas '. In addition, he reiterated that belligerents have an obligation to take precautions to ensure that the objective to be attacked is not the civilian population as well as in the choice of weapons and methods to be used. The purpose would be to reduce to a minimum or avoid entirely harming civilian populations in the vicinity of a military objective.[20]

[18] See the communication from the High Commissioner of Refugees in A/7720 p. 47 n. 60 & p. 93.

[19] A/7720, paras 133–44; A/8052, para. 42.

[20] A/7720, para. 143; A/8052, para. 42 (a), (e), & (f).

As for the humanitarian protection of prisoners of war, the Secretary-General considered the Third Geneva Convention of 1949 to be ' generally . . . sound ', but he pointed out that at present the question whether a person qualifies for the protection of the Convention is unilaterally decided upon by the capturing power, and that there might be advantages in allowing an international agency ' to advise and give guidance ' on the eligibility of persons for POW status. Other suggestions were that prisoners should not be interrogated until they have received medical attention; that all brutal methods of interrogation, including the giving of drugs, alcohol, or similar agents, and deprivation of food and rest, should be prohibited; and that the power to impose the death sentence on prisoners ' should be exercised with the greatest moderation and if possible prohibited altogether '. U Thant suggested that, even in guerrilla fighting, persons should not be sentenced to death merely for acts, such as killing their enemy in open fight, which may reasonably be expected of combatants and which are committed in accordance with the laws and customs of war. In the case of internal conflicts, he favoured the gradual elimination of capital punishment inflicted on combatants solely on the ground of having espoused the cause of either party to the conflict.[21]

The humanitarian protection of combatants raises many acutely difficult questions. Some of these arise from the near impossibility of distinguishing between a ' ruse of war ', which is permitted under the Hague Regulations (Art. 24), and to ' kill or wound treacherously ', which are among the acts ' especially prohibited ' (Art. 23(b)). A more precise rule is needed on this. It is also necessary to clarify the prohibition of ' the improper wearing of military insignia and uniform ', as well as the prohibition of declaring that ' no quarter ' will be given, which is a negative obligation only (A/8052, paras 101–3 & 108–9).

The Secretary-General considered that the Hague Regulations should be updated and adapted to modern conditions,

[21] A/7720, para. 181; A/8052, paras 104–7, 111 (c), 114–21, 182, 184, 190, 191 (c) (ii), & 191 (e). See also MML, paras 104, 222, & 224 and FM27-10, paras 71a, 93, & 175-184.

either by their revision as a whole, by the preparation of ' an additional Protocol to the Geneva Convention [*sic*], or an independent international instrument '. The elaboration or amendment should define and if possible extend the definition of protected combatants; define what is inadmissible as ' treacherous ' conduct; elaborate the existing prohibition of killing or wounding the disabled enemy; define how a combatant can clearly make known his intention to surrender; and replace the rule forbidding the declaration that ' no quarter ' will be given by the positive obligation to proclaim ' that the disabled enemy will be protected under the laws and customs of war '. The Secretary-General admitted the ' practical difficulties and complexity of the task ' and he emphasized the need for international procedures to verify the implementation of both existing and any new provisions (A/8052, paras 111–13).

Both civilians and combatants would benefit from the prohibition of weapons or methods of war which cause unnecessary suffering, which are ' especially prohibited ' under Article 23 (e) of the Hague Regulations. The Secretary-General noted in 1969 that this problem must be dealt with in large measure by means of arms control and disarmament, but he pointed out that incendiary weapons such as napalm cause needless suffering unless their use is accompanied by ' special precautions ', and he tentatively suggested that ' the legality or otherwise of the use of napalm ' called for special study (A/7720, paras 183–201). This proposal was repeated in 1970, the Secretary-General then favouring the idea of a study of ' the precise effects of the use of napalm on human beings and the living environment . . . with a view to curtailing or abolishing such uses of the weapons in question as might be established as inhumane ' (A/8052, paras 122–6 & 152). In 1971 the General Assembly authorized the preparation of an expert report on napalm and other incendiary weapons, and all aspects of their possible use.

Perhaps the most difficult group of questions concerned conflicts not of an international character, guerrilla fighting, and the use of armed force by groups struggling for freedom from oppressive government or alien rule. The Secretary-General had emphasized in his first report that while the distinction between international and internal conflicts may be of great importance from the point of view of international law, this may not be the case when it comes to the securing of humanitarian standards. He also pointed out that the ' traditional distinction between international war formally declared . . . and purely internal conflicts [had become] less clear '. A matter for further study should concern the elaboration of a new international instrument providing protection for civilians in those internal armed conflicts ' of international concern ' (A/7720, paras 104, 131, 168–77).[22]

U Thant elaborated this proposal in some detail in 1970, dealing in the main with the need to clarify and strengthen common Article 3 of the Geneva Conventions. On one point, there seemed to be substantial agreement among the experts he had consulted. While foreign military intervention can have the effect of transforming an internal conflict into an international one, it is often difficult to assess whether intervention is in fact taking place, especially if it is covert or in the guise of ' volunteers ' or mercenaries. Another difficulty of definition arises because common Article 3 comes into effect only in the case of ' armed ' conflict, and some experts would like to see the application of Article 3 in certain situations of conflict where there has been no actual recourse to weapons. One possibility would be to widen the expression ' armed conflict ' so as to cover the operations of ' any movement which . . . aims at overthrowing the Government by the use of arms, changing the form or structure of the State by modifying the Constitution or basic laws of the State or part thereof '. The Secretary-General also reported the opinion of certain experts who would regard all ' struggles for self-determination, and liberation from colonial and foreign rule . . . as international ' (A/8052, paras 130–47), if not necessarily inter-state.

One difficulty about giving protection to persons engaged in non-international conflicts, as indeed in all conflicts, is that the wider the definition of those claiming the benefits of combatant status, the wider the definition of those who may be legitimately attacked. The Secretary-General took the expression used in common Article 3, ' persons taking no active part in the hostilities ', and asked which persons, in addition to those

[22] See also the proposals of Denmark and Norway, A/7720, pp. 74–5 & 81–2.

named in Article 3 for illustrative purposes, should be regarded as ' not actively participating in the hostilities '. He proposed that the protection of Article 3 should apply to all those whose conduct and activities have no relation to the conduct of hostilities, those whose assistance or participation was given under duress, and those who ' merely express opinions criticizing the Government or favouring the objectives of the uprising '. He also suggested that Article 3 should be extended so as to afford protection to medical and relief personnel; to allow the free passage of food, clothing, and medical supplies; and to allow detainees the right to send and receive family messages and to receive relief (A/8052, paras 148–56).

The Secretary-General's first report (paras 202–27) considered the general problem of securing effective implementation of agreed norms, and this problem was considered in greater detail in the 1970 report (paras 157–62, 185–6, & 238–58). Reference has already been made to the proposal that an international agency might in some circumstances advise whether persons claiming POW status do in fact qualify for the protection given by the Third Geneva Convention. The Secretary-General noted that determining whether a given situation comes within the purview of Article 3, that is to say, is an internal conflict, is ' complex and delicate '. Among his suggestions for dealing with this was that advice on this point should be available from ' some international body . . . offering full guarantees of competence, independence and impartiality ' (paras 116, 157–62, & 191(e)).

Guerrilla warfare may be an element of an international conflict, as was the case of the underground and partisan movements in the second world war, or it may be resorted to in civil and other internal wars. The Secretary-General suggested in his first report that an expert study should be made to advise whether new rules are needed to confer the status of ' protected ' combatants upon guerrilla fighters not eligible for protection under the Geneva Conventions, but he pointed out that the possibility of doing this depends to a large extent on whether the guerrillas themselves are seen to apply humanitarian norms (paras 158–67). In his second report, U Thant suggested that if guerrilla groups do not have adequate facilities for holding prisoners, they might hand them over to an allied or neutral state. Guerrillas should afford full respect and freedom of action to medical and relief personnel (paras 166–7 & 181). He commented that ' the international provisions in force concerning the definition of protected combatants contain discrepancies, are not always precise enough and may lend themselves to difficulties of interpretation '. He reiterated his proposal for a study in order to ' ascertain and clarify ' the meaning of existing texts, to bring them into better harmony with each other, and to broaden their scope so as to cover certain categories of combatants not now protected. In addition, he put forward for study his own tentative suggestions for broadening the definition or interpretation of privileged combatants in international conflicts (paras 89–98, 174–80, 183, 189, 191 (b) (i), 191 (e) & (f)).

Among the Secretary-General's other suggestions for further consideration was that Article 23 of the Hague Regulations, which lists acts which are especially forbidden, should be construed or amended so as to prohibit ' the killing or harming of all persons who participate actively in international conflicts, at the time of surrender or capture ' (paras 107, 111, 168–73, 191 (a)).

An important section of the 1969 report dealt with the role of Protecting Powers. U Thant suggested that there was a pressing need for measures to improve and strengthen the system of international supervision and assistance to parties to armed conflicts in their observance of humanitarian norms. Max Petitpierre has written that the Geneva Conventions are ' almost devoid of sanctions ' and Telford Taylor, writing in a wider context, has commented that the laws of war are ' erratically if not capriciously enforced '.[23] Among U Thant's proposals were the following: (a) widening the effective choice of methods of supervision and assistance available to the parties; (b) establishment of a new organ or organization for supervision and assistance; (c) extension of the role of Protecting Powers to additional humanitarian functions; (d) recourse to international organizations as substitute for Protecting Powers; (e) creation of official panels of states willing to act as

[23] Petitpierre, in *IRRC*, Feb. 1971, p. 74; Taylor, p. 39.

Protecting Powers. In addition, the General Assembly or the International Conference of the Red Cross might, by resolution, emphasize the fact that Protecting Powers, in addition to safeguarding the interests of the parties, are agents of the international community (A/7720, paras 202–24).

In his second report, U Thant suggested that these questions should receive further study, and he emphasized that this section of his report was necessarily of a tentative character, merely outlining alternative possibilities, with emphasis on co-operation with the governments concerned (A/8052, paras 186, 191 (d), & 240–7). Any new organ or agency should help in applying not only the existing rules of the Geneva Conventions but also the norms set by UN human-rights instruments. It might also undertake tasks arising from any new international instruments, such as advising on those eligible for POW status and whether an internal conflict exists, as well as administering and verifying civilian sanctuaries. The CICR would not necessarily be able to assume additional functions beyond its present humanitarian responsibilities. The role of Protecting Power embraces diplomatic and political functions, and the CICR might find the role of conciliator or mediator more congenial than acting as representative of one of the belligerents or of the international community. Perhaps the UN, he suggested, constituted ' the most authentic and comprehensive expression of the international community '. If a UN organ or agency were created, it would need to have a degree of autonomy so that it could act independently and impartially. The executive head should be guided by a committee of highly qualified personalities of international renown and unquestioned integrity.

The final substantive question dealt with in the Secretary-General's two reports concerned medical and relief assistance—a matter raised also in a communication from India. U Thant suggested in 1969 that guidelines should be formulated aimed at improving the efficiency, strengthening the co-ordination, and expanding the scope of relief activities in situations of armed conflict. If a UN body were created as an organ of protection as suggested above, either the UN organ, or a non-UN humanitarian organization, might act as co-ordinator between various relief agencies (A/7720, paras 153–5, 225–7, & pp. 77–8). This would, of course, require careful handling so as to avoid overlapping with the CICR.

In his second report, U Thant suggested that the UN might ' in appropriate cases ' co-ordinate and execute relief activities. This might necessitate the creation of an autonomous organization, guided by ' a committee of highly qualified personalities of international renown and unquestioned integrity ... who would adequately represent the major legal and social systems of the world ' (paras 42 (j), 44, & 247–8). It might be possible in due course to integrate such relief activities with the UN programme for dealing with natural disasters.[24]

A programme as ambitious as that outlined by the Secretary-General in his two reports would need:

1. Wide dissemination and publicity for existing humanitarian instruments, especially to military personnel (a point stressed by India, Norway, and WHO.[25]

2. More effective implementation of existing instruments, including improved means of reporting and verification.[26]

3. A review of existing reservations to humanitarian conventions to see whether any of these reservations can now be withdrawn.[27]

4. Expert studies on several important matters, such as civilian sanctuaries, the effects of using napalm on human beings and the living environment, the effects of terror bombing and the possibility of defining limits, the humanitarian protection of civilians in internal armed conflicts, the humanitarian protection of guerrilla fighters, and an extended use of Protecting Powers.[28]

5. The preparation of amendments or protocols to existing instruments, or of entirely new instruments.[29]

These two reports were considered in 1970 at twenty-two meetings of the General Assembly's Main Committee concerned with social, humanitarian, and cultural subjects. The debate

[24] E/4994, 13 May 1971 (mimeo.).
[25] A/7720, paras 117–21, pp. 77–8, 81–2, 96–7; A/8050, paras 251–6.
[26] A/7720, paras 109–227; A/8050, paras 238–50.
[27] A/7720, para. 116; A/8050, para. 257.
[28] A/7720, paras 142, 166, & 177; A/8050, paras 83–7, 126, & 186.
[29] A/7720, paras 130–2; A/8050, paras 18, 163–5, & 192–3.

was complicated by repeated attempts on the part of some representatives to discuss particular armed conflicts, especially those in South-east Asia and the Middle East, and also, though to a lesser extent, the question of guerrilla fighters in Southern Africa. In the end, however, on 9 December 1970, the Assembly was able to approve five separate resolutions.

The first (2673 (XXV)) dealt with the protection of journalists engaged on dangerous missions in areas of armed conflict; it was adopted by 85 votes to none, with 32 abstentions (mainly Communist or Afro-Asian states) and 10 absentees. It recalled those provisions of the Geneva Conventions of 1949 affording ' certain types of protection . . . to journalists ' and, *inter alia*, invited ECOSOC to request the Commission on Human Rights at its next session and ' as a matter of priority ' to consider the possibility of preparing a draft international agreement to be adopted ' as soon as possible ', to ensure the protection of journalists engaged on dangerous missions (this had arisen because of the disappearance of seventeen foreign journalists in Cambodia earlier in 1970). The abstaining states made it clear that they did not object to the principle of devising better measures to protect journalists, but they questioned whether this matter needed such high priority, and they wished to ensure that only bona fide journalists should be protected and not persons engaging in political or military activities under cover of the journalistic profession.

The second resolution (2674 (XXV)) had been introduced by the Sudan and co-sponsored by Ceylon, India, and the Soviet Union. It condemned countries which engage in aggressive wars and disregard the principles of the Geneva Conventions of 1949 and the Geneva CBW Protocol of 1925; affirmed that ' participants in resistance movements and freedom-fighters in Southern Africa and territories under colonial and alien domination and foreign occupation ' should, if arrested, be treated as POWs; and recognized the need to develop additional international instruments providing for the protection of ' civilian populations and freedom-fighters '. Two states corrected their votes after the result had been announced; taking these corrections into account, the resolution was adopted by 76 votes (mainly Afro-Asian and Communist states) to 1 (Portugal), with 38 states abstaining (mainly Western and Latin American) and 12 absentees.

The third resolution (2675 (XXV)) had originally been submitted by Norway, and was adopted by 109 votes to none, with 18 states abstaining or absent.[30] It affirmed eight basic principles for the protection of civilian populations in armed conflicts, ' without prejudice to their future elaboration within the framework of progressive development of the international law of armed conflict ' (for text, see App. V, pp.187-8).

The fourth resolution (2676 (XXV)), sponsored by the United States and 11 other Members, was adopted by 67 votes to 30, with 30 abstentions or absentees.[31] It, *inter alia*, called on all parties to an armed conflict to comply with the Geneva Convention relating to POWs; endorsed the continuing efforts of the CICR to secure the effective application of the Convention; requested the Secretary-General ' to exert all efforts to obtain humane treatment for prisoners of war '; and urged compliance with particular provisions of the Convention regarding the repatriation of sick and wounded prisoners, and humane treatment of prisoners not repatriated.

The fifth resolution (2677 (XXV)), which was introduced by the UK and co-sponsored by 12 other states, was approved by 111 votes to none, with 16 states abstaining or absent. It called upon all parties to any armed conflict to observe the rules laid down in the Hague Conventions of 1899 and 1907, the Geneva CBW Protocol of 1925, the Geneva Conventions of 1949, ' and other humanitarian rules applicable in armed conflicts '; urged states which had not already done so to adhere to ' those Conventions '; expressed the hope that the expert conference to be convened in 1971 by the CICR would ' consider further what development is required in existing humanitarian laws applicable to armed conflicts and that it will make specific recommendations . . . for consideration by Governments '; requested the Secretary-General to invite governments to comment on his two reports, to transmit relevant UN documents

[30] When the vote was taken on this resolution in Committee, the Communist states, except Romania and Yugoslavia, had abstained.

[31] In Committee, the Communist states had voted against it, and the abstainers had been mainly Afro-Asian states.

to the CICR, to present to the autumn 1971 session of the General Assembly the comments of governments, and to report on the results of the CICR expert conference ' and on any other relevant developments '; and decided ' to consider this question again, in all its aspects ' at the 26th General Assembly session in the autumn of 1971.

It will be noted that although the Assembly adopted these resolutions, it did not in 1970 act upon most of the Secretary-General's specific proposals. It took no decision on his proposals for wide dissemination and publicity for existing humanitarian instruments or on more effective means of reporting on and verification of the implementation of existing instruments. Expert studies were not requested on civilian sanctuaries, terror bombing, the protection of civilians in internal armed conflicts, the protection of guerrilla fighters, or an extended use of Protecting Powers. The only new instrument specifically requested was that relating to the protection of journalists. In 1971, however, the Assembly urged states to review reservations to existing international instruments and authorized a study of napalm.

One can only speculate that the majority of delegations wished to postpone action on U Thant's other proposals until the CICR had completed the next stage of its work.

Human Rights in territories occupied by Israel

While discussions have been taking place on these and other proposals, the world has not been free of armed conflict. There has been fighting in South-east Asia, between Federal Nigeria and former Biafra, between Honduras and El Salvador, between India and Pakistan, and in the Middle East. There has been military intervention in Czechoslovakia, and allegations of attacks on or incursions into Guinea, Haiti, Senegal, and Zambia. There have been reports of military skirmishes between Kurds and government forces in Iraq. Dissident groups have fought against government forces in Chad, the Sudan, Ethiopia, Thailand, the Yemen, Jordan, Ceylon, Burma, and Morocco, and guerrillas have operated in Southern Africa and Latin America. There have been hijackings and kidnappings. A UN peace-keeping force has been functioning in Cyprus, and

UN observers have been stationed in Kashmir and in the Suez Canal area.

In some of these cases, the UN has exercised humanitarian responsibilities (Nigeria–Biafra, the Middle East, India and East Pakistan); in some there has been UN conciliation, mediation, or the exercise of good offices (Cyprus, the Middle East); in some, UN organs have engaged in debate or passed resolutions (Czechoslovakia, Guinea, Haiti, Senegal, Southern Africa, Zambia, India-Pakistan). But it is unprecedented for UN organs to decide to investigate directly the application of humanitarian principles during armed conflict or in occupied territory after the cessation of hostilities, as happened after the 1967 war in the Middle East. There have, in fact, been two different UN bodies of inquiry, which on the face of things has been an unnecessary duplication of effort. One body, which was established by the General Assembly in 1968, is the Special Committee to Investigate Israeli Practices Affecting the Human Rights of the Population of the Occupied Territories (hereafter referred to as the Special Committee). The other body was set up by the Human Rights Commission in 1969 and is known as the Special Working Group of Experts established under resolution 6 (XXV) of the Commission on Human Rights (hereafter referred to as the Working Group).

It would be tedious to recount in detail the work of these two bodies, but some information is necessary about the circumstances in which they were set up. On 14 June 1967, immediately after the Six-Day War, the Security Council resolved to recommend to the governments concerned ' the scrupulous respect of the humanitarian principles ' contained in the Geneva Conventions of 1949 (res. 237 (S/7968/Rev. 3). On 4 July 1967 the General Assembly welcomed this resolution ' with great satisfaction ' (res. 2252 (ES-V)).

On 27 September 1968 the question of territory occupied by Israel was debated in the Security Council at the request of Pakistan and Senegal, and the Council resolved to ask the Secretary-General to send a Special Representative ' to the Arab territories under military occupation by Israel ' and asked the government of Israel to receive him and ' to cooperate with him and to facilitate his work ' (res. 259). On 14 October the

Secretary-General reported that Israel was not prepared to co-operate with the proposed mission unless its mandate were to include the treatment of both Arabs and Jews in all the states which had taken part in the June war. U Thant therefore reported that he was unable to give effect to the Security Council resolution.[32]

In spite of this rebuff, the General Assembly resolved on 19 December 1968 to establish the Special Committee already referred to, the membership to be determined by the President of the General Assembly. The government of Israel was asked to receive the Committee, co-operate with it and facilitate its work, and the Committee was asked to report ' as soon as possible and whenever the need arises thereafter ' (2443 (XXIII)).

Before the Special Committee could be appointed, the President of the 1968 Assembly session, Emilio Arenales of Guatemala, had died following an operation for a brain tumour, and the question arose as to how the committee should be appointed. The government of Israel has alleged (and there is no reason to doubt the truth of this) that before his death

the late President [of the General Assembly] approached a large number of Member States . . . but, at the time of his death, had not been successful . . . on account of the refusal of a great many Member States to accept such an invitation. . . . The States which refused . . . acted in full awareness of the real nature of the resolution [of the General Assembly], as being a transparent political manoeuvre. . . .

In the communication addressed to the Ambassador of Israel . . . on 6 March 1969, the late President of the General Assembly himself expressed his view that the establishment at that juncture of the special committee would add ' further causes of friction to the already tense situation in the Middle East '.[33]

The situation facing the UN upon the death of Arenales was not covered by the General Assembly's Rules of Procedure, nor were there any exact precedents. U Thant, acting under the article of the Charter which designates him as ' chief administrative officer of the Organization ', felt that he had no

[32] S/8851 (*SCOR*, 23rd yr, Suppl. Oct.–Dec. 1968), pp. 74–6.
[33] Communication of 28 May 1969, reproduced in A/7495, 28 May 1969, pp. 3–5, & A/7495/Add. 1, 19 June 1969, pp. 3–4 (mimeo.).

alternative but to consult the 126 Members in writing, with the following result [34]: 25 states did not reply; 4 ' abstained '; 3 favoured convening a special session of the Assembly to decide on another method for constituting the Special Committee; 13 (plus one second preference), favoured postponing the matter until the next session due to convene four months later; 81 favoured the adoption of an ad hoc procedure. Of these, 64 (plus 2 second preferences) favoured designating one of the Vice-Presidents to make the appointment; 12, ' in line with the spirit . . . of the rules of procedure ', wished to invite the government of Guatemala to designate the chairman of its delegation for the next session and ask him to make the appointment; and 5 were willing to accept either of these procedures.

The Secretary-General noted that ' more than an absolute majority ' preferred a procedure which was ' consonant with the spirit ' of the Charter and rules of procedure, i.e. the designation of one of the Vice-Presidents to undertake the appointment.[35] Accordingly, a meeting of all the Vice-Presidents of the previous General Assembly session (the Vice-Presidents are states, not individuals) was held on 23 June 1969, and they decided to entrust the appointment of the Special Committee to Dr Luis Alvarado of Peru.[36] On 12 September 1969, four days before the 1969 session of the Assembly was due to convene, it was announced that Ceylon, Somalia, and Yugoslavia had agreed to serve on the Special Committee.[37]

Israel strongly objected to the procedure adopted to deal with this unprecedented situation, as well as to the composition of the Committee:

In view of the one-sided character of the resolution [of the General Assembly] . . . all [sic] uncommitted States that were approached refused to serve on the Committee. The only countries willing to become members of the Committee were Somalia, Yugoslavia and Ceylon. All three have no diplomatic relations with Israel. . . .

[34] A/7495/Add. 2, 24 June 1969, Annex II (mimeo.).
[35] Ibid. Annex I, paras 7 & 9.
[36] Ibid. paras 2–3.
[37] A/7495/Add. 3; see also A/8089, 16 Nov. 1970, paras 3–6.

Somalia even denies Israel's right to independence and sovereignty (A/8164, 13 Nov. 1970, p. 2).

It is not from the report of the Special Committee that one discovers the ostensible reason for Israel's attitude of non-co-operation, but from one of her letters of protest. Israel, it appears, was not being merely perverse, but considered that any UN inquiry into human rights in the Middle East should not be confined to Arabs in territory occupied by Israel, but should apply also to the Jewish minorities in Arab states.

The resolution was objectionable *inter alia* because it contained an adverse prejudgement of the facts the committee was supposed to investigate, and because it took no account of the persecution of Jewish minorities in certain Arab countries . . . (A/7495, 28 May 1969, p. 3; mimeo.).[38]

Meanwhile, the problem of the occupied territories had been raised in the Commission on Human Rights, which on 27 February 1968 had requested the Secretary-General to keep it informed about the application of the Universal Declaration of Human Rights and the four Geneva Conventions in territories occupied by Israel, as well as affirming the right of those who had left ' to return . . . without delay ' (res. 6 (XXIV)). The Secretary-General's report (E/CN.4/999), issued on 6 February 1969, consisted of a digest of various UN decisions and reports relating to the humanitarian needs of the people following the June war, together with the summary of a reply from the government of Israel on the return to the West Bank of those who had fled.[39]

After the Commission on Human Rights had considered U Thant's report, on 4 March 1969 it set up the Working Group mentioned earlier, asking it to investigate allegations that Israel had violated the Fourth Geneva Convention of 1949 relating to the Protection of Civilian Persons in Time of War (res. 6 (XXV)). The Working Group had six members appointed as individuals, the identical membership of an ad hoc Group which had previously reported on conditions in Southern Africa. Before the Working Group could report to its parent

---

[38] See also S/8607 & S/8653 (*SCOR*, 23rd yr, Suppl. Apr.–June 1968), pp. 177–8 & 243–4; S/8699 (ibid. Suppl. July–Sept. 1968), pp. 73–95, paras 4–10 & 14.
[39] S/8153 (*SCOR*, 22nd yr, Suppl. July–Sept. 1967), pp. 294–6.

body, however, another General Assembly session had been held, only to learn that the Assembly's Special Committee, which had only just come into existence, had been unable to do more than elect a chairman.[40] A resolution (2546 (XXIV)) in stronger terms was adopted by the Assembly on 11 December, which recorded ' grave concern ' at reports of violations of human rights in territories occupied by Israel; condemned such practices as collective punishment, destruction of homes, and deportations; called upon Israel ' to desist forthwith from its reported repressive practices '; and asked the Special Committee to ' take cognizance ' of the Assembly's new resolution on the matter.

At this stage, then, there existed two UN bodies to investigate the application of humanitarian principles in territories occupied by Israel: the Special Committee appointed by the General Assembly, and the Working Group appointed by the Commission on Human Rights. Not surprisingly, both bodies received full co-operation from Arab governments and the Arab League. Besides holding meetings in New York and Geneva, the two bodies paid separate visits to Amman, Beirut, Cairo, and Damascus. Each heard over 100 witnesses, most of them in open meeting. Both bodies consulted representatives of the CICR and visited refugee camps in Syria and Jordan. Both also asked the Commissioner-General of UNRWA to provide information. The Commissioner-General expressed his understanding and sympathy with the needs and purposes of the Working Group, but he doubted whether its requests fell ' within the terms of the [Agency's] mandate, or are consistent with the activities as conducted at present by UNRWA '.[41] The Special Committee suggested in its report that the work of UNRWA should be ' amplified and intensified in scope ', and that organizations of this kind should be authorized to ' make . . . information available, without condition, to investigating bodies '.

The failure of UNRWA to disclose information regarding conditions prevailing in the occupied territories . . . might appear to be a dereliction of a humanitarian duty. If, however, the policies of

[40] A/7826, 5 Dec. 1969, paras 16-21 (mimeo.).
[41] E/CN.4/1016 & Adds. 1-5, 20 Jan.–20 Feb. 1970, ch. 1, para. 12.

UNRWA preclude the organization from furnishing any evidence
. . . , the Special Committee must either accept the situation . . . or
seek some change of policy.[42]

It should be added that on several occasions, the Secretary-
General has relied on the reports of UNRWA for information
connected with human rights in occupied territories.[43]

Neither investigating body was able to visit territory occupied
by Israel, which considered the activities of the Working Group
to be ' a purely propaganda exercise ', and informed it that
there was no basis for co-operation. Israel took the same view
of the Special Committee: ' The history of this matter has from
the beginning been tainted with political bias and procedural
irregularity '; and she therefore refused to co-operate.[44]

Besides hearing witnesses, the two bodies examined documentation including, in the case of the Working Group, specific
Egyptian complaints of violations of the Geneva Conventions.[45]
The Working Group stated that it was ' not in a position to
verify juridically the allegations which were received ' and that
the evidence presented to it was ' one-sided ', because of Israel's
refusal to recognize or co-operate with it. Nevertheless, the
Group had felt able to evaluate the evidence proffered. The
Special Committee also felt that, despite the absence of co-
operation on the part of Israel, it had created ' a basis upon
which a responsible opinion can be given '.[46]

The Working Group issued its report in January and February 1970. It was of the opinion that the Fourth Geneva Convention of 1949 was being violated; that persons were being
detained without trial; that houses and villages had been
destroyed after the cease-fire; and that people had been expelled
or transferred from their homes. It recommended that the
Fourth Convention be fully implemented; that allegations of

[42] A/8089, 26 Oct. 1970, pp. 4–6, & paras 11 & 53 (mimeo.).

[43] S/8001, pp. 271–5 & S/8021, pp. 299–30 (SCOR, 22nd yr, Suppl. Apr.–June
1967); S/8124, pp. 199–209 & S/8133, pp. 220–1 (ibid. Suppl. July–Sept. 1967).

[44] E/CN.4/1016, ch. 1, para. 9; UN Press Release HR/408, 17 Feb. 1970;
A/8089, para. 11.

[45] S/8064 (A/6759), SCOR, 22nd yr, Suppl. July–Sept. 1967, pp. 95–9; S/8588
(A/7099), ibid. 23rd yr, Suppl. Apr.–June 1968, pp. 164–5. See also the complaint
of Jordan in S/9897, 3 Aug. 1970 (mimeo.).

[46] E/CN.4/1016/Add. 2, ch. IV, para. 1; A/8089, p. 5.

torture, looting, and pillage should be investigated by the Israel authorities and those found responsible suitably punished; that deported or transferred persons should be allowed to return home under UN supervision; that detainees should be brought to trial at an early date; that confiscated property taken in a manner inconsistent with the Geneva Convention should be restored to its owners; and that the Israel anthorities should refrain from demolishing houses for reasons not provided for in the Convention, and should provide compensation in all cases of demolished houses in violation of the Convention.[47]

The Special Committee, in its report, sought to define the human rights which the Security Council on 4 June 1967 had described as 'essential and inalienable' (res. 237). The Committee concluded that these rights are those affirmed in the Universal Declaration of Human Rights and those deriving from the express provisions of the 1949 Geneva Conventions (A/8089, paras 33–9). The Committee's general verdict was that the situation of the refugees in the occupied territories was 'grim'. Among particular allegations that human rights were being violated in the occupied territories were the following.[48]

There was 'little reason to doubt' that Israel 'hoped to enervate the [Arab] community by depriving it of intelligent and active leadership' by means of deportations and expulsions, thereby reducing it 'to a state of passive subservience'. There was 'considerable evidence' of infringements of the right of persons living in the occupied areas to remain there and of the right of those who fled to return to their homes. Israel had been pursuing 'a policy of collective and area punishments . . . imposed indiscriminately'. While not contesting the right of the occupying power under the Fourth Geneva Convention to restrict the freedom of those who pose a threat to security, the Committee considered that this power was 'being abused in that it is exercised too freely'. Individuals were being held in detention 'for indefinite, prolonged periods' and 'administrative detainees and ordinary prisoners are treated alike'. The Committee heard several allegations of destruction of houses and buildings ('in many instances . . . unwarranted') and

[47] Ibid. chs IV & V.
[48] A/8089, p. 5 and paras 61, 72, 77, 110–11, 128–31, & 133.

confiscation and expropriation of property. Although such destruction is prohibited by the Fourth Geneva Convention ' except where such destruction is rendered absolutely necessary by military operations ' (Art. 53), Israel had ' unscrupulous recourse ' to military necessity in carrying out ' this wanton destruction '. Evidence had also been presented of ' widespread looting '.

The Committee concluded that Israel had been violating human rights in the occupied territories; ' the fundamental violation . . . lies in the very fact of occupation '. The weight of international public opinion should be brought to bear to persuade the Israel government to desist from the violations. The General Assembly should recommend to the states whose territory is occupied ' that they appoint immediately either a neutral State or States, or an international organization which offers all guarantees of impartiality and effectiveness, to safeguard the human rights of the population '. Israel should be called upon ' to accept such an arrangement and to provide all the facilities necessary '. It recommended that there should be ' a further and more thorough study of . . . the entire question of the protection of human rights in occupied territories ', and asked that ' sufficient professional and other staff ' should be assigned to the Committee should it be necessary to visit the Middle East again.[49] The Special Committee issued two further reports in 1971.[50]

On 13 November 1970 a brief statement was circulated by the government of Israel (A/8164, mimeo.) commenting on the Committee's first report. Israel reiterated her objection to the procedure followed in setting up the Committee, which had resulted in its serving as ' a tool of Arab propaganda '. The Committee had ' proceeded to organize a spectacle of hearing " evidence " from . . . pre-selected, coached and rehearsed witnesses '. In the case of one witness, Israel provided detailed information to refute the Committee's allegation. This witness, a resident of Gaza, had alleged that he had been given an anaesthetic and castrated by an Israel doctor. Israel contended that the witness had undergone two operations performed by Arab

[49] Ibid. pp. 5–6, & paras 145–6, 152–3, & 155.
[50] A/8389, 5 Oct. 1971, & A/8389/Add.1, 9 Dec. 1971 (mimeo.).

surgeons for the removal of his testicles before the June war. She maintained that her Mission to the UN possessed a copy of a report by Professor Muhamad Safawat, dated 28 July 1966, stating that the hope of the witness for a transplant operation was illusory (A/8089, para. 104).

But to demonstrate that one charge was false was not to undermine the main tenor of the Special Committee's report. Indeed, Israel's 4-page reply to a report of some 130 pages showed how contemptuously Israel viewed the activities of the Committee. She considered the report to be 'an organized propaganda exercise' from which no valid conclusions could be drawn (A/8164).

The two UN reports were submitted to the parent bodies in 1970. The Human Rights Commission approved its Working Group's report on 23 March (res. 10 (XXVI)). Israel was condemned for refusing to apply the Fourth Geneva Convention, and called on to take measures to rectify the situation. The Group was commended and its mandate extended, and Israel was asked to receive it and co-operate with it. ECOSOC later took note of the report of the Human Rights Commission, and the Secretary-General also brought the matter to the attention of the General Assembly and the Security Council.[51]

The Special Committee's report was issued on 26 October 1970, and on 18 November, at the request of Iraq, the General Assembly decided to place it on its agenda, the item becoming the 101st of the 1970 session. When the report was being considered, a representative of the Palestinian Arabs was permitted to address the Assembly's Special Political Committee ' without such authorization implying any recognition of the delegation ' (A/8257, 11 Dec. 1970, para. 4).

A resolution sponsored by 8 Afro-Asian states was adopted in the Special Political Committee, and was approved in plenary on 15 December by 52 votes to 20, with 55 abstentions or absences (res. 2727 (XXV)). The UK abstained in both Committee and plenary. By the resolution, the Assembly asked the Special Committee to continue its work ' pending the early

[51] E/4816, ch. XI, paras 184–99 & ch. XXIII, pp. 79–82 (*ECOSOCOR*, 48th sess., suppl. 5); ECOSOC res. 1504 (XLVIII), 27 May 1970; S/9888, 27 July (mimeo.).

termination of Israeli occupation of Arab territories ', to consult the CICR, and to report ' as soon as possible and whenever the need arises '. Israel was again asked to receive and cooperate with the Committee, and it was decided to resume consideration of the matter in 1971.

When the Human Rights Commission met in 1971, it renewed its attack on Israel for disregarding human rights in the occupied territories and adopted a resolution condemning Israel for specified violations and calling upon her to comply with the Fourth Geneva Convention; the CICR was urged to cooperate with UN organs.[52]

Meanwhile, the Security Council has continued to receive written complaints from Arab states about the treatment of civilians in the occupied territories, to which Israel has issued a number of written replies.

[52] UN Press Release HR/115, 26 Mar. 1971, pp. 12–13 (certain paragraphs of the resolution are reproduced twice in the Press Release).

ARMS CONTROL AND DISARMAMENT

*Warfare may in the past have been
associated with victory; and occasionally with
peace. It is clear that it can no longer result in
either. Let the Decade of Disarmament therefore bring with it an increasing realization
that whatever it costs, whatever presumed
advantages have to be ceded, the political
settlement of international differences will in
the end always prove less costly and less
dangerous than any settlement brought about
by the force of arms. With this realization,
may the nations of the world during the
Disarmament Decade finally embark on the
reduction and elimination of the dreaded means
of their destruction. Nothing less will rescue
mankind from international anarchy and war.*

Declaration by the Nobel Peace Prize
Laureates presented to the President of
the 25th session of the General Assembly

GOVERNMENTS, when they are serious about it and not just
indulging in propaganda, pursue arms control and disarmament because they believe that this is one way of increasing
national and international peace and security. Public opinion
is often sceptical or indifferent: the discussions seem endless,
the achievements meagre, and in periods of acute international
tension, it may seem more urgent to come to grips with the
political difficulties of which arms are only a symptom.

There are, however, some other considerations. Arms are
sometimes an intrinsic source of tension—witness the Cuban
missile crisis and the difficulties over the now almost forgotten
MLF. Arms races are always expensive and usually de-
stabilizing. Moreover, the very process of negotiating about
disarmament provides a means of communication between
potential adversaries about those policies and actions which
give rise to anxiety and often to over-reaction. It is increasingly
recognized that the exchange of information during disarmament negotiations helps the parties to adjust those defence

postures which the other side finds provocative, and to do so without impairing the security of one's own side.

The vast subject of arms control and disarmament, whether limited or general, partial or complete, becomes more complex every year, and many governments now have special sections or departments which specialize in arms control and disarmament, whereas only twenty years ago, most professional diplomats privately regarded the matter with scorn, whatever they may have had to say in public. And it still remains true that, in many parts of the world, defence ministries and general staffs think of disarmament as a plot to weaken their own side while the potential enemy improves his position.

In this chapter I want to illustrate the problem of prohibitions and restrains in war by considering the efforts which have been made to control chemical, germ, and nuclear weapons. It can be argued that if one despairs of abolishing war in any conceivable future, then it is more important to seek to promote agreement on general principles of restraint rather than to attempt to control particular weapons. Indeed, A. L. Burns, in the perceptive essay cited on p. 39, maintains that very few of the prohibitions and permissions of the traditional code regarding the just use of force ' are susceptible of being embodied in treaties or agreements, explicit or implicit '. He may well be right. Even a total ban on a weapon, covering every phase from research and development to actual use in war, cannot alter the fact that once it has been invented, it cannot be disinvented. How to make it has become part of mankind's permanent stock of knowledge.

At the same time the groups of weapons I have chosen to consider arouse especial revulsion in the public mind, and chemical and nuclear weapons have actually been used in war. Moreover, it is difficult to use these weapons in accordance with the twin principles of discrimination and proportion, so that there are particular reasons for regarding the abolition or control of them as a matter of great urgency.

Chemical and bacteriological (biological) weapons

Chemical weapons are usually defined as those chemical agents employed for their toxic effects on man, animals, or plants. This definition is intended to *exclude* incendiary and smoke weapons, which exert their primary effects through physical force, fire, deprivation of air, or reduced visibility, and which are considered by the authors of a recent UN report as better classified with high explosives.[1] This report includes among chemical weapons incapacitating agents (tear and harassing gases) and defoliants and herbicides. Some gases, such as CS, are used in aerosol form, and since 2 February 1970 British official spokesmen have sometimes referred to them as ' smokes '. One is reminded of the opening sentence of the standard British lecture on air-raid precautions during the second world war. ' Gases are of three kinds: solids, liquids, and vapours.'

What most people call ' germ warfare ' was referred to in the Geneva Protocol of 1925 as ' bacteriological methods of warfare '. There are, however, living organisms, in addition to bacteria, which can be used as weapons. To avoid misunderstanding, the UN now generally uses the term ' bacteriological (biological) weapons ' (A/7575/Rev. 1, para. 18). A further complication arises when the term ' biological agent ' is used, since it might reasonably be held that man is a biological agent.

The attempt to prohibit the use of chemical and germ weapons in war by means of specific legal instruments began just over a century ago with the St Petersburg Declaration of 29 November–11 December 1868.[2] Before the middle of the nineteenth century the law of war was entirely customary, and it is still necessary to distinguish between legal obligations of a contractual nature which derive from international treaties, and obligations which are part of customary international law. One difficulty in the CBW field is that some of the basic texts are ambiguous or inconsistent on this point.

Looking back more than a century, the St Petersburg Declaration seems to have been more important for the general

---

[1] A/7575/Rev. 1 & S/9292/Rev. 1, *Chemical and Bacteriological (Biological) Weapons and the Effects of their Possible Use: Report of the Secretary-General*, 1969, para. 18; *Health Aspects of Chemical and Biological Weapons: Report of a WHO Group of Consultants*, 1970 (hereafter cited as *WHO Report*), p. 12.

[2] *Docs re. 1st Hague Peace Conference*, pp. 30–1.

principles it enuniated than for its specific provision—the prohibition of ' any projectile of a weight below 400 grammes [about 14 ounces], which is either explosive or charged with fulminating [flashing] or inflammable substances '.

The Declaration's Preamble states the need for civilized nations to agree on technical limits ' at which the necessities of war ought to yield to the requirements of humanity '. There follow five principles, of which the first reads somewhat quaintly in the age of nerve gases and thermonuclear missiles: ' Considering that the progress of civilization should have the effect of alleviating as much as possible the calamities of war.' The second by implication affirmed the immunity of non-combatants from direct attack: ' the only legitimate object which States should endeavour to accomplish during war is to weaken the military forces of the enemy '. The remaining three principles were concerned with the protection of wounded combatants:

Considering . . . that for this purpose [weakening the enemy's military forces] it is sufficient to disable the greatest possible number of men;

That this object would be exceeded by the employment of arms which uselessly aggravate the suffering of disabled men, or render their death inevitable;

That the employment of such arms would, therefore, be contrary to the laws of humanity.

It should be noted that the Declaration banned only projectiles *less* than the specified weight, on the ground that small projectiles would cause unnecessary suffering. Larger shells were permitted, because it was considered that the amount of suffering they caused was not disproportionate to the military advantages of employing them.

The next document bearing on CBW is the Brussels Declaration of 27 August 1874. This Declaration included the important statement which was later to become the second basic principle of the Hague Conventions: ' The laws of war do not recognize in belligerents an unlimited power in the adoption of means of injuring an enemy ' (Art. 12). The Brussels Declaration also stated as ' especially forbidden ' the use of ' poison or poisoned weapons ' (Art. 13 (a)).

The Regulations annexed to Hague Convention (II) of 1899 repeated the 1874 ban on unlimited warfare: ' The right of belligerents to adopt means of injuring the enemy is not unlimited ' (Art. 22). The use of ' poison or poisoned arms ' was again declared to be ' especially prohibited ', as was the use of ' arms, projectiles, or material of a nature to cause superfluous injury ' (Art. 23 (a) & (e)). There was also concluded at the 1899 Hague Conference a separate declaration banning, on a reciprocal basis, the use of ' projectiles *the sole object of which* is the diffusion of asphyxiating or deleterious gases ' (my italics).[3] Britain ratified the 1899 Declaration on poisonous gases on 30 August 1907.

Hague Convention (IV) of 18 October 1907 was an improved version of Convention (II) of 1899 on the laws and customs of war. The preamble to it, and to the Convention of 1899 which it replaced, included the so-called Martens Clause, part of which was incorporated in the four Geneva Red Cross Conventions of 1949. The Martens Clause declares that until a more complete code of the laws of war is issued, the parties declare that in cases not covered by the Regulations annexed to the Conventions, inhabitants and belligerents remain under the protection of ' the principles of the law of nations, as they result from the usages established among civilized peoples, from the laws of humanity, and the dictates of the public conscience '.[4] The 1907 Convention also reaffirmed that belligerents do not have the right to adopt unlimited means of injuring the enemy (Art. 22), and it was again declared to be ' especially forbidden ' to employ poison or poisonous weapons, or to use arms, projectiles, or material calculated to cause unnecessary suffering (Art. 23 (a) & (e)).

During the first world war, 6,000 tons of lachrymators and 7,000 tons of respiratory irritant gases were used.[5] The postwar treaties carried the attempt to prohibit chemical and germ

---

[3] *The Hague Declaration (IV, 2) of 1899 concerning asphyxiating gases* (Washington, CEIP, 1915), pam. no. 8.

[4] I have used the 1907 English wording, which is also used in the Geneva Conventions of 1949.

[5] *The Control of Chemical and Biological Weapons* (New York, CEIP, 1971) (hereafter cited as *Carnegie CBW Rep.*), pp. 65–6.

weapons a stage further, the wording used being significant in two respects. First, the weapons prohibited were defined as ' asphyxiating, poisonous or other [in French, *similaires*] gases and all analogous liquids, materials or devices [*procédés*] '.[6] This was the wording destined to be used in the Geneva CBW Protocol of 1925. Secondly, the peace treaties asserted without qualification that the use of the specified weapons was prohibited: ' The use of ... *being prohibited*, their manufacture and importation are strictly forbidden in ... ' (my italics). Were the drafters of the treaties asserting that all employment of chemical weapons in war was contrary to customary international law? That is the view of some international lawyers, although if it was in 1919 an established rule of international law, it had been but recently breached.[7]

The same wording, ' asphyxiating, poisonous or other gases and all analogous liquids, materials or devices ', was used in Article V of the Washington Naval Treaty of 6 February 1922, which was, however, never ratified by France and consequently did not enter into effect. The treaty declared that the use in war of the specified substances had been ' justly condemned by the general opinion of the civilized world '; it asserted that a prohibition of the use in war of the specified substances had been ' declared in treaties to which a majority of the civilized powers are parties '; in order that the prohibition should be ' universally accepted as a part of international law, binding alike on the conscience and practice of nations ', the parties assented to the prohibition and agreed to be bound by it ' as between themselves '; and the parties invited ' all other civilized nations to adhere thereto '.

The 1922 wording was followed in all important respects in the Geneva Protocol of 17 June 1925, but the parties agreed also ' to extend this prohibition [of the use of the specified chemical agents in war] to the use of bacteriological methods of warfare '. The 1922 reference to treaties ' to which a majority

[6] Versailles Treaty, 28 June 1919, Art. 171. The treaties with Austria (St Germain-en-Laye), Bulgaria (Neuilly-sur-Seine) and Hungary (Trianon) added ' flame-throwers ' and changed ' analogous ' to ' similar '.

[7] *Development of International Legal Limitations on the Use of Chemical and Biological Weapons*, report prepared for the US Arms Control and Disarmament Agency (1968), ii.70 (mimeo.).

of the civilized powers are parties ' was retained, except that
' civilized ' was dropped, and it was also omitted from the
reference to additional accessions. Moreover, instead of simply
inviting other states to adhere, the 1925 Protocol commits the
parties to exerting every effort to induce other states to accede.[8]
It should be noted that the 1925 Protocol was a by-product of a
convention on the supervision of the international trade in
arms, ammunition, and implements of war, which never came
into force.

Nobody would now claim that the Geneva Protocol was well
drafted, either in English or French. It is by no means clear
which paragraphs of the section relating to chemical weapons
are declaratory of customary international law, and which are
solely of a contractual nature. The fact that the chemical part
is simply extended to bacteriological warfare would be easier
to interpret if the chemical part were itself unambiguous. There
is a great deal in the Protocol for lawyers to argue about, but
the layman will not go far wrong if he regards the Protocol as a
no-first-use treaty, confined to the use of the specified agents in
war. The Protocol does not prevent research, manufacture,
stockpiling, transfer, training, or—in practice—reprisals, and
it does not ban the use of the specified substances in non-war
situations. Needless to say, non-parties to the Protocol, and
parties released from their obligations under it because of a
breach by an adversary, remain bound by the customary law
applicable in armed conflicts.

Britain did not ratify the Geneva Protocol until 9 April 1930.
A good many states, including Britain, ratified with a reservation of reciprocity, which in Britain's case reads as follows: [9]

The said Protocol is only binding on His Britannic Majesty as
regards those Powers and States which have both signed and ratified
the Protocol, or have finally acceded thereto; The said Protocol
shall cease to be binding on His Britannic Majesty towards any
Power at enmity with him whose armed forces, or the armed forces

[8] 94 LNTS, 2138.
[9] The text of all reservations can be found in A/AC.50/3 (report of the Committee
of Twelve), 3 Aug. 1951 (mimeo.), pp. 53–7, and in Hearings before the Subcommittee on National Security Policy and Scientific Developments of the
Committee on Foreign Affairs of the US House of Representatives, 18 Nov.–19
Dec. 1969, pp. 271–4.

of whose allies, fail to respect the prohibitions laid down in the said Protocol.

No state has ratified or acceded ' with a reservation limiting the types of chemical weapons to which it applies '.[10]

Before ratifying the Geneva Protocol, any government must ask itself precisely what substances are to be prohibited in war. The British government's conclusion on this matter was made clear in Parliament on 18 February 1930: ' Smoke screens are not considered as poisonous and do not, therefore, come within the terms of the Geneva Gas Protocol. Tear gases and shells producing poisonous fumes are, however, prohibited under the Protocol.' [11] This statement was to assume considerable importance forty years later. The fact was that the United States, which had played a leading part in the 1925 deliberations, took the view in 1930 that governments could not be expected to bind themselves ' to refrain from the use in war, against an enemy, of agencies [tear gases] which they have adopted for peace-time use against their own population '.[12]

The draft disarmament treaty being considered in 1930 contained an undertaking, subject to reciprocity, to abstain from the use in war of ' asphyxiating, poisonous or similar [other] gases, and of all analogous liquids, substances or processes [materials or devices] '.[13] On 18 November 1930 Britain submitted to the Preparatory Commission for the Disarmament Conference a memorandum to the effect that, basing itself on the English text, the British government took the view that the prohibition of the use of gases in war included lachrymatory gases. Other delegations were invited to express their opinions on this point.[14] France submitted the rather tart comment:

[10] *Carnegie CBW Rep.*, p. 13.

[11] HC/Deb., cols 1169–70. In a later statement in Parliament the reference to smoke-screens was made more precise. ' Smoke-screens . . . , in so far as they do not contain poisonous elements, are not within the scope of the [Geneva] Protocol ', (ibid.) 24 Nov. 1930, col. 878.

[12] The Hon. Hugh Gibson, 20th mtg of the Preparatory Commission for the Disarmament Conference, 2 Dec. 1930 (LN) doc. IX, Disarmament. 1931.IX.I, p. 312. The US accepts that it is 'especially forbidden' to use 'poison or poisoned weapons' in war (see FM27-10, paras 37, 504a).

[13] Wording of Geneva Protocol of 1925 in square brackets.

[14] Cmd 3747 (1930).

'All the texts at present in force or proposed . . . are identical.'
The Geneva Protocol and the proposed treaty referred to the
use of gases in war, and did not preclude the use of appliances
discharging irritant gases for maintaining internal order.
France was of the opinion that the prohibitions 'apply to all
gases employed with a view to toxic action on the human
organism, whether the effects of such action are a more or less
temporary irritation of certain mucous membranes or whether
they cause serious or even fatal lesions'. French military regulations specifically prohibited the use in war of irritant gases,
and these were defined as gases causing tears, sneezing, etc.[15]

The British memorandum and the French note were discussed in Geneva on 2 December 1930, and there was virtual
unanimity in support of the Anglo-French view. Twenty-eight
states had ratified the Geneva Protocol. None stated their
opposition to the Anglo-French view, either in 1930 or subse-
quently.[16] The delegates of Canada, China, Czechoslovakia,
Italy, Japan, Romania, the Soviet Union, Spain, Turkey, and
Yugoslavia agreed with Britain and France that the prohibition
contained in the Geneva Protocol and the draft treaty applied
to tear gases; only the United States, not a party to the
Protocol, expressed reservations, for the reason mentioned
above.[17]

It so happened that a parliamentary question on the
definition of poisonous elements under the Geneva Protocol
was due to be answered in the House of Commons a fortnight
after the Geneva debate. As background for answering the
question, E. H. Carr, then in the Foreign Office, wrote a
minute on the complication arising from the fact that 'the
Americans and others do not regard the prohibition as extend-
ing to tear gas, which apparently is *harmless to health*' (my
italics). Among those initialling the minute without dissent
were Sir Robert Vansittart and Hugh Dalton.[18] In his reply

[15] LN doc. IX, p. 311.

[16] *Carnegie CBW Rep.*, pp. 11–12.

[17] LN doc. IX, pp. 311–14.

[18] In am indebted to David Carlton, author of *MacDonald versus Henderson*, for
this information. The file containing the minute is in the PRO, ref. W 13568 in
FO 371/14974.

to the question, Arthur Henderson simply said that the exact substances which are prohibited ' are not defined, either in the Gas Protocol or elsewhere '.[19]

The significance of the Carr minute did not become fully apparent until much later—indeed, not until 1970, when the British government interpreted the prohibition contained in the Geneva Protocol as not being applicable to CS. The tear gas available in 1930 was CN; Corson and Stoughton had synthesized CS in 1928, but it was not developed for use until the 1950s. CS has ' a more potent irritant action than CN but [is] less likely to cause complete incapacity than such agents as the arsenical sternutators [sneezing agents] ' (e.g. Adamsite).[20] It seems clear from Carr's minute that it was known to the British government in 1930 (the year Britain ratified the Geneva Protocol) that there existed tear gases not harmful to human health. But Michael Stewart, replying to a written parliamentary question on 2 February 1970, said that ' modern technology has developed CS smoke which, unlike the tear gases available in 1930, is considered to be not significantly harmful to man in other than wholly exceptional circumstances '.[21] While it is true that CS was not ' available ' in 1930, it was known to the British government at that time that gases with the characteristics of CS existed.

The 1930 view that the prohibition of gases in war included tear gases continued to be the British position after 1930, and when Britain put forward a draft disarmament treaty on 16 March 1933 it was provided: (a) that the prohibition of the use of chemical weapons in war shall apply to the use of any natural or synthetic substance, such as ' toxic, asphyxiating, lachrymatory, irritant or vesicant [blistering] substances ' (Art. 48); (b) that parties to the treaty would be required to inform the proposed disarmament commission of ' lachrymatory substances intended . . . for police operations ' (Art. 54); (c) that smoke or fog used for screening purposes was not included in the prohibition of chemical weapons, ' provided that such smoke or fog is not liable to

[19] HC/Deb., 17 Dec. 1930, col. 1290.
[20] *WHO Report*, Annex 1, p. 54.
[21] HC/Deb., 2 Feb. 1970, col. 18.

produce harmful effects under normal conditions of use' (Art. 48 (c)).[22]

On 8 June 1933 the Disarmament Conference decided to accept the British draft as a basis for future work, but as Hitler strengthened his grip in Germany, the interwar disarmament effort lapsed into futility.

In the first twenty years of debate and negotiation on disarmament after the second world war, chemical and germ weapons were rarely referred to. Only two developments interrupted the relative indifference to the CBW problem. First, in 1952 the Soviet Union and other Communist states alleged that the United States had used germ weapons in Korea. The Security Council placed two items on its agenda:

Question of an appeal to States to accede to and ratify the Geneva Protocol of 1925 (proposed by the Soviet Union);

Question of a request for investigation of alleged bacterial warfare (proposed by the United States).

On the first item, a Soviet proposal to appeal to states to ratify or accede to the Geneva Protocol was not adopted (1 vote in favour, 10 abstentions), and a US proposal to refer the matter to the UN Disarmament Commission was withdrawn. On the second item, the Soviet Union vetoed two proposals, one of which would have asked the CICR to investigate the charges, and the other would have condemned the fabrication and dissemination of false charges.[23] Both of the items remain on the list of matters of which the Security Council is seized.

It is perhaps worth noting that a Soviet academician was a member of the UN group of experts which in 1969 stated that there is no military experience of the use of bacteriological (biological) agents as weapons of war (A/7575/Rev. 1, para. 38).

The second postwar development was Protocol no. III of 23 October 1954,[24] modifying and completing the Brussels Treaty of 17 March 1948. By this Protocol, West Germany undertook

[22] LN doc. 1933, IX.10, pp. 488–9.

[23] *SCOR*, 7th yr, 577—90th mtgs (18 June–9 July 1952); suppl. Apr.–June 1952, pp. 17 (S/2671) & 21–68 (S/2684). The text of the vetoed proposals is given in my *Voting in the Security Council*, pp. 175–7.

[24] 211 UNTS, 364, Annex II, s. 11.

not to manufacture atomic, biological, and chemical weapons in its territory. Chemical weapons were defined as ' any equipment or apparatus, expressly designed to use, for military purposes, the asphyxiating, toxic, irritant, paralysant, growth-regulating, anti-lubricating or catalysing properties of any chemical substance ', other than chemical substances required for peaceful civilian purposes.

Interest in the CBW problem revived in the mid-1960s partly because of allegations that Egyptian forces had used poison gas in the Yemen and the knowledge that American and other forces had used tear and harassing gases as well as anti-plant chemicals in S. E. Asia. The matter was discussed by the General Assembly on 5 December 1966, which approved a Hungarian proposal, amended in language though not in substance, which called for strict observance of ' the principles and objectives ' of the Geneva Protocol (res. 2162B (XXI)).

British policy at this time had three prongs.
1. To persuade non-parties to the Geneva Protocol of 1925 to accede. At the time of the General Assembly decision of 15 December 1966, the CICR informed U Thant that 48 states were parties to the Protocol (A/6597, mimeo.). Four and a half years later the number of parties had just about doubled.[25]
2. To separate biological from chemical weapons, on the ground that the former had never been used in war and a total ban could be imposed immediately. Britain therefore put forward a draft convention designed to prohibit not only the use of biological weapons in war, but also research directed towards production of biological weapons, manufacture, acquisition, and possession, and to eliminate stocks.[26] Two features of this

[25] It is not easy to be absolutely certain how many states are now parties to the Protocol. It would appear that on 28 June 1971, 87 UN Members (counting the USSR and the Byelorussian and Ukrainian Republics as 3 parties) and 5 non-UN Members were parties, making a total of 92. In addition, the USA regarded 8 UN Members which were once colonial territories as having succeeded to the obligations of the former metropolitan power. The three Baltic states were parties prior to their incorporation in the USSR.

[26] ENDC/255, 10 July 1969. Revised drafts were submitted in 1969 and 1970: see ENDC/255/Rev. 1, 26 Aug. 1969, annexed to A/7741, DC/232, 3 Nov. 1969 (mimeo.), & CCD/255/Rev. 2, annexed to A/8059, DC/233, 11 Sept. 1970 (mimeo.).

draft convention deserve mention. First, the convention would prohibit not only first-use of biological weapons, but also second-use as well. Secondly, it provided for the automatic investigation of complaints of violations by means of standing machinery under the UN Secretary-General, without prior authorization by the Security Council in any particular case, but with reports to it. A draft resolution by which the Security Council would authorize the Secretary-General to establish the necessary machinery was proposed. The draft convention also contained provisions for strengthening existing restraints on the use of chemical weapons, and explicitly stated that the new convention would in no way limit or derogate from the obligations of the Geneva Protocol.

3. The third element in British policy was to ask the Secretary-General to have a technical report prepared on chemical weapons, thus taking up an idea first mooted by Malta in 1967. The General Assembly widened the proposal to include biological weapons as well, and U Thant accordingly appointed 14 consultant experts, 5 from North Atlantic Treaty countries (including France), 4 from Warsaw Pact countries, and one each from Ethiopia, India, Japan, Mexico, and Sweden. The British member was Sir Solly Zuckerman.

This is not the place even to summarize the technical information contained in the unanimous UN report, or that in a companion WHO study, but five particular conclusions of the UN experts may be mentioned.[27]

1. Many countries have the potential to produce C or B weapons, and ordinary delivery systems can be adapted to deliver chemical agents.

2. 'Civilians would be even more vulnerable than the military.'

3. 'Whatever military reasons might be advanced for the use of these weapons, and whatever their nature, whether incapacitating or lethal, there would be significant risk of escalation.'

4. The outstanding characteristic of these weapons, which

[27] A/7575/Rev. 1, esp. paras 10, 13, 337, 340, 342–3, 345, 368–9, 3 1, 374–7; see also *WHO Report.*

constitutes their special danger, is their ' variability, amounting under some circumstances to unpredictability '; they are ' potentially unconfined in their effects, both in space and time '; their use could have ' irreversible effects on the balance of nature ' and ' could open the door to hostilities which could become less controlled, and less controllable than any war in the past '.

5. Not only would the use of these weapons be ' profoundly dangerous '; ' their very existence . . . contributes to international tension without compensating military advantages. They generate a sense of insecurity not only in countries which might be potentially belligerent, but also in those which are not.' The only remedy is ' the earliest effective elimination '.

The Secretary-General accepted the report in its entirety and, in transmitting it to governments, urged states:

1. to accede to the Geneva Protocol of 1925;

2. to make a clear affirmation that the prohibition in the Geneva Protocol ' applies to the use in war of all chemical, bacteriological and biological agents (including tear gas and other harassing agents), which now exist or which may be developed in the future ';

3. to reach agreement to halt the development, production, and stockpiling of all C and B agents for war purposes, and to achieve their elimination from military arsenals (A/7575/Rev. 1, p. xii).

The first and third of U Thant's points coincided with British policy. The second point coincided with what had been assumed by the public to have been British policy for forty years.

On 26 August 1969 the substance of U Thant's second proposal was incorporated in a working paper submitted to the Geneva disarmament committee by Sweden and eleven other non-aligned states,[28] and the working paper, after slight revision, was later submitted as a draft resolution to the General Assembly.

When U Thant's proposals were made public on 2 July 1969,

[28] ENDC/265, 26 Aug. 1969, annexed to A/7741, DC/232, 3 Nov. 1969

Britain's minister for disarmament reacted cautiously (and with prescience) to the second point: ' I fear that it may be difficult to secure the unanimous agreement of all the parties to the Protocol [to U Thant's interpretation of it]. . . .[M]ight not our failure to agree throw doubt on the continued validity of the Protocol? ' [29] British reservations increased as the weeks went by, particularly when British troops had to use CS in Northern Ireland, the first instance of the use of tear gas for riot control within the UK.

The non-aligned draft resolution declared that the Geneva Protocol embodied 'the generally recognized rules of international law ', and that any use of chemical or biological agents in international armed conflicts would be contrary to the Geneva Protocol. When it was put to the vote in December 1969, Britain abstained, ostensibly on the ground that it was beyond the competence of the General Assembly to interpret international treaties. The resolution was adopted nonetheless by 80 to 3 (Australia, Portugal, USA), with 26 abstentions (res. 2603A (XXIV), 16 Dec. 1969).

Seven more weeks were to elapse, however, before the British government made clear precisely what its reservations were. On 2 February 1970, replying to a seemingly innocuous request in the House of Commons to make a statement on disarmament, the Foreign Secretary said he would like to explain the government's view regarding the use of tear gases in war. He quoted the conclusion of the second Labour government in 1930 that smoke screens did not come within the Geneva Protocol; he maintained that CS is far less toxic than the screening smokes which the 1930 statement excluded; and he expressed the government's view that CS ' and other such gases ' should be regarded as outside the prohibition of use in war contained in the Geneva Protocol. The next day the Prime Minister added that CS ' has been newly discovered or invented—whatever is the right phrase—since 1930 '.[30]

Until the files are opened in thirty years' time, we cannot be sure why the Labour government reached this decision.

[29] Foreign & Commonwealth Office, *Arms Control and Disarmament: Notes on Current Developments*, 10 Nov. 1969, p. 16.
[30] HC Deb., 2 Feb. 1970, cols 17–18; 3 Feb. 1970, cols 209–12.

Many ordinary citizens no doubt took much the same view as did the United States in 1930—that it would be absurd not to use in war a chemical substance which British troops were using for riot control in the UK in time of peace. Lord Chalfont, who was minister for disarmament during the latter phase of this unhappy story, has suggested that this was not the only or even the main argument that carried weight: ' The military pragmatists and the realists had won a victory. The options so dear to the defence planners had been kept open.' [31]

Opposition to the decision announced on 2 February was based on three main considerations. First, there is in practice an important distinction between use in peace and use in war. Tear gas is used in peace under strict controls and to avoid using more lethal weapons; the purpose is to reduce injuries and save lives.[32] In war, it may also be used in conjunction with other weapons to increase the lethal effectiveness of the latter.[33] Whatever may have been the original intention of the American authorities, it is beyond any doubt that tear gases have been used in South-east Asia to enhance the effectiveness of conventional anti-personnel weapons. But the most grave danger in war is the risk of escalation from gases which merely irritate to those that kill (e.g. nerve gases).

The second objection was to the method used to reinterpret an international treaty. Britain had taken the view when ratifying the Geneva Protocol in 1930 that the Protocol banned the use of tear gases in war, and had played a leading part in trying to persuade other countries to take the same view. The unilateral reinterpretation of an international treaty undermines the effort to build world order. The offence was compounded in this case because it followed so closely on U Thant's appeal and the vote of a substantial majority in the General Assembly urging states to respect the traditional view of the obligations contained in the Geneva Protocol.

The third objection followed naturally from the second.

---

[31] ' The CS Gas Muddle ', *New Statesman*, 31 July 1970, p. 109.

[32] The two reports of the Himsworth Committee on the use of CS for riot control purposes in Northern Ireland were issued as Cmnds 4173 (1969) & 4775 (1971).

[33] *WHO Report*, p. 12, n. 4.

Britain had been establishing a reputation as a country genuinely committed to arms control and disarmament. When Britain first proposed separating biological from chemical weapons, and dealing with the former by means of an immediate and total ban, there were critics who said that the ulterior motive for this ploy was to make it easier for the United States to continue using harassing gases and anti-plant chemicals in Vietnam. The effect of the British proposal to separate biological from chemical weapons, said the critics, would not be to strengthen the Geneva Protocol but to weaken it. British ministers denied this charge and pointed to the paragraph in Britain's proposal on biological weapons to the effect that its purpose was to reinforce the Protocol, but critics of British policy maintained that the government's claim that it wished to strengthen the Protocol lacked plausibility after 2 February 1970.

The British government can at any time return to the traditional interpretation of the Geneva Protocol. If doubts should exist regarding the precise scope of the Protocol, an authoritative opinion could be secured from the International Court of Justice. This is the course of action favoured by Judge Philip Jessup, a former member of the Court.[34]

While all this had been happening in Britain, the Nixon Administration had been conducting a review of its policy on CBW, and on 25 November 1969 the President announced that he was asking the Senate to advise and consent to US ratification of the Geneva Protocol of 1925. In addition, Nixon announced that the United States was taking a number of unilateral steps regarding CBW.

1. The United States would not be the first to use incapacitating or lethal *chemical* weapons.

2. The United States renounced entirely the use of all *biological* weapons, would destroy stocks of such weapons, and would discontinue research on biological warfare except for research on ' defensive measures such as immunization and safety measures '. Nixon also stated his support for the British draft convention on biological weapons, but would ' seek . . . to

[34] *Carnegie CBW Rep.*, pp. 28–30 & 123.

clarify specific provisions of the draft to assure that necessary safeguards are included '.[35] The US Administration let it be known that it did not regard the chemicals being used in South-east Asia as coming within the scope of the ' no first use ' commitment. On 14 February 1970 it was announced that the US ban on biological weapons would also apply to the so-called biological toxins, which are chemicals even though ' the technology of their production resembles that of biological agents '.[36] Toxins are not capable of reproduction.

There was an unaccountable delay in the submission of the Geneva Protocol to the US Senate, and when it was eventually transmitted nine months later, there was attached to the President's Message the text of a letter from Secretary of State William P. Rogers. This proposed that the United States should ratify the Protocol with a reservation which would permit retaliatory use of chemical weapons but would leave without any reservation the prohibition of biological weapons. The letter continued: ' It is the United States' understanding of the Protocol that it does not prohibit the use in war of riot-control agents and chemical herbicides.' [37]

On 15 April 1971 Senator Fulbright, chairman of the Senate Foreign Relations Committee, wrote to President Nixon to explain that while the Committee attached great importance to the Protocol, ' many of us are reluctant to proceed further toward its ratification on the basis of the understandings and interpretations which have been attached to it by the Secretary of State '. If it was not possible to ratify without restrictive interpretations, ' many Members [of the Committee] now consider that it would be in the interest of the United States . . . to postpone further action on the Protocol '. Senator Fulbright asked President Nixon to re-examine the proposed interpretation by which tear gas and herbicides would be excluded from the prohibition contained in the Protocol.[38]

While these deliberations and decisions were taking place in Britain and the United States, the processes of debate in New

[35] US Press Release USUN—174(69), 25 Nov. 1969.
[36] *WHO Report*, p. 12, n. 2.
[37] Message from the President of the United States transmitting the [Geneva] Protocol . . . , 19 Aug. 1970, p. (vi).
[38] *Congressional Record—Senate*, 8 June 1971, S8486–7.

York and negotiation in Geneva followed their normal course. In 1969 the Warsaw Pact UN Members together with Mongolia had put forward a draft convention to prohibit the development, production, and stockpiling of both chemical and bacteriological (biological) weapons. The draft was submitted directly to the General Assembly in New York although the Geneva negotiating committee was in session at the time, arousing suspicions that there was an element of propaganda in the Communist tactics. A revised Communist draft was submitted to the Assembly a year later. In April 1970 Hungary, Mongolia, and Poland submitted to the Geneva committee a proposal for dealing with alleged violations of a comprehensive CBW treaty, a proposal which clearly drew heavily on the complaints procedure contained in the UK draft convention on biological weapons. Mongolia also proposed that special government agencies might be established to enforce compliance with prohibitions on C and B weapons in a manner similar to that in the 1961 Single Convention on Narcotic Drugs.[39] Several other ideas were put forward in Geneva for enforcing, or explaining why it was impossible to enforce, a CBW treaty.[40]

Thus when the General Assembly took up the question of CBW on 7 December 1970 there was no lack of technical and political background material. The Assembly decided (res. 2662 (XXV)), without a dissenting vote, to remit the problem to the Geneva committee, commending as a 'basic approach' the ideas of the non-aligned countries.[41] These ideas included emphasis on the urgency and importance of dealing with CBW, the desirability of continuing to deal with C and B weapons together, and the necessity of both national and international verification 'which would complement and supplement each other'.

[39] A/7655, 19 Sept. 1969; A/8136, 23 Oct. 1970; CCD/285, 14 Apr. 1970, annexed to A/8059, DC/233, 11 Sept. 1970; CCD/P.464, 14 Apr. 1970, paras 49–50. At the request of Spain (28 Nov. 1932), the League of Nations Secretariat had conducted a study of analogies between the problem of the traffic in narcotic drugs and that of the trade in and manufacture of arms (see Conf. doc. D.159 (4 May 1933) in LN 1935.IX.4, pp. 494–502).

[40] See in particular the proposals of Canada, Czechoslovakia, Italy, Japan, Morocco, Sweden, the UAR, UK, & USA, annexed to A/8059.

[41] CCD/310, 25 Aug. 1970, annexed to ibid.

But a surprise lay in store for the Geneva committee. On 30 March 1971 the Soviet delegate, acting for all the Communist states, submitted a draft convention dealing with biological weapons only. He explained that the Soviet Union would still have preferred to link chemical and biological weapons in one treaty, but because of ' the reluctance of the United States and other Western Powers to renounce chemical warfare ' and ' desiring to break the deadlock ', the Communist group of countries were ready to prohibit the development, production, and stockpiling of bacteriological weapons and toxins, and their means of delivery, and to destroy all stocks. Prohibition of use in war would continue to be covered by the Geneva Protocol. The draft convention contained a commitment to negotiate in good faith on equivalent measures for chemical weapons (CCD/PV. 505, pp. 22–40 & CCD/325). On 5 August 1971 there was a further surprise, for the United States and the Soviet Union submitted a *joint* draft convention to ban biological weapons.

These moves embarrassed the non-aligned members of the committee, which had supported the earlier Soviet insistence that chemical and biological weapons should be dealt with simultaneously. There were, however, sufficient common features between the Soviet proposal and the earlier British draft to make it possible for the committee to submit an agreed text for the approval of the General Assembly. Nevertheless, the enthusiasts for general and complete disarmament and the cynics made common cause in denouncing this as one more example of agreeing to ban an activity which no state in its right mind had any intention of conducting. Those who welcomed the new move argued that it is precisely when nobody wishes to develop or use an obscene means of warfare, like the deliberate spreading of disease, that it should be prohibited by international treaty.

Nuclear weapons

While the manufacture of C and B weapons is within the capacity of many countries, that of nuclear and thermonuclear weapons is, at the time of writing, a monopoly of five states. Nuclear weapons and the means of their delivery are not cheap. The two superpowers spent about 9 per cent of their GNP on defence in 1969.[42] That, in absolute terms, represented about $80,000 m. for the United States and about $39,000 m. for the Soviet Union.

But there is an even greater moral scandal than the nuclear arms competition of the superpowers. A typical European country spends about 3 per cent of its GNP on defence; that was the case in 1969 for Belgium, Bulgaria, Denmark, West Germany, Hungary, Italy, the Netherlands, Norway, and Poland. Yet nine countries of Asia, the Middle East, and Africa spent over 10 per cent of their GNP on defence in 1969, and two of them actually spent one-quarter of the GNP.[43] A consultative group appointed by the UN Secretary-General estimated that the world spent $120,000 m. on defence in 1961; by 1969 the figure had reached $200,000 m.[44]

The two superpowers are now engaged in bilateral discussions designed to curb the strategic arms race. One method of achieving this result, though by no means the only one, would be ' a comprehensive freeze on all missile tests ' plus a freeze on ' currently deployed forces at present levels and types of weapons . . . [and] a simultaneous ban on ABM systems or at least a limitation that prevents rapid expansion '.[45] But the attempt to control nuclear weapons has taken more than one form. There have, in fact, been five different but connected approaches.

1. *Prohibition of the placing of nuclear weapons in particular regions or environments.* The Antarctica Treaty, signed on 1 December 1959, prohibits ' any measures of a military nature . . . as well as the testing of any type of weapon ' in Antarctica, and nuclear explosions and the disposal of radioactive waste are expressly forbidden.[46] The Outer Space Treaty, signed on 27 January 1967, prohibits the placing in orbit of ' any objects carrying

---

[42] ISS, *The Military Balance 1970–1* (London, 1970), p. 110. [43] Ibid. pp. 110–11.
[44] E/5393, 28 Feb. 1962, para. 8 (mimeo.); William Epstein, *Disarmament: Twenty-Five Years of Effort* (Toronto, 1971), p. 39. See also A/8469, 22 Oct. 1971 (mimeo.), para. 2.
[45] Joshua Lederberg, ' A Freeze on Missile Testing ', *B. Atomic Scientists*, Mar. 1971, p. 43; Herbert Scoville, Jr., ' The Limitation of Offensive Weapons ', *Scientific American*, Jan. 1971, p. 25.
[46] 402 UNTS, 71. The text of the treaty can also be found in H. J. Taubenfeld, ' A treaty for Antarctica ', *International Conciliation*, Jan. 1961, pp. 318–22.

nuclear weapons or any other kinds of weapons of mass destruction ', as well as installing such weapons on celestial bodies or
stationing them in outer space.[47] The Treaty of Tlatelolco,
signed on 14 February 1967, together with two Additional
Protocols, is designed to prohibit the receipt, storage, installation, deployment, and possession of nuclear weapons in Latin
America, as well as testing, use, manufacture, production, or
acquisition.[48] A draft treaty to prohibit the emplacement of
nuclear weapons and other weapons of mass destruction on the
sea-bed and the ocean floor was laid before the General
Assembly in 1970, and was approved by 104 votes to 2, with 21
states abstaining or absent.[49] It was opened for signature on
11 February 1971 and has been signed by 80 states (June 1971).
The Assembly in November 1961 called upon all UN Members
to refrain from testing, storing, or transporting nuclear weapons
in Africa, and to consider and respect the continent as a de-
nuclearized zone (res. 1652 (XVI)); and in December 1965 it
reaffirmed this call (res. 2033 (XX)). On 27 May 1971 the Soviet
Union proposed that a treaty be prepared which would ban the
placing in orbit around the moon of any objects carrying
nuclear weapons or any other kinds of weapons of mass destruction, or the installation of such weapons on the surface of the
moon or in its subsoil.[50]

Nuclear-free zones have been proposed for other regions,

[47] Text annexed to GA res.2222 (XXI), 19 Dec. 1966; see also Cmnds 3198
(1967) & 3519 (1968).

[48] Text in *GAOR*, 22nd sess., Annexes, agenda item 91, pp. 3–10. See also
Cmnds 3615 (1968) & 4409 (1970). On 7 December 1970 the Assembly voted by
104 : 0, with France and the USSR among the abstainers, deploring the fact that
some nuclear-weapon states (i.e. the USSR, France, and China) had not signed
Protocol II whereby nuclear-weapon states would agree that the treaty should be
' fully respected . . . in all its express aims and provisions ' and that such states
would not contribute to violations of the treaty or use or threaten to use nuclear
weapons against parties to the treaty (res. 2666 (XXV)). On 4 January 1971 the
USSR assured Mexico that she would respect the status of those Latin American
states which turn their territories into completely nuclear-free zones, provided that
other nuclear powers undertake the same commitments. The USSR would, at the
same time, reserve the right to reconsider her undertaking in the event of any
nuclear-free Latin American state perpetrating or being an accomplice to aggression (S/10250/Rev. 1, 8 July 1971, p. 3 (mimeo.)).

[49] Text of the treaty as approved by the General Assembly is annexed to GA
res. 2660 (XXV), 7 Dec. 1970.

[50] A/8391, 4 June 1971, Annex Art. II (2).

including the Nordic area, Central Europe, the Balkans, the Adriatic, the Mediterranean, the Middle East, and Asia and the Pacific. Poland has put forward several proposals for Central Europe, including the Rapacki plan (1957) to prohibit production and stockpiling of nuclear weapons in Poland, Czechoslovakia, and both parts of Germany; and the Gomulka plan (1964) for a freeze of nuclear weapons in the same region.

2. *Prohibition of the testing of nuclear weapons.* One special feature of nuclear weapons is that simply to test them above ground or in the oceans releases radiation which causes somatic damage to some people now living and genetic damage to generations yet unborn. A total prohibition on all testing of nuclear weapons, if it could be generally accepted and effectively enforced, would prove a formidable barrier to any increase in the number of states possessing their own nuclear weapons (horizontal proliferation), and would also prevent the further sophistication of nuclear weapons by countries already possessing them (vertical proliferation). So far it has not been possible to ban all testing of nuclear weapons, but a partial test-ban treaty, prohibiting tests in the atmosphere, in outer space, and under water was signed on 5 August 1963.[51] More than 100 states have ratified the treaty (June 1971), but two nuclear-weapon states (France and China) are among the non-parties.[52]

3. *Prohibition of the horizontal proliferation of nuclear weapons.* The attempt to stop the horizontal proliferation of nuclear weapons began with an Irish proposal in 1958 and culminated in the non-proliferation treaty of 1968. This was accompanied by a resolution of the Security Council of 19 June 1968 on security assurances and three virtually identical statements made in the Council on 17 June 1968 by the Soviet,

[51] 480 UNTS, 43.

[52] On 7 December 1970 the General Assembly requested the Geneva disarmament committee ' as a matter of urgency ' to continue its efforts to agree on a treaty to ban underground tests (res. 2663 (XXV)). Ostensibly the failure to agree on a comprehensive test ban is due to differences between the USA and the USSR on whether on-site inspection is needed to deter cheating. The truth is that the superpowers wish to continue testing and claim that a total test ban depends on significant progress in SALT. Another view, however, is that SALT cannot succeed without a prior ban on all tests.

UK, and US representatives.[53] The Board of the International Atomic Energy Agency approved the safeguards agreements required under the NPT on 20 April 1971. Neither China nor France has ratified, but France has declared that it will in practice respect the treaty provisions. Among the countries which might be considered as potential nuclear-weapon powers but which are non-signatories of the treaty are Argentina, Brazil, Chile, India, Israel, Pakistan, Portugal, South Africa, and Spain.

The NPT contains three sets of obligations. The nuclear-weapon states undertake not to transfer nuclear weapons to any recipient whatsoever, or to assist or encourage non-nuclear-weapon states to manufacture, acquire, or control such weapons. The non-nuclear-weapon states undertake not to manufacture or acquire nuclear weapons, and to accept the safeguards system of the IAEA. All parties agree to co-operate in the development of the peaceful uses of nuclear energy, including nuclear explosions for peaceful purposes, and to negotiate further measures of nuclear disarmament. It should be noted that quite apart from obligations under the NPT, West Germany has agreed not to manufacture atomic weapons ' in its territory '.[54]

It has sometimes been said that the NPT is ' discriminatory ' in that it seeks to freeze permanently a situation in which five states possess nuclear weapons, while all other parties have to accept the inferior status of not having such weapons and of being subject to IAEA controls. There is no denying the force of this, but it must at the same time be said that non-nuclear-weapon states derive advantages from the treaty; if that were not so, sixty-six of them would not have ratified it and a further thirty-three would not have signed it (June 1971). Moreover, the UK and the United States have agreed to submit to the safeguards arrangements, subject only to exclusions for reasons of national security.

There were a number of important milestones during the ten-year effort to conclude the NPT. One was the report on nuclear

[53] Text of treaty annexed to res. 2373 (XXII), 18 June 1968; also in Cmnd 4474 (1970). Text of security assurances in SC. res 255, 19 June 1968, & S/PV. 1430, 17 June 1968, pp. 11–15, 17–20, 22–25.
[54] Protocol (III), 23 Oct. 1954, 211 UNTS, 364.

weapons prepared in 1967 by a group of twelve consultant experts at the request of the General Assembly (A/6865, 10 Oct. 1967, mimeo.). Sir Solly Zuckerman was a member of this group.

The experts pointed out that air warfare has made it possible to destroy cities without first defeating the defending armies. Large megaton nuclear weapons have a greater destructive power than all of the conventional explosive that has ever been used in warfare since the invention of gunpowder, and the two superpowers in 1967 possessed more than enough destructive power to eliminate all mankind. The distinction sometimes made between tactical and strategic nuclear war would in practice be likely to be meaningless.

It can be firmly stated that were nuclear weapons to be used in this [tactical] way, they could lead to the devastation of the whole battle zone. . . . Circumstances such as these would be incompatible with the continued conduct of military operations within the zones of devastation. . . . [T]he destruction and disruption which would result from so-called tactical nuclear war would hardly differ from the effects of strategic war in the area concerned.

Moreover, the disastrous effects of all-out nuclear war could not be confined to the powers engaged in that war (A/6865, paras 1, 14, 31, 35, 40, & 81).

Once the nuclear arms race begins, ' no size of programme ever satisfies '. Having acquired an unsophisticated nuclear-weapons system, a country is driven inexorably to produce more sophisticated and less vulnerable means of delivery. The experts calculated that six countries had the economic and financial resources to ' go nuclear ' at a small high-quality level, and another twenty countries at a more modest level (paras 45, 56, & 74).[55]

Spiralling arms races, concluded the experts, have no end and lead to phases of ' major insecurity '. The goal should be the total elimination of stocks and a ban on use. ' The ultimate question for the world to decide . . . is what short-term interests it is prepared to sacrifice, in exchange for an assurance of survival and security ' (paras 42, 80, 91–2).

[55] In the light of more recent studies, I suggest that these estimates should be increased to at least 9 and 21 respectively.

The other event on the road to the NPT was an important, if sometimes confusing, conference of non-nuclear-weapon states held in Geneva in 1968.[56] The non-nuclear-weapon states were being asked to renounce a military option. In return for this, they called for ' greater commitments and assistance to them by the nuclear powers in the fields of security, of the peaceful uses of nuclear energy, and of peaceful nuclear explosions, and also for greater disarmament efforts by the nuclear powers '.[57]

4. *Attempts to achieve vertical nuclear disarmament*. The NPT contains a specific undertaking by the parties ' to pursue negotiations in good faith on . . . cessation of the nuclear arms race and . . . nuclear disarmament '. The treaty had, in fact, been concluded at a crucial stage in the development of nuclear weapons. The two superpowers, then in a period of strategic nuclear balance, were technically able to proceed to a new and expensive level of sophistication. MIRVs provide increased offensive capability while ABM systems give improved defensive capability. These two weapons systems act and react on each other. Dr Herbert York has put it like this:

ABM and MIRV are thus inseparable; each one requires and inspires the other. Separately or in combination, they create uncertainty in each of the nuclear powers about the capability and even the intentions of the other. These uncertainties eventually lead in turn to fear, over-reaction, and further increases in the number and types of all kinds of weapons, defensive as well as offensive.[58]

Both superpowers were on the point of embarking on these technical advances, the results of which would almost certainly be to leave them relatively neither more nor less secure, but at vast expense. The arguments for and against improving first-strike capability and acquiring the capacity to penetrate ABM defences, which are important purposes of MIRVs, and for and against providing ABM defence of missile sites and/or cities, are highly technical and beyond the scope of this study. Suffice it to note that the United States and the Soviet Union saw enough common interest in trying to halt the nuclear arms race to

[56] The final document of the conference was issued as A/7277, 1968.
[57] Epstein, p. 23.
[58] Hearings before the Subcommittee on Arms Control, International Law and Organization of the US Senate Cttee on Foreign Relations, 8 Apr. 1970, p. 61.

agree in 1969 to begin the bilateral strategic arms talks. All the indications are that the talks, which opened in Helsinki on 17 November 1969, got off to a businesslike start. On 20 May 1971 the two superpowers issued the following joint statement:

The Governments of the United States and the Soviet Union, after reviewing the course of their talks on the limitation of strategic armaments, have agreed to concentrate this year [1971] on working out an agreement for the limitation of the deployment of anti-ballistic missile systems (ABM's). They have also agreed that, together with concluding an agreement to limit ABM's, they will agree on certain measures with respect to the limitation of offensive strategic weapons.

The two sides are taking this course in the conviction that it will create more favourable conditions for further negotiations to limit all strategic arms. These negotiations will be actively pursued.[59]

It is not yet clear whether these aims will be achieved by agreements in express terms, or by tacit understandings. A number of countries have expressed fears that SALT might put a quantitative limit on nuclear-weapons systems, while leaving the nuclear arms race unrestricted in qualitative terms.

China and France have adopted a posture of studied indifference to SALT, but for Britain a successful outcome of the talks would have momentous implications. As suggested above, one possible outcome would permit the superpowers to deploy ABM systems on a limited scale. What would be the future of the strategic nuclear element of the British deterrent in a world of limited ABM systems? Would Britain have to replace her submarine-launched Polaris A-3 missiles with multiple-warhead missiles of the Poseidon type?

5. *Prohibition of use of nuclear weapons.* How useful is it to agree to ban the use of any weapon while some states are allowed to continue research and development, to manufacture and stock-pile, and to train their forces in the use of that weapon? The hard-headed realist is no doubt tempted to question the useful-ness of paper promises, and yet the ' ban-the-bomb ' slogan has at times had an undoubted appeal in some countries, and it must be admitted that nuclear weapons have characteristics which justify treating the question of their control differently from that

[59] US Embassy Press Release.

L

of controlling conventional weapons. From a moral point of view, the crucial fact is that the use of nuclear weapons, whether for offence or defence, would release radiation which would harm innocent people—not only enemy civilians but allied and neutral and one's own civilians as well. No scientist can say with assurance precisely how much damage is caused by the radiation arising from nuclear explosions. In 1956, when nuclear weapons were measured in kilotons rather than megatons, a committee of the British Medical Research Council reported that contamination of the atmosphere as a result of large-scale nuclear war ' could not fail to increase for many generations the load of distress and suffering that individuals *and all human societies* would be called upon to support' (my italics).[60] The very fact of uncertainty about the exact amount of harm is itself a ground for caution.

Nuclear weapons have such destructive power that it is difficult to use them discriminately against military targets only. It is true that tactical nuclear weapons have been developed for battlefield use, but it would be folly to regard these weapons as ' merely a more modern and effective form of second world war artillery '. Douglas Dodds-Parker, in his report for the WEU, defined a tactical nuclear weapon as one which, if used, would be unlikely to provoke a strategic response. This is a subjective definition, and Dodds-Parker later pointed out that ' it might not always be clear to an enemy whether he was being struck by " tactical " or " strategic " weapons '.[61] The difficulty of distinguishing between tactical and strategic use was also stressed by the UN experts who reported in 1967. In such conditions, it is impossible to escape from the risk of escalation.

Moreover, the nuclear powers have been careful not to commit themselves never to use strategic nuclear weapons in such a way as to kill large numbers of civilians. Robert McNamara, for example, defined the strategic policy of the

[60] Cmd 9780, (1956), para. 290; see also the reports of the UN Scientific Committee on the Effects of Atomic Radiation, issued in 1958 and subsequent years.

[61] WEU Ass., *State of European Security: the Tactical Use of Nuclear Weapons and the Defence of Western Europe*, 14th ord. sess., 1st pt, doc. 440, 2 May 1968, paras 6, 23, & 39.

United States in 1968 as being to possess an Assured Destruction Capability. He considered that an effective US capability would be the possibility of destroying one-fifth to one-quarter of the Soviet population and one-half of Soviet industrial capacity.[62] I find it impossible to conceive of a targeting policy having that effect which does not include a conditional intention to attack cities.

As a broad generalization, one may say that weapons are neutral; moral and political issues arise only when someone intends, threatens, or decides to use them. At the same time nuclear weapons are of such magnitude that one can understand why the possibility of their use should give rise to feelings of revulsion if not indignation, and why it seems reasonable to make efforts to prohibit or restrict their use.

In the early days of the UN, the problem revolved mainly around the Soviet slogan about banning the bomb, which was widely regarded at the time as a propaganda ploy. Serious debate and negotiation about disarmament date from 1954, when the Soviet Union agreed to take as a basis for discussion a comprehensive Anglo-French plan for verified disarmament by stages.

In 1961, as a result of an initiative by Ethiopia, it was decided to separate the question of *the use* of nuclear weapons from other disarmament matters. On 24 November 1961 the General Assembly adopted a resolution (1653 (XVI)) declaring that the use of nuclear or thermonuclear weapons is ' contrary to the spirit, letter and aims of the United Nations and, as such, a direct violation of the Charter of the United Nations . . . [and] contrary to the rules of international law and to the laws of humanity '. Any state using such weapons would be ' acting contrary to the laws of humanity and . . . committing a crime against mankind and civilization '. U Thant was asked to consult governments with a view to convening a conference for signing a convention banning the use of such weapons.

Britain and the United States opposed this decision on the ground that deterrence depends on a determination to respond to aggression at whatever level is necessary, and that there

[62] Statement to the Senate Armed Services Committee, 1 Feb. 1968 (*Survival*, Apr. 1968, pp. 106–14).

should be no abrogation of the right of self-defence. The Western view was that paper promises not to use weapons which you possess and are training your armed forces to use are no substitute for concrete measures of arms control or disarmament. The official British report on the UN session commented:

Feeling ran high on this draft resolution. The United States, the United Kingdom and a number of other Western delegations, while sharing the anxiety of the sponsors to avoid nuclear war, argued that this aim could not be achieved by this means but only by agreement on comprehensive disarmament, which would include nuclear disarmament. Meanwhile they must retain their undoubted right under the Charter and in international law to use nuclear weapons in self-defence if necessary.[63]

The fact was that Western governments wished to leave open the possibility of using nuclear weapons in response to a conventional attack. The real weakness of the resolution was not the one they stressed. It was, as the CICR pointed out, that it did not cover the case of reprisals.[64]

The Soviet government has always adopted a simple view of this problem in its public pronouncements: that a convention to prohibit the use of nuclear weapons would be an important step on the road to their complete abolition. If the Geneva Protocol of 1925 banning chemical and germ weapons in war has served a useful purpose, why not have a similar ban on the use of nuclear weapons?

It may be useful to summarize at this point what is known of the Chinese attitude. After the first nuclear test explosion in China in 1964, the Chinese government issued a statement which repeated Chairman Mao's saying that the atom bomb is a paper tiger and denounced the partial test ban as ' a big fraud to fool the peoples of the world '. It declared that China would ' never at any time and under any circumstance be the first to use nuclear weapons ' and that she has consistently advocated ' the complete prohibition and thorough destruction of nuclear weapons through international consultations '.[65] The Chinese government has several times proposed the

[63] Cmnd 1791 (1962), para. 123. For the US position, see FM27-10, para. 35.
[64] Memo. on Protection, Annex 2, pp. 4-5.
[65] Full text in *Survival*, Jan.-Feb. 1965, pp. 8-9.

convening of a world conference to consider the prohibition and destruction of nuclear weapons.[66]

The UN item regarding a non-use convention was continued by each regular session of the General Assembly from 1961 to 1967.[67] From time to time other proposals for a ban on particular uses have been made. On 27 May 1965 the Soviet Union introduced in the UN Disarmament Commission a draft resolution, which was not pressed to a vote, supporting the idea of a non-use convention, and inviting nuclear-weapon states ' to declare . . . that they will not be the first to use nuclear weapons ' (DC/219). On 1 February 1966 she stated that she was prepared ' to assume immediately an obligation not to be the first to use nuclear weapons, provided that the other nuclear Powers do likewise ', and in 1967 she submitted to the General Assembly a draft convention by which states would undertake not to use, threaten to use, or incite other states to use nuclear weapons.[68] A number of third world countries have proposed a ban on the threat or use against non-nuclear states.[69] The present status of the matter is that the Assembly on 8 December 1967 invited states ' to examine ' the Soviet draft convention to prohibit use ' and such other proposals as may be made ', and referred the matter to the negotiating committee in Geneva (res. 2289 (XXII)). Seventy-seven Members voted in favour of this decision (46 Afro-Asians, 10 Communists, 16 Latin American and Caribbean states, 4 European neutrals, plus Spain), the NATO countries being among the 29 abstainers.

[66] See *Survival*, July 1966, pp. 229 & 235; Jan. 1967, pp. 3–5; Aug. 1957, pp. 269–70; see also *New York Times*, 2 Nov. 1970. On 23 June 1971 the Soviet government proposed that a conference of the five nuclear powers should be held to consider the entire range of measures relating to nuclear disarmament (S/10236 & A/8328). For a full Chinese statement, see A/PV.1983, 15 Nov. 1971 (mimeo), pp. 97-8.

[67] Res. 1801 (XVII), 14 Dec. 1962 & 1909 (XVIII), 27 Nov. 1963; *GAOR*, 19th sess., annex 9, p. 6; 20th sess., annexes, agenda item 29; res. 2164 (XXI), 5 Dec. 1966, & 2289 (XXII) 8 Dec. 1967.

[68] ENDC/167, 3 Feb. 1966, annexed to A/6390, DC/228, 30 Aug. 1966; A/6834 (GAOR, 22nd sess., annexes, agenda item 96); ENDC/227, 16 July 1968, annexed to A/7189, DC/231, 4 Sept. 1968; ENDC/P.402, 10 Apr. 1969, paras 44–68.

[69] See e.g. Pakistan's proposal at the Conference of Non-Nuclear-Weapon States in 1968, in *Final Document of the Conference*, A/7277 (*GAOR*, 23rd sess., agenda item 96, pp. 58–60). See also A/CDNF.35/Doc. 8, 9 July 1968, prepared by Prof. Jaroslav Zourek.

Some states would have liked to have used the UN silver jubilee in 1970 to conclude an international convention to prohibit the use of nuclear weapons,[70] but there was insufficient support for the adoption of such a convention. The Declaration (res. 2627 (XXV)) adopted on that occasion merely expressed the pious hope of concluding new arms-control agreements and ' moving forward from arms limitation to a reduction of armaments and disarmament everywhere, particularly in the nuclear field '.

The never-ending competition in the development of nuclear weapons shows how an arms race acquires a momentum of its own. The technical experts feel impelled to transform each new theoretical possibility into an actuality, and decide afterwards what its military justification should be. To a foreigner, it has often seemed as if the ABM debate in the United States has not been a search for a weapons-system to counter a specific threat, but a search for a rationale to justify a weapons-system which was thought to be technically feasible. Discussion about nuclear ' superiority ' over possible adversaries can easily be unrelated to actual military needs.[71] Each side, on the basis of incomplete or faulty intelligence, over-reacts to the supposed developments on the other side. Both the United States and the Soviet Union, insuring against a technological breakthrough by the other, have acquired a massive strategic ' overkill ' capacity.

It is sometimes said that as a country acquires a nuclear capability, so its leaders inevitably develop an enhanced sense of international responsibility. If a direct connection between the two processes were proved beyond all doubt, then the NPT would seem to be an unmitigated disaster, since it denies to the vast majority of countries a sure means of achieving an enhanced sense of international responsibility.

The paradox is that nuclear weapons are not there to be used, but to deter their use by others. The superpowers cannot use their nuclear strength for day-to-day political purposes—to

[70] A/7690 (*GAOR*, 24th sess., annexes, agenda item 25), para. 22.
[71] See Walter I. Slocombe, *Political Implications of Strategic Parity* (Adelphi Paper no. 77) (London, 1971).

change or maintain the status of Berlin, to bring pressure to bear on the parties to the Middle East conflict, to prevent a neighbour (Czechoslovakia, say, or the Dominican Republic) from developing dangerous political tendencies. It is said that when North Korea seized the *Pueblo* on 23 January 1968 the only US aircraft which could be summoned for assistance were armed with nuclear weapons. Power is the ability to persuade others to behave in ways they had not intended, but excessive power may well be unusable.

Although the central strategic balance is relatively stable at the time of writing the nuclear powers realize that deterrence alone is not enough: they have to face the possibility that deterrence may fail, whether by accident, miscalculation, or sheer lunacy. In a multilateral alliance, who should decide when deterrence has failed, when to resort to tactical or strategic nuclear weapons? How can the risks of escalation be minimized?

Nuclear strategy has acquired an esoteric intellectual framework and jargon of its own, but the possibility of nuclear war is too serious a matter to be left to the pundits in the think-tanks. The ordinary citizen is entitled to basic information about the nuclear weapons now available, and the implications of using them, and he is entitled to decide in time of peace on any limits within which he wishes his government to operate in the event that deterrence should fail. A crucial moral question is whether there are any circumstances in which a civilized government would be right to use strategic nuclear weapons against enemy cities and civilian areas. Simply to ask the question may be thought to weaken the credibility of deterrence, but if it is a proper question for governments to ask and answer *in private* (which it surely is), it is difficult to maintain that it is an improper question for ordinary citizens to ask and try to answer *in public*.

For myself, I can only say that I accept the fact that nuclear weapons cannot be disinvented. I consider that the security of mankind requires their immediate control and ultimate abolition. I believe that to the extent that Britain has influence, it should be to insist that such weapons shall never be used against enemy cities or civilian areas, whatever the provocation.

The General Assembly declared ten years ago (res. 1653 (XVI), 24 Nov. 1961) that the suffering and destruction resulting from the use of nuclear and thermonuclear weapons would necessarily be indiscriminate, and that therefore to use such weapons would be a crime against mankind and civilization. The resolution may not have been legally binding, but I find it morally persuasive.

EPILOGUE

To me the most urgent problem of our time is the problem of discovering a way of over- coming evil without becoming another form of evil in the process.

Laurens van der Post, letter in *The Times*, 23 Nov. 1970.

I HAVE tried to show that there is no single panacea for prevent- ing indiscriminate and excessive violence in armed conflict. I do not accept that aggression is an ineradicable human drive, a ' universal trait of the social life of humans '.[1] But Lorenz has shown that man does have characteristics which make him a dangerous creature; in particular, lack of natural weapons, and lack of strong inhibitions against injuring his own kind. And man becomes more of a danger to himself as his capacity to injure, kill, and destroy by ' unnatural ' means increases.[2]

The non-pacifist will doubtless continue to look to some version of the Just War doctrine to provide guidelines regarding the just use of armed force. Admittedly, the doctrine has been more elegant in theory than useful in practice. Robert W. Tucker rightly notes that in the vast literature devoted to the problem of war in Christian thought, there has been little inquiry into the relation of doctrine to practice.[3] The fact that the principle of non-combatant immunity is increasingly difficult to apply in practice is not, in itself, a reason for re- nouncing it. And it must be admitted that the principle of proportionality is no less difficult to apply; ' the criteria . . . are very subjective and elusive '.[4] But even if one were to accept that the Just War doctrine is not an adequate guide to the conduct of military operations in the second half of the

[1] Stanislav Andreski, ' Origins of War ', in J. D. Carthy & F. J. Ebling, eds, *Natural History of Aggression* (London, 1964), p. 129.

[2] *On Aggression* (London, 1967), p. 207.

[3] *Just War and Vatican Council II: a Critique* (New York, 1966), p. 9, n. 3.

[4] T. R. Weber, *Modern War and the Pursuit of Peace* (New York, 1968), p. 16.

twentieth century, it seems to me that Pictet goes too far when he describes the doctrine as ' baneful '.[5]

For the pacifist, the problem is not the drawing up of guide-lines regarding the just use of armed force, since he believes that resort to armed force always creates more problems than it solves. For him, the problem is whether the renunciation of armed force is compatible with responsible citizenship in a substantially non-pacifist world. Is pacifism a vocation for the few, analogous to the vocation of celibacy, a commitment and testimony to another way of life; or is it a doctrine which can be translated into workable policies which could be put before the electorate as practicable alternatives to those present policies which depend, in the last resort, on willingness to threaten or use military power? This was the problem which worried George Orwell and to which he returned time and again in his writings. ' Pacifism [he wrote to the Rev. Iorwerth Jones in 1941] refuses to face the problem of government and pacifists think always as people who will never be in a position of control.'[6]

The humanitarian effort to protect the innocent and to prevent unnecessary suffering in armed conflict is a task in which pacifist and non-pacifist can unite. Progress in the future does not require the maintenance of the traditional distinction between the Law of The Hague and the Law of Geneva. The CICR has accepted a special responsibility to strive for the continual improvement of humanitarian international law, but its responsibility is not exclusive; the UN, in its work to secure universal respect for and observance of human rights, has a parallel role. Arms control and disarmament, whether by express agreement or tacit understanding, are also required.

In the long run, however, there is no substitute for an informed and enlightened public opinion. Reinhold Niebuhr emphasized that society, as a corporate entity, has found it almost impossible to operate according to the same ethical norms as the individual, but Pope John XXIII was satisfied with no less. ' The same moral law [he wrote in *Pacem in terris*],

---

[5] *R. Internat. Commiss. Jurists*, Mar. 1969, p. 25.
[6] *Collected Essays, Journalism and Letters of George Orwell*, ed. Sonia Orwell & Ian Angus (London, 1970), ii.136.

which governs the relations between individual human beings, serves also to regulate the relations of political Communities with one another.' That is why the Martens Clause places such confidence in the usages established among civilized peoples, the laws of humanity, and the dictates of the public conscience.

APPENDIX I

EXTRACTS FROM SOME INTERNATIONAL DECLARATIONS AND RESOLUTIONS ON THE USE OF FORCE, 1945–1970

(a) *Judgment of the Nuremberg Tribunal, 1946*[1]

In the opinion of the Tribunal, the solemn renunciation of war as an instrument of national policy necessarily involves the proposition that such a war is illegal in international law; and that those who plan and wage such a war, with its inevitable and terrible consequences, are committing a crime in so doing. War for the solution of international controversies undertaken as an instrument of national policy certainly includes a war of aggression, and such a war is therefore outlawed by the Pact [of Paris of 1928]. . . .

(b) *General Assembly resolution 290 (IV) on the Essentials of Peace, 1 December 1949*

The General Assembly . . .

Calls upon every nation:

2. *To refrain* from threatening or using force contrary to the Charter;

3. *To refrain* from any threats or acts, direct or indirect, aimed at impairing the freedom, independence or integrity of any State, or at fomenting civil strife and subverting the will of the people in any State. . . .

(c) *General Assembly resolution 380 (V), Peace through Deeds, 17 November 1950*

The General Assembly . . .

Solemnly reaffirms that, whatever the weapons used, any aggression, whether committed openly, or by fomenting civil strife in the interest of a foreign Power, or otherwise, is the gravest of all crimes against peace and security throughout the world. . . .

(d) *Declaration of the Bandung Conference on World Peace and Co-operation, 24 April 1955*[2]

. . . Nations should practise tolerance, live together in peace with

[1] A/C.6/L.537, 30 Oct. 1963, p. 61 (mimeo.).
[2] Ibid. p. 26.

158

one another as good neighbours, and develop friendly cooperation on the basis of . . . refraining from acts or threats of aggression or the use of force against the territorial integrity or political independence of any country. . . .

(e) *General Assembly Declaration (res. 2131 (XX)) on the Inadmissibility of Intervention in the Domestic Affairs of States and the Protection of their Independence and Sovereignty, 21 December 1965*

1. No State has the right to intervene, directly or indirectly, for any reason whatever, in the internal or external affairs of any other State. Consequently, armed intervention and all other forms of interference or attempted threats against the personality of the State or against its political, economic and cultural elements, are condemned.

2. No State may use or encourage the use of economic, political or any other type of measures to coerce another State in order to obtain from it the subordination of the exercise of its sovereign rights or to secure from it advantages of any kind. Also, no State shall organize, assist, foment, finance, incite or tolerate subversive, terrorist or armed activities directed towards the violent overthrow of the régime of another State, or interfere in civil strife in another State.

3. The use of force to deprive peoples of their national identity constitutes a violation of their inalienable rights and of the principle of non-intervention.

(f) *General Assembly resolution 2160 (XXI) on Strict Prohibition of the Threat or Use of Force in International Relations, and the Right of Peoples to Self-determination, 30 November 1966*

The General Assembly . . . Reaffirms that:

(a) States shall strictly observe, in their international relations, the prohibition of the threat or use of force against the territorial integrity or political independence of any State, or in any other manner inconsistent with the purposes of the United Nations. Accordingly, armed attack by one State against another or the use of force in any other form contrary to the Charter of the United Nations constitutes a violation of international law giving rise to international responsibility;

(b) Any forcible action, direct or indirect, which deprives peoples under foreign domination of their right to self-determination and freedom and independence and of their right to determine freely their political status and pursue their economic, social and cultural development constitutes a violation of the Charter of the United Nations. Accordingly, the use of force to deprive peoples of their national identity, as prohibited by the Declaration on the Inadmissibility of Intervention in the Domestic Affairs of States and the Protection of Their Independence and Sovereignty contained in General Assembly resolution 2131 (XX), constitutes a violation of their inalienable rights and of the principle of non-intervention. . . .

(g) *Declaration of the UN Conference on the Law of Treaties on the Prohibition of Military, Political or Economic Coercion in the Conclusion of Treaties, 22 May 1969* [3]

The United Nations Conference on the Law of Treaties . . . Solemnly condemns the threat or use of pressure in any form, whether military, political, or economic, by any State in order to coerce another State to perform any act relating to the conclusion of a treaty in violation of the principles of the sovereign equality of States and freedom of consent. . . .

(h) *General Assembly Declaration of Principles of International Law concerning Friendly Relations and Cooperation among States in accordance with the Charter (res. 2625 (XXV)), 24 October 1970*

Every State has the duty to refrain in its international relations from the threat or use of force against the territorial integrity or political independence of any State, or in any other manner inconsistent with the purposes of the United Nations. Such a threat or use of force constitutes a violation of international law and the Charter of the United Nations and shall never be employed as a means of settling international issues.

A war of aggression constitutes a crime against the peace, for which there is responsibility under international law.

In accordance with the purposes and principles of the United Nations, States have the duty to refrain from propaganda for wars of aggression.

Every State has the duty to refrain from the threat or use of force to violate the existing international boundaries of another State or as a means of solving international disputes, including territorial disputes and problems concerning frontiers of States.

Every State likewise has the duty to refrain from the threat or use of force to violate international lines of demarcation, such as armistice lines, established by or pursuant to an international agreement to which it is a party or which it is otherwise bound to respect.

[3] A/7697, 10 Oct. 1969 (mimeo.), Annex.

Nothing in the foregoing shall be construed as prejudicing the positions of the parties concerned with regard to the status and effects of such lines under their special régimes or as affecting their temporary character.

States have a duty to refrain from acts of reprisal involving the use of force.

Every State has the duty to refrain from any forcible action which deprives peoples referred to in the elaboration of the principle of equal rights and self-determination of their right to self-determination and freedom and independence.

Every State has the duty to refrain from organizing or encouraging the organization of irregular forces or armed bands, including mercenaries, for incursion into the territory of another State.

Every State has the duty to refrain from organizing, instigating, assisting or participating in acts of civil strife or terrorist acts in another State or acquiescing in organized activities within its territory directed towards the commission of such acts, when the acts referred to in the present paragraph involve a threat or use of force.

The territory of a State shall not be the object of military occupation resulting from the use of force in contravention of the provisions of the Charter. The territory of a State shall not be the object of acquisition by another State resulting from the threat or use of force. No territorial acquisition resulting from the threat or use of force shall be recognized as legal. Nothing in the foregoing shall be construed as affecting:

(a) Provisions of the Charter or any international agreement prior to the Charter régime and valid under international law; or

(b) The powers of the Security Council under the Charter.

All States shall pursue in good faith negotiations for the early conclusion of a universal treaty on general and complete disarmament under effective international control and strive to adopt appropriate measures to reduce international tensions and strengthen confidence among States.

All States shall comply in good faith with their obligations under the generally recognized principles and rules of international law with respect to the maintenance of international peace and security, and shall endeavour to make the United Nations security system based upon the Charter more effective.

Nothing in the foregoing paragraphs shall be construed as enlarging or diminishing in any way the scope of the provisions of the Charter concerning cases in which the use of force is lawful.

(i) *General Assembly Declaration (res. 2734 (XXV)) on the Strengthening of International Security, 16 December 1970*

The General Assembly . . .

Solemnly reaffirms that every State has the duty to refrain from the threat or use of force against the territorial integrity and political independence of any other State, and that the territory of a State shall not be the object of military occupation resulting from the use of force in contravention of the provisions of the Charter, that the territory of a State shall not be the object of acquisition by another State resulting from the threat or use of force, that no territorial acquisition resulting from the threat or use of force shall be recognized as legal and that every State has the duty to refrain from organizing, instigating, assisting or participating in acts of civil strife or terrorist acts in another State. . . .

APPENDIX II

COMMENTS OF THE ILC ON THE SEVEN NUREMBERG PRINCIPLES, 1950[1]

Principle I

Any person who commits an act which constitutes a crime under international law is responsible therefor and liable to punishment.

98. This principle is based on the first paragraph of article 6 of the Charter of the Nürnberg Tribunal which established the competence of the Tribunal to try and punish persons who, acting in the interests of the European Axis countries, whether as individuals or as members of organizations, committed any of the crimes defined in sub-paragraphs (*a*), (*b*) and (*c*) of article 6. The text of the Charter declared punishable only persons ' acting in the interests of the European Axis countries ' but, as a matter of course, Principle I is now formulated in general terms.

99. The general rule underlying Principle I is that international law may impose duties on individuals directly without any interposition of internal law. The findings of the Tribunal were very definite on the question whether rules of international law may apply to individuals. ' That international law imposes duties and liabilities upon individuals as well as upon States ', said the judgment of the Tribunal, ' has long been recognized '. It added: ' Crimes against international law are committed by men, not by abstract entities, and only by punishing individuals who commit such crimes can the provision of international law be enforced.'

Principle II

The fact that internal law does not impose a penalty for an act which constitutes a crime under international law does not relieve the person who committed the act from responsibility under international law.

100. This principle is a corollary to Principle I. Once it is admitted that individuals are responsible for crimes under international law, it is obvious that they are not relieved from their international responsibility by the fact that their acts are not held to be crimes under the law of any particular country.

101. The Charter of the Nürnberg Tribunal referred, in express

---

[1] A/1316 (*GAOR*, 5th sess., suppl. 12), footnotes (except at para. 119) omitted.

terms, to this relation between international and national responsibility only with respect to crimes against humanity. Sub-paragraph (c) of article 6 of the Charter defined as crimes against humanity certain acts ' whether or not [committed] in violation of the domestic law of the country where perpetrated '. The Commission has formulated Principle II in general terms.

102. The principle that a person who has committed an international crime is responsible therefor and liable to punishment under international law, independently of the provisions of internal law, implies what is commonly called the ' supremacy ' of international law over national law. The Tribunal considered that international law can bind individuals even if national law does not direct them to observe the rules of international law, as shown by the following statement of the judgment: ' . . . the very essence of the Charter is that individuals have international duties which transcend the national obligations of obedience imposed by the individual State.'

Principle III

The fact that a person who committed an act which constitutes a crime under international law acted as Head of State or responsible Government official does not relieve him from responsibility under international law.

103. This principle is based on article 7 of the Charter of the Nürnberg Tribunal. According to the Charter and the judgment, the fact that an individual acted as Head of State or responsible government official did not relieve him from international responsibility. ' The principle of international law which, under certain circumstances, protects the representatives of a State ', said the Tribunal, ' cannot be applied to acts which are condemned as criminal by international law. The authors of these acts cannot shelter themselves behind their official position in order to be freed from punishment . . . .' The same idea was also expressed in the following passage of the findings: ' He who violates the laws of war cannot obtain immunity while acting in pursuance of the authority of the State if the State in authorizing action moves outside its competence under international law.'

104. The last phrase of article 7 of the Charter, ' or mitigating punishment ', has not been retained in the formulation of Principle III. The Commission considers that the question of mitigating punishment is a matter for the competent Court to decide.

Principle IV

The fact that a person acted pursuant to order of his Government or of a superior does not relieve him from responsibility under international law, provided a moral choice was in fact possible to him.

105. This text is based on the principle contained in article 8 of the Charter of the Nürnberg Tribunal as interpreted in the judgment. The idea expressed in Principle IV is that superior orders are not a defence provided a moral choice was possible to the accused. In conformity with this conception, the Tribunal rejected the argument of the defence that there could not be any responsibility since most of the defendants acted under the orders of Hitler. The Tribunal declared: ' The provisions of this article [article 8] are in conformity with the law of all nations. That a soldier was ordered to kill or torture in violation of the international law of war has never been recognized as a defence to such acts of brutality, though, as the Charter here provides, the order may be urged in mitigation of the punishment. The true test, which is found in varying degrees in the criminal law of most nations, is not the existence of the order, but whether moral choice was in fact possible.'

106. The last phrase of article 8 of the Charter ' but may be considered in mitigation of punishment, if the Tribunal determines that justice so requires ', has not been retained for the reason stated under Principle III, in paragraph 104 above.

Principle V

Any person charged with a crime under international law has the right to a fair trial on the facts and law.

107. The principle that a defendant charged with a crime under international law must have the right to a fair trial was expressly recognized and carefully developed by the Charter of the Nürnberg Tribunal. The Charter contained a chapter entitled: ' Fair Trial for Defendants ', which for the purpose of ensuring such fair trial provided the following procedure:

' *a.* The indictment shall include full particulars specifying in detail the charges against the defendants. A copy of the indictment and of all the documents lodged with the indictment, translated into a language which he understands, shall be furnished to the defendant at a reasonable time before the trial.

' *b.* During any preliminary examination or trial of a defendant he shall have the right to give any explanation relevant to the charges made against him.

' *c.* A preliminary examination of a defendant and his trial shall be conducted in, or translated into, a language which the defendant understands.

' *d.* A defendant shall have the right to conduct his own defence before the Tribunal or to have the assistance of counsel.

' *e.* A defendant shall have the right through himself or through his counsel to present evidence at the trial in support of his defence, and to cross-examine any witness called by the prosecution.'

108. The right to a fair trial was also referred to in the judgment itself. The Tribunal said in this respect: ' With regard to the constitution of the Court all that the defendants are entitled to ask is to receive a fair trial on the facts and law.'

109. In the view of the Commission, the expression ' fair trial ' should be understood in the light of the above-quoted provisions of the Charter of the Nürnberg Tribunal.

Principle VI

The crimes hereinafter set out are punishable as crimes under international law :

a. *Crimes against peace :*

(i) *Planning, preparation, initiation or waging of a war of aggression or a war in violation of international treaties, agreements or assurances ;*

(ii) *Participation in a common plan or conspiracy for the accomplishment of any of the acts mentioned under* (i).

110. Both categories of crimes are characterized by the fact that they are connected with ' war of aggression or war in violation of international treaties, agreements or assurances '.

111. The Tribunal made a general statement to the effect that its Charter was ' the expression of international law existing at the time of its creation '. It, in particular, refuted the argument of the defence that aggressive war was not an international crime. For this refutation the Tribunal relied primarily on the General Treaty for the Renunciation of War of 27 August 1928 (Kellogg-Briand Pact) which in 1939 was in force between sixty-three States. ' The nations who signed the Pact or adhered to it unconditionally ', said the Tribunal, ' condemned recourse to war for the future as an instrument of policy, and expressly renounced it. After the signing of the Pact, any nation resorting to war as an instrument of national policy breaks the Pact. In the opinion of the Tribunal, the solemn

renunciation of war as an instrument of national policy necessarily involves the proposition that such a war is illegal in international law; and that those who planned and waged such a war, with its inevitable and terrible consequences, are committing a crime in so doing. War for the solution of international controversies undertaken as an instrument of national policy certainly includes a war of aggression, and such a war is therefore outlawed by the Pact.'

112. In support of its interpretation of the Kellogg-Briand Pact, the Tribunal cited some other international instruments which condemned war of aggression as an international crime. The draft of a Treaty of Mutual Assistance sponsored by the League of Nations in 1923 declared, in its article 1, ' that aggressive war is an international crime '. The Preamble to the League of Nations Protocol for the Pacific Settlement of International Disputes (Geneva Protocol), of 1924, ' recognizing the solidarity of the members of the International Community ', stated that ' a war of aggression constitutes a violation of this solidarity, and is an international crime ', and that the contracting parties were ' desirous of facilitating the complete application of the system provided in the Covenant of the League of Nations for the pacific settlement of disputes between the States and of ensuring the repression of international crimes '. The declaration concerning wars of aggression adopted on 24 September 1927 by the Assembly of the League of Nations declared, in its preamble, that war was an ' international crime '. The resolution unanimously adopted on 18 February 1928 by twenty-one American Republics at the Sixth (Havana) International Conference of American States, provided that ' war of aggression constitutes an international crime against the human species '.

113. The Charter of the Nürnberg Tribunal did not contain any definition of ' war of aggression ', nor was there any such definition in the judgment of the Tribunal. It was by reviewing the historical events before and during the war that it found that certain of the defendants planned and waged aggressive wars against twelve nations and were therefore guilty of a series of crimes.

114. According to the Tribunal, this made it unnecessary to discuss the subject in further detail, or to consider at any length the extent to which these aggressive wars were also ' wars in violation of international treaties, agreements, or assurances '.

115. The term ' assurances ' is understood by the Commission as including any pledge or guarantee of peace given by a State, even unilaterally.

116. The terms 'planning' and 'preparation' of a war of aggression were considered by the Tribunal as comprising all the stages in the bringing about of a war of aggression from the planning to the actual initiation of the war. In view of that, the Tribunal did not make any clear distinction between planning and preparation. As stated in the judgment, 'planning and preparation are essential to the making of war'.

117. The meaning of the expression 'waging of a war of aggression' was discussed in the Commission during the consideration of the definition of 'crimes against peace'. Some members of the Commission feared that everyone in uniform who fought in a war of aggression might be charged with the 'waging' of such a war. The Commission understands the expression to refer only to high-ranking military personnel and high State officials, and believes that this was also the view of the Tribunal.

118. A legal notion of the Charter to which the defence objected was the one concerning 'conspiracy'. The Tribunal recognized that 'conspiracy is not defined in the Charter'. However, it stated the meaning of the term, though only in a restricted way. 'But in the opinion of the Tribunal', it was said in the judgment, 'the conspiracy must be clearly outlined in its criminal purpose. It must not be too far removed from the time of decision and of action. The planning, to be criminal, must not rest merely on the declarations of a party programme such as are found in the twenty-five points of the Nazi Party, announced in 1920, or the political affirmations expressed in *Mein Kampf* in later years. The Tribunal must examine whether a concrete plan to wage war existed, and determine the participants in that concrete plan.'

b. *War crimes:*

Violations of the laws or customs of war which include, but are not limited to, murder, ill-treatment or deportation to slave-labour or for any other purpose of civilian population of or in occupied territory, murder or ill-treatment of prisoners of war, of persons on the seas, killing of hostages, plunder of public or private property, wanton destruction of cities, towns, or villages, or devastation not justified by military necessity.

119. The Tribunal emphasized that before the last war the crimes defined by article 6 (*b*) of its Charter were already recognized as crimes under international law. The Tribunal stated that such crimes were covered by specific provisions of the Regulations annexed to The Hague Convention of 1907 respecting the Laws and Customs of War on Land and of the Geneva Convention of 1929 on

the Treatment of Prisoners of War. After enumerating the said provisions, the Tribunal stated: ' That violation of these provisions constituted crimes for which the guilty individuals were punishable is too well settled to admit or [*sic*] argument.' [2]

c. *Crimes against humanity:*

Murder, extermination, enslavement, deportation and other inhuman acts done against any civilian population, or persecutions on political, racial or religious grounds, when such acts are done or such persecutions are carried on in execution of or in connexion with any crime against peace or any war crime.

120. Article 6 (*c*) of the Charter of the Nürnberg Tribunal distinguished two categories of punishable acts, to wit: first, murder, extermination, enslavement, deportation and other inhuman acts committed against any civilian population, before or during the war, and second, persecution on political, racial or religious grounds. Acts within these categories, according to the Charter, constituted international crimes only when committed ' in execution of or in connexion with any crimes within the jurisdiction of the Tribunal '. The crimes referred to as falling within the jurisdiction of the Tribunal were crimes against peace and war crimes.

121. Though it found that ' political opponents were murdered in Germany before the war, and that many of them were kept in concentration camps in circumstances of great horror and cruelty ', that ' the policy of persecution, repression and murder of civilians in Germany before the war of 1939, who were likely to be hostile to the Government, was most ruthlessly carried out ', and that ' the persecution of Jews during the same period is established beyond all doubt ', the Tribunal considered that it had not been satisfactorily proved that before the outbreak of war these acts had been committed in execution of, or in connexion with, any crime within the jurisdiction of the Tribunal. For this reason the Tribunal declared itself unable to ' make a general declaration that the acts before 1939 were crimes against humanity within the meaning of the Charter '.

122. The Tribunal did not, however, thereby exclude the possibility that crimes against humanity might be committed also before a war.

123. In its definition of crimes against humanity the Commission

[2] During its discussion on the crime of killing hostages, the Commission took note of the fact that the Geneva Conventions of 12 August 1949, and more specifically article 34 of the Convention relative to the protection of civilian persons in time of war, prohibit the *taking* of hostages.

has omitted the phrase ' before or during the war ' contained in article 6 (c) of the Charter of the Nürnberg Tribunal because this phrase referred to a particular war, the war of 1939. The omission of the phrase does not mean that the Commission considers that crimes against humanity can be committed only during a war. On the contrary, the Commission is of the opinion that such crimes may take place also before a war in connexion with crimes against peace.

124. In accordance with article 6 (c) of the Charter, the above formulation characterizes as crimes against humanity murder, extermination, enslavement, etc., committed against ' any ' civilian population. This means that these acts may be crimes against humanity even if they are committed by the perpetrator against his own population.

Principle VII

Complicity in the commission of a crime against peace, a war crime, or a crime against humanity as set forth in Principle VI is a crime under international law.

125. The only provision in the Charter of the Nürnberg Tribunal regarding responsibility for complicity was that of the last paragraph of article 6 which reads as follows: ' Leaders, organizers, instigators and accomplices participating in the formulation or execution of a common plan or conspiracy to commit any of the foregoing crimes are responsible for all acts performed by any persons in execution of such a plan.'

126. The Tribunal, commenting on this provision in connexion with its discussion of count one of the indictment, which charged certain defendants with conspiracy to commit aggressive war, war crimes and crimes against humanity, said that, in its opinion, the provision did not ' add a new and separate crime to those already listed '. In the view of the Tribunal, the provision was designed to ' establish the responsibility of persons participating in a common plan ' to prepare, initiate and wage aggressive war. Interpreted literally, this statement would seem to imply that the complicity rule did not apply to crimes perpetrated by individual action.

127. On the other hand, the Tribunal convicted several of the defendants of war crimes and crimes against humanity because they gave orders resulting in atrocious and criminal acts which they did not commit themselves. In practice, therefore, the Tribunal seems to have applied general principles of criminal law regarding complicity. This view is corroborated by expressions used by the Tribunal in assessing the guilt of particular defendants.

APPENDIX III

CICR DRAFT RULES FOR THE LIMITATION OF THE DANGERS INCURRED BY THE CIVILIAN POPULATION IN TIME OF WAR, SEPTEMBER 1956[1]

Preamble

All nations are deeply convinced that war should be banned as a means of settling disputes between human communities.

However, in view of the need, should hostilities once more break out, of safeguarding the civilian population from the destruction with which it is threatened as a result of technical developments in weapons and methods of warfare,

The limits placed by the requirements of humanity and the safety of the population on the use of armed force are restated and defined in the following rules.

In cases not specifically provided for, the civilian population shall continue to enjoy the protection of the general rule set forth in Article 1, and of the principles of international law.

Chapter I. — Object and Field of Application

ARTICLE 1

Object

Since the right of Parties to the conflict to adopt means of injuring the enemy is not unlimited, they shall confine their operations to the destruction of his military resources, and leave the civilian population outside the sphere of armed attacks.

This general rule is given detailed expression in the following provisions:

ARTICLE 2

Field of application

The present rules shall apply:

(a) In the event of declared war or of any other armed conflict, even if the state of war is not recognized by one of the Parties to the conflict.

(b) In the event of an armed conflict not of an international character.

[1] 2nd ed., Apr. 1958, pp. 7–15 & 72–3.

ARTICLE 3

Definition of term ' attacks '

The present rules shall apply to acts of violence committed against the adverse Party by force of arms, whether in defence or offence. Such acts shall be referred to hereafter as ' attacks '.

ARTICLE 4

Definition of term ' civilian population '

For the purpose of the present rules, the civilian population consists of all persons not belonging to one or other of the following categories:

(a) Members of the armed forces, or of their auxiliary or complementary organizations.

(b) Persons who do not belong to the forces referred to above, but nevertheless take part in the fighting.

ARTICLE 5

Relation with previous Conventions

The obligations imposed upon the Parties to the conflict in regard to the civilian population, under the present rules, are complementary to those which already devolve expressly upon the Parties by virtue of other rules in international law, deriving in particular from the instruments of Geneva and The Hague.

Chapter II. — Objectives barred from Attack

ARTICLE 6

Immunity of the civilian population

Attacks directed against the civilian population, as such, whether with the object of terrorizing it or for any other reason, are prohibited. This prohibition applies both to attacks on individuals and to those directed against groups.

In consequence, it is also forbidden to attack dwellings, installations or means of transport, which are for the exclusive use of, and occupied by, the civilian population.

Nevertheless, should members of the civilian population, Article 11 notwithstanding, be within or in close proximity to a military objective they must accept the risks resulting from an attack directed against that objective.

ARTICLE 7

Limitation of objectives which may be attacked

In order to limit the dangers incurred by the civilian population, attacks may only be directed against military objectives.

Only objectives belonging to the categories of objective which, in view of their essential characteristics, are generally acknowledged to be of military importance, may be considered as military objectives. Those categories are listed in an annex to the present rules [p. 177].

However, even if they belong to one of those categories, they cannot be considered as a military objective where their total or partial destruction, in the circumstances ruling at the time, offers no military advantage.

Chapter III. — Precautions in Attacks on Military Objectives

ARTICLE 8

Precautions to be taken in planning attacks

The person responsible for ordering or launching an attack shall, first of all:

(a) make sure that the objective, or objectives, to be attacked are military objectives within the meaning of the present rules, and are duly identified.

When the military advantage to be gained leaves the choice open between several objectives, he is required to select the one, an attack on which involves least danger for the civilian population:

(b) take into account the loss and destruction which the attack, even if carried out with the precautions prescribed under Article 9, is liable to inflict upon the civilian population.

He is required to refrain from the attack if, after due consideration, it is apparent that the loss and destruction would be disproportionate to the military advantage anticipated:

(c) whenever the circumstances allow, warn the civilian population in jeopardy, to enable it to take shelter.

ARTICLE 9

Precautions to be taken in carrying out the attack

All possible precautions shall be taken, both in the choice of the weapons and methods to be used, and in the carrying out of an attack, to ensure that no losses or damage are caused to the civilian population in the vicinity of the objective, or to its dwellings, or that such losses or damage are at least reduced to a minimum.

In particular, in towns and other places with a large civilian population, which are not in the vicinity of military or naval operations, the attack shall be conducted with the greatest degree of precision. It must not cause losses or destruction beyond the immediate surroundings of the objective attacked.

The person responsible for carrying out the attack must abandon or break off the operation if he perceives that the conditions set forth above cannot be respected.

ARTICLE 10

Target-area bombing

It is forbidden to attack without distinction, as a single objective, an area including several military objectives at a distance from one another where elements of the civilian population, or dwellings, are situated in between the said military objectives.

ARTICLE 11

' Passive ' precautions

The Parties to the conflict shall, so far as possible, take all necessary steps to protect the civilian population subject to their authority from the dangers to which they would be exposed in an attack—in particular by removing them from the vicinity of military objectives and from threatened areas. However, the rights conferred upon the population in the event of transfer or evacuation under Article 49 of the Fourth Geneva Convention of 12 Aug. 1949 are expressly reserved.

Similarly, the Parties to the conflict shall, so far as possible, avoid the permanent presence of armed forces, military material, mobile military establishments or installations, in towns or other places with a large civilian population.

ARTICLE 12

Civil Defence bodies

The Parties to the conflict shall facilitate the work of the civilian bodies exclusively engaged in protecting and assisting the civilian population in case of attack.

They can agree to confer special immunity upon the personnel of those bodies, their equipment and installations, by means of a special emblem.

ARTICLE 13

Intentional exposure to danger

Parties to the conflict are prohibited from placing or keeping members of the civilian population subject to their authority in or near military objectives, with the idea of inducing the enemy to refrain from attacking those objectives.

Chapter IV. — Weapons with Uncontrollable Effects
ARTICLE 14

Prohibited methods of warfare

Without prejudice to the present or future prohibition of certain specific weapons, the use is prohibited of weapons whose harmful effects—resulting in particular from the dissemination of incendiary, chemical, bacteriological, radioactive or other agents—could spread to an unforeseen degree or escape, either in space or in time, from the control of those who employ them, thus endangering the civilian population.

This prohibition also applies to delayed-action weapons, the dangerous effects of which are liable to be felt by the civilian population.

ARTICLE 15

Safety measures and devices

If the Parties to the conflict make use of mines, they are bound, without prejudice to the stipulations of the VIIIth Hague Convention of 1907, to chart the mine-fields. The charts shall be handed over, at the close of active hostilities, to the adverse Party, and also to all other authorities responsible for the safety of the population.

Without prejudice to the precautions specified under Article 9, weapons capable of causing serious damage to the civilian population shall, so far as possible, be equipped with a safety device which renders them harmless when they escape from the control of those who employ them.

Chapter V. — Special Cases
ARTICLE 16

' *Open towns* '

When, on the outbreak or in the course of hostilities, a locality is declared to be an ' open town ', the adverse Party shall be duly notified. The latter is bound to reply, and if it agrees to recognize the locality in question as an open town, shall cease from all attacks on the said town, and refrain from any military operation the sole object of which is its occupation.

In the absence of any special conditions which may, in any particular case, be agreed upon with the adverse Party, a locality, in order to be declared an ' open town ', must satisfy the following conditions:

(a) it must not be defended or contain any armed force;

(b) it must discontinue all relations with any national or allied armed forces;

(c) it must stop all activities of a military nature or for a military purpose in those of its installations or industries which might be regarded as military objectives;

(d) it must stop all military transit through the town.

The adverse Party may make the recognition of the status of ' open town ' conditional upon verification of the fulfilment of the conditions stipulated above. All attacks shall be suspended during the institution and operation of the investigatory measures.

The presence in the locality of civil defence services, or of the services responsible for maintaining public order, shall not be considered as contrary to the conditions laid down in Paragraph 2. If the locality is situated in occupied territory, this provision applies also to the military occupation forces essential for the maintenance of public law and order.

When an ' open town ' passes into other hands, the new authorities are bound, if they cannot maintain its status, to inform the civilian population accordingly.

None of the above provisions shall be interpreted in such a manner as to diminish the protection which the civilian population should enjoy by virtue of the other provisions of the present rules, even when not living in localities recognized as ' open towns '.

ARTICLE 17

Installations containing dangerous forces

In order to safeguard the civilian population from the dangers that might result from the destruction of engineering works or installations—such as hydro-electric dams, nuclear power stations or dikes—through the releasing of natural or artificial forces, the States or Parties concerned are invited:

(a) to agree, in time of peace, on a special procedure to ensure in all circumstances the general immunity of such works where intended essentially for peaceful purposes:

(b) to agree, in time of war, to confer special immunity, possibly on the basis of the stipulations of Article 16, on works and installations which have not, or no longer have, any connexion with the conduct of military operations.

The preceding stipulations shall not, in any way, release the Parties to the conflict from the obligation to take the precautions required by the general provisions of the present rules, under Articles 8 to 11 in particular.

Chapter VI. — Application of the Rules[2]

ARTICLE 18

Assistance of third parties

States not involved in the conflict, and also all appropriate organizations, are invited to co-operate, by lending their good offices, in ensuring the observance of the present rules and preventing either of the Parties to the conflict from resorting to measures contrary to those rules.

ARTICLE 19

Trial and judicial safeguards

All States or Parties concerned are under the obligation to search for and bring to trial any person having committed, or ordered to be committed, an infringement of the present rules, unless they prefer to hand the person over for trial to another State or Party concerned with the case.

The accused persons shall be tried only by regular civil or military courts; they shall, in all circumstances, benefit by safeguards of proper trial and defence at least equal to those provided under Articles 105 and those following of the Geneva Convention relative to the Treatment of Prisoners of War of 12 Aug. 1949.

ARTICLE 20

Diffusion and details of application

All States or Parties concerned shall make the terms of the provisions of the present rules known to their armed forces and provide for their application in accordance with the general principles of these rules, not only in the instances specifically envisaged in the rules, but also in unforeseen cases.

Draft Annex: List of Categories of Military Objectives according to Article 7, paragraph 2

I. The objectives belonging to the following categories are those considered to be of generally recognized military importance:

[2] Articles 18 and 19, dealing with the procedure for supervision and sanctions, are merely given as a rough guide and in outline; they will naturally have to be elaborated and supplemented at a later stage.

(1) Armed forces, including auxiliary or complementary organizations, and persons who, though not belonging to the above-mentioned formations, nevertheless take part in the fighting.

(2) Positions, installations or constructions occupied by the forces indicated in sub-paragraph (1) above, as well as combat objectives (that is to say, those objectives which are directly contested in battle between land or sea forces including airborne forces).

(3) Installations, constructions and other works of a military nature, such as barracks, fortifications, War Ministries (e.g. Ministries of Army, Navy, Air Force, National Defence, Supply) and other organs for the direction and administration of military operations.

(4) Stores of arms or military supplies, such as munition dumps, stores of equipment or fuel, vehicles parks.

(5) Airfields, rocket launching ramps and naval base installations.

(6) Those of the lines and means of communication (railway lines, roads, bridges, tunnels and canals) which are of fundamental military importance.

(7) The installations of broadcasting and television stations; telephone and telegraph exchanges of fundamental military importance.

(8) Industries of fundamental importance for the conduct of the war:

(a) industries for the manufacture of armaments such as weapons, munitions, rockets, armoured vehicles, military aircraft, fighting ships, including the manufacture of accessories and all other war material;

(b) industries for the manufacture of supplies and material of a military character, such as transport and communications material, equipment for the armed forces;

(c) factories or plants constituting other production and manufacturing centres of fundamental importance for the conduct of war, such as the metallurgical, engineering and chemical industries, whose nature or purpose is essentially military;

(d) storage and transport installations whose basic function it is to serve the industries referred to in (a)–(c);

(e) installations providing energy mainly for national defence, e.g. coal, other fuels, or atomic energy, and plants producing gas or electricity mainly for military consumption.

(9) Installations constituting experimental, research centres for experiments on and the development of weapons and war material.

II. The following, however, are excepted from the foregoing list:

(1) Persons, constructions, installations or transport which are protected under the Geneva Conventions I, II, III, of 12 Aug. 1949;

(2) Non-combatants in the armed forces who obviously take no active or direct part in hostilities.

III. The above list will be reviewed at intervals of not more than ten years by a group of Experts composed of persons with a sound grasp of military strategy and of others concerned with the protection of the civilian population.

APPENDIX IV

DRAFT PROTOCOLS ADOPTED AT THE CONFERENCE OF GOVERNMENT EXPERTS, 24 MAY–12 JUNE 1971[1]

1. To the Fourth Geneva Convention of 12 August 1949 relative to the protection of wounded and sick civilian persons in time of war

PREAMBLE

The Parties, while solemnly reaffirming the provisions of the Fourth Geneva Convention of August 12, 1949, relative to the protection of civilian persons in time of war, have agreed to the following additional provisions.

Art. 1 : Application of the Protocol

The provisions of this Protocol shall apply to all cases specified in article 2 of the aforesaid Fourth Convention and, with the exception of articles 8 and 10, paragraph 3 and 4 of this Protocol, to the whole of the populations of the countries in conflict.

Art. 2 : Terms

In this Protocol the expression:

(a) ' Protected Person ' means all those persons specified as protected persons in the four Geneva Conventions;

(b) ' Medical Establishments and Units ' means hospitals and other fixed medical establishments, medical and pharmaceutical stores of fixed medical establishments, mobile medical units, blood transfusion centres and other installations designed for medical purpose;

(c) ' Medical Transportation ' means transportation of wounded, sick, infirm, maternity cases, medical personnel, medical equipment and supplies by ambulances or by any other means of transportation excluding aircraft transportation.

(d) ' Medical Personnel ' means persons regularly and solely engaged in the operation and administration of medical establishments and units, including the personnel engaged in the search for,

[1] Experts' Rpt., pp. 29-31; also reproduced in A/8370, 2 Sept. 1971 (mimeo.), Annexes.

removal and transporting of and caring for wounded and sick, the infirm and maternity cases.

(e) ' Distinctive Emblem ' means the distinctive emblem of the red cross (red crescent, red lion and sun) on a white background.

Art. 3: Protection and care

All wounded and sick, whether non-combatants or combatants rendered *hors de combat*, as well as the infirm, expectant mothers and maternity cases, shall be the object of special protection and respect.

In all circumstances these persons shall be treated humanely and shall receive medical care and attention necessitated by their condition with the least possible delay, and without any adverse distinction or discrimination founded on race, colour, caste, nationality, religion, political opinion, sex, birth, wealth or any other similar criteria.

Art. 4: Respect for persons

Any unjustified act or omission which endangers the health or physical or mental well-being of any protected person is prohibited.

Consequently, all experiments on and treatment of protected persons, including removal or transplant of organs, not intended to provide them with medical relief are prohibited. This prohibition applies even if the protected persons concerned have given consent to such experiments.

Art. 5: Civilian medical establishments and units

Civilian medical establishments and units may in no circumstances be attacked, but shall at all times be respected and protected by the Parties to the conflict.

The Parties to a conflict shall provide these medical establishments and units with certificates identifying them for the purposes of this Protocol.

With authorization from the State, medical establishments and units shall be marked by means of the distinctive emblem.

In order to obviate the possibility of any hostile action, Parties to the conflict shall as far as military considerations permit take the necessary steps to make known the location of medical establishments and units and mark them with the aforesaid distinctive emblem in such manner as to be clearly visible to the adverse forces.

The responsible authorities shall ensure that the said medical establishments and units are, as far as possible, situated in such a manner that attacks against military objectives cannot imperil their safety.

Art. 6: Discontinuance of protection of civilian medical establishments and units

The protection to which civilian medical establishments and units are entitled shall not cease unless they are used to commit, outside their humanitarian duties, acts harmful to the enemy. Protection may, however, cease only after due warning has been given, naming, in all appropriate cases, a reasonable time-limit, and after such warning has remained unheeded.

The fact that sick or wounded members of the armed forces are nursed in these medical establishments and units, or the presence of small arms and ammunition taken from such combatants which have not yet been handed to the proper service, shall not be considered to be acts harmful to the enemy.

Art. 7: Civilian medical transportation

Ambulances and other vehicles used for medical transportation and serving civilian medical establishments and units shall be respected and protected at all times. They shall bear a certificate from the competent authority testifying to their medical nature.

Other means of transport used in isolation or in convoy, whether on land or on waterways, temporarily assigned for medical transportation, shall be respected and protected while being used for the aforesaid purpose.

With the consent of the competent authority, all vehicles and means of transportation mentioned above shall be provided with the distinctive emblem. However, the means of transportation mentioned in paragraph 2 above may display the distinctive emblem only while performing their humanitarian mission.

The provisions of article 6 shall also be applicable to medical transportation.

Art. 8: Requisition

The right of the Occupying Power to requisition civilian medical establishments and units, their movable and immovable assets as well as the services of their medical personnel, shall not be exercised except temporarily and only when there is urgent necessity for the care of protected persons and then on condition that suitable arrangements are made in due time for the care and treatment of the patients and for the needs of the civilian population for hospital accommodation.

The material and stores of medical establishments and units cannot be requisitioned so long as they are necessary for the needs of the civilian population.

Art. 9: Civilian medical personnel

Civilian medical personnel duly recognized or authorized by the State and regularly and solely engaged in the operation and administration of medical establishments and units and the duly authorized personnel of the National Red Cross Societies employed in the medical treatment of the protected persons, as well as the personnel engaged in the search for, removal and transporting of and caring for wounded and sick, the infirm and maternity cases, shall be respected and protected.

The aforesaid medical personnel shall be recognizable by means of an identity card bearing the photograph of the holder and embossed with the stamp of the responsible authority, and also by means of a stamped armlet which they shall wear on the left arm while carrying out their duties. This armlet shall be issued by the State and shall bear the distinctive emblem.

As far as possible, every assistance shall be given to the aforesaid personnel in order that they may carry out their humanitarian mission to the best of their ability. In particular they shall be permitted access to all places where their services may be required, subject to such supervisory and safety measures as may be considered necessary by the Parties to the conflict.

If the aforesaid personnel fall into the hands of the adverse party they shall be given all facilities necessary for the performance of their mission. In no circumstances shall they be compelled or required to perform any work outside their medical duties.

The management of each medical establishment and unit shall at all times hold at the disposal of the competent national or occupying authorities an up-to-date list of such personnel.

Art. 10: Protection in the discharge of medical duties

In no circumstances shall the exercise of medical activities, consistent with professional rules, be considered an offence, no matter who the beneficiary may be.

In no circumstances shall medical personnel be compelled by any authority to violate any provision of the Geneva Conventions of August 12, 1949 for the protection of war victims, or of this Protocol.

No medical personnel shall be required to perform acts or do work which violates professional rules.

No medical personnel shall be compelled to inform an occupation authority of the wounded and sick under their care, unless failure to do so would be contrary to the regulations concerning the notification of communicable diseases.

Art. 11 : *The role of the population*

The civilian and military authorities shall permit the inhabitants and relief societies, even in invaded or occupied areas, spontaneously to collect and care for wounded or sick, of whatever nationality.

The civilian population shall respect these wounded and sick, and in particular abstain from offering them violence.

No one may ever be molested or convicted for having nursed or cared for military or civilian wounded or sick.

Art. 12 : *Use of the distinctive emblem*

The Parties shall take all necessary measures to ensure the proper use of the distinctive emblem and to prevent and repress any misuse thereof.

2. To Article 3 of the Geneva Conventions of 12 August 1949 relative to the protection of wounded and sick in armed conflicts not international in character

Art. 1 : *Protection and care*

All wounded and sick, whether non-combatants or combatants rendered *hors de combat*, as well as the infirm, expectant mothers and maternity cases, shall be the object of special protection and respect.

In all circumstances these persons shall be treated humanely and shall receive medical care and attention necessitated by their condition with the least possible delay, and without any adverse distinction or discrimination founded on race, colour, caste, nationality, religion, political opinion, sex, birth, wealth or any other similar criteria.

Any unjustified act or omission which endangers the health or physical or mental well-being of any person referred to in the first paragraph is prohibited.

Art. 2 : *Search and recording*

At all times and particularly after an engagement, parties to the conflict shall without delay take all possible measures to search for and collect the wounded and the sick, to protect them against pillage and ill-treatment and to ensure their adequate care.

Parties to the conflict shall communicate to each other or, when this is not possible, publish all details of wounded, sick and dead of the adverse party in their hands.

Art. 3: Role of the population

The civilian population shall in particular respect the wounded and the sick and abstain from offering them violence.

No one may ever be molested or convicted for having nursed or cared for the wounded or sick.

Art. 4: Medical and religious personnel

Military and civilian medical personnel as well as chaplains and others performing similar functions shall be, in all circumstances, respected and protected during the period they are so engaged. If they should fall into the hands of the adverse party they shall be respected and protected. They shall receive all facilities to discharge their functions and shall not be compelled to perform any work outside their professional duties.

Art. 5: Medical establishments and transportation

Fixed establishments and mobile medical units, both military and civilian, which are solely intended to care for the wounded and the sick shall under no circumstances be attacked; they and their equipment shall at all times be respected and protected by the parties to the conflict.

Transportation of wounded and sick, or of medical personnel or equipment shall be respected and protected in the same way as mobile medical units.

Art. 6: Evacuation

The parties to the conflict shall endeavour to conclude local arrangements for the removal from areas where hostilities are taking place of wounded or sick, infirm, expectant mothers and maternity cases.

Art. 7: Medical assistance by other States or by impartial humanitarian organizations

An offer of medical assistance by another State or by an impartial humanitarian organization to aid in the relief of persons suffering as a consequence of the conflict shall not be considered as an unfriendly act or have any effect on the legal status of the parties to the conflict.

An offer by another State to receive wounded, sick or infirm persons, expectant mothers and maternity cases on its territory shall not be considered as an unfriendly act or have any effect on the legal status of the parties to the conflict.

Art. 8: *The distinctive emblem*

The emblem of the red cross (red crescent, red lion and sun) on a white background is retained as the distinctive emblem of the medical services of the parties to a conflict. It shall not be used for any other purposes and shall be respected in all circumstances.

Art. 9: *Legal status of the parties to a conflict*

The application of the preceding provisions shall not affect the egal status of the parties to the conflict.

APPENDIX V

BASIC PRINCIPLES FOR THE PROTECTION OF CIVILIAN POPULATIONS IN ARMED CONFLICTS, 9 DECEMBER 1970 (RES. 2675 (XXV)) APPROVED BY THE UN GENERAL ASSEMBLY

The General Assembly

Noting that in the present century the international community has accepted an increased role and new responsibilities for the alleviation of human suffering in any form and in particular during armed conflicts,

Recalling that to this end a series of international instruments has been adopted, including the four Geneva Conventions of 1949,

Recalling further its resolution 2444 (XXIII) of 19 December 1968 on respect for human rights in armed conflicts,

Bearing in mind the need for measures to ensure the better protection of human rights in armed conflicts of all types,

Noting with appreciation the work that is being undertaken in this respect by the International Committee of the Red Cross,

Noting with appreciation the reports of the Secretary-General on respect for human rights in armed conflicts,

Convinced that civilian populations are in special need of increased protection in time of armed conflicts,

Recognizing the importance of the strict application of the Geneva Convention relative to the Protection of Civilian Persons in Time of War of 12 August 1949,

Affirms the following basic principles for the protection of civilian populations in armed conflicts, without prejudice to their future elaboration within the framework of progressive development of the international law of armed conflict:

1. Fundamental human rights, as accepted in international law and laid down in international instruments, continue to apply fully in situations of armed conflict.

2. In the conduct of military operations during armed conflicts, a distinction must be made at all times between persons actively taking part in the hostilities and civilian populations.

187

3. In the conduct of military operations, every effort should be made to spare civilian populations from the ravages of war, and all necessary precautions should be taken to avoid injury, loss or damage to civilian populations.

4. Civilian populations as such should not be the object of military operations.

5. Dwellings and other installations that are used only by civilian populations should not be the object of military operations.

6. Places or areas designated for the sole protection of civilians, such as hospital zones or similar refuges, should not be the object of military operations.

7. Civilian populations, or individual members thereof, should not be the object of reprisals, forcible transfers or other assaults on their integrity.

8. The provision of international relief to civilian populations is in conformity with the humanitarian principles of the Charter of the United Nations, the Universal Declaration of Human Rights and other international instruments in the field of human rights. The Declaration of Principles for International Humanitarian Relief to the Civil Population in Disaster Situations, as laid down in resolution XXVI adopted by the twenty-first International Conference of the Red Cross, shall apply in situations of armed conflict, and all parties to a conflict should make every effort to facilitate this application.

INDEX

ABMs, 146–7, 152
Acheson, D., 41
Africa, Southern, irregular fighters in, 84, 108; UN and, 114
African National Congress (ANC), 84
aggression, definition of, 48–9, 53
Alaric, 3
Algeria, 97
Alvarado, L., 113
Ambrose, St, 4–6, 9
Anne, Queen, 22
Antarctica Treaty (1959), 141
Aquinas, Thomas, St, 6, 9–12, 15–16, 25, 32, 34, 38
Arabs, and territories occupied by Israel, 72–4, 111–20
Arenales, E., 112
arms control, 121–54, *see also* bacteriological weapons; chemical weapons; gas (poison); nuclear weapons
Arnobius of Sicca, 3
atomic weapons, *see* nuclear weapons
Augustine, St, 3, 6–10, 12, 15–16, 27, 34, 38
Australia, 52, 135
Austria, 99
Ayala, B., 25

bacteriological (biological) weapons, prohibitions, 81, 94; control of, 122–4, 126, 133–4, 139; alleged use in Korea, 131; UK proposes total ban, 132–3, 137; US renounces, 137–8, 140; Soviet draft convention on, 140
Bandung Conference on World Peace and Cooperation, 158
Beirut, airport attacked, 56
Berlin, 153
Bettenson, H., cited, 4n.
Biafra, Red Cross in, 71
Bindschedler-Robert, Denise, cited, 54n., 66n., 68, 79, 80, 85n., 86n., 88n.
biological weapons, *see* bacteriological weapons
Briand-Kellogg Pact, *see* Paris, Pact of
Britain, *see* United Kingdom
British Council of Churches, 19
British Medical Research Council, 148
Brown, P., 6

Brussels Declaration (1874), 63–4, 83, 93, 124
Brussels Treaty (1948), 131

Cajetan, T. de Vio, 10, 25
Calvin, John, 15–18, 25
Cambodia, 108
Carnegie, Endowment for Internat. Peace, CBW report, 124n., 137n.
Carnegie, A., 67
Carr, E. H., 129–30
Celsus, 1
Ceylon, 108, 113
Chalfont, Lord, 136
chaplains, protection for, 61, 185
chemical weapons: prohibition, 81; control of, 122–5; Geneva CBW Protocol, 126–7, 130, 132, 139–40; UK policy on, 132, 137; UN policy on, 133; US policy on, 137–8; *see also* gas (poison)
China, as nuclear power, 142n., 143–4, 147, 150–1
Christian church, attitude to war, 1–23; Grotius on, 26–8, 31, 35
Cicero, M.T., 5
civilians: protected by Geneva Conventions, 59, 62, 67, 70, 169–70, 172; Red Cross and, 70, 75–9, 82, 171–9; UN resolutions on, 81, 93; and acts of resistance, 84; and human rights, 99–100, 102, 109, 181–3, 187–8; Israel and, 124; role of, 185
colonial wars, 93, 97, 108
combatants, protection of, 99, 101–2, 181
Comité International de la Croix Rouge (CICR), *see* Red Cross
Conference of Government Experts (1971), draft protocols, 180–6
Conference of non-nuclear weapons states, Geneva (1968), 146, 151n.
Congo, UN forces in, 96
conscription, 36–7
Constantine, Emperor, 3, 4, 28
Convention on the non-applicability of Statutory Limitations to War Crimes and Crimes against Humanity (1970), 51, 53
CS gas, 123, 130, 135, 137

189

United Nations—*continued*
Disarmament Commission, 131, 151
ECOSOC, 51, 89n., 98, 108, 119
Emergency forces, 96, 110–11
General Assembly: on war crimes,
42, 52–3; and Nuremberg principles, 43, 47–8, 50; and ILC's
draft code, 48–50; and W. Germany's war crimes law, 50–1; on
violations during armed conflicts,
52; and civilian protection 75, 77,
92–4, 97, 187–8; and irregular
fighters, 82; and Protecting Powers,
105; and U Thant's reports, 107–8,
110; and Israel, 111–13, 115,
118–19; and CBW, 132–4, 136,
139–40; control of nuclear
weapons, 142–5, 149–52, 154
High Commissioner for Refugees, 95,
100n.
International Law Commission: and
Nuremberg principles, 42–8, 50,
(quoted), 163–70; draft codes of
offences against peace and security,
42, 47–50; and international jurisdiction, 47, 49–50; rejects proposals to codify laws of war, 91
Scientific Committee on the Effects
of Atomic Radiation, 148n.
Security Council: and war crimes,
52; and reprisals, 55; and CICR,
71; and peace-keeping, 91; and
Israel, 111–12, 117, 119–20; and
alleged germ warfare, 131; and
nuclear control, 143; powers, 161
Special Committee on Friendly
Relations and Cooperation among
States, 54
Special Committee to Investigate
Israeli practices, 111–19
Special Political Committee of the
General Assembly, 119
UNESCO, 65–6, 94–5
UNRWA, 115–16
WHO, 123n., 130n., 133, 136n.,
138n.
USA: non-member of League, 41; at
UN, 52, 94, 109, 175; and Cuba
missiles, 70; ban on use of gas, 127,
129, 136; and alleged germ warfare,
131; CBW policy, 137–8; and
Geneva Protocols, 137–8; defence
expenditure, 141; and nuclear

USA—*continued*
weapons control, 143n., 144, 146,
149–50; and SALT 147; strategic
policy and capacity, 148–9, 152–3
Arms Control and Disarmament
Agency, 126n.
House Foreign Affairs Committee,
127n.
Senate Foreign Relations Committee,
Subcommittee on Arms Control
146n.
War Dept, Interim Committee, 38

Vansittart, Sir R., 129
Vatican Council, 2nd, 15, 19
Versailles, Treaty of (1919), 126n.
Viet Cong, 84
Vietnam, war in, 50; chemical weapons
used in, 132, 137
Vietnam, North, and POWs, 94
Vietnam, South, 93
Vio, T. de, *see* Cajetan, T. de Vio
Vitoria, F. de, 9, 11–14, 24–5

war: attempts to outlaw, 39–40, 91;
crimes, 42–50, 163–70; and international criminal jurisdiction, 48–9,
51; statutory limitations on war
crimes, 50–1; indiscriminate, 75;
internal, 88–9, 96, 102–4, 110;
declarations of, 89; in period 1945–
68, 92, *see also* Just War
Washington Naval Treaty (1922), 126
Western European Union (WEU), 148
Whewell, William, 25, 28n.
World Conference on Religion and
Peace, 20n.
World Council of Churches, 19–20
World Veterans' Federation, 83, 85
wounded: protection for, 58–9, 61, 67,
181, 184; Red Cross and, 70;
repatriation of, 109
Wright, Quincy, 55

Yemen, gas in, 132
York, H., 146
Yugoslavia, 109n., 113

Zimbabwe African National Union
(ZANU), 84
Zimbabwe African People's Union
(ZAPU), 84
Zuckerman, Sir S., 133, 145